Global Health Disputes and Disparities

T0264899

Global Health Disputes and Disparities explores inequalities in health around the world, looking particularly at the opportunity for, and limitations of, international law to promote population health by examining its intersection with human rights, trade, and epidemiology, and the controversial issues of legal process, religion, access to care, and the social context of illness.

Using a theoretical framework rooted in international law, this volume draws on a wide range of rich empirical data to assess the challenges facing the field, including international legal treaty interpretation, and specific issues related to the application of law in resolving pressing issues in gender, access to care, and social determinants of health. In doing so, it illustrates the challenges for implementing rights-based approaches to address health disparities, with profound implications for future regulations and policymaking. It includes both interviews with leading scholars, as well as a variety of case studies from prominent international forums, including formal claims brought before the Human Rights Council and the Committee on the Elimination of All Forms of Discrimination Against Women, as well as regional and national experiences, drawn from disputes in India, Indonesia, South Africa, and the USA.

This volume is an innovative contribution to the burgeoning fields of global health and human rights, and will be of interest to students and researchers in public health, global health, law, and sociology interested in the social determinants of health and social justice from both theoretical and practical perspectives.

Dhrubajyoti (Dru) Bhattacharya is the Director of the Health Policy track in the Master of Public Health program at Loyola University Chicago, Assistant Professor of Health Policy at Loyola University Chicago Stritch School of Medicine, and Visiting Professor of Law at Loyola University Chicago School of Law, USA.

Routledge Studies in Public Health

Global Health Disputes and Disparities

A critical appraisal of international law and population health

Dru Bhattacharya

Routledge
Taylor & Francis Group

LONDON AND NEW YORK

First published 2013
by Routledge
2 Park Square, Milton Park, Abingdon, Oxon, OX14 4RN

Simultaneously published in the USA and Canada
by Routledge
711 Third Avenue, New York, NY 10017

First issued in paperback 2017

Routledge is an imprint of the Taylor & Francis Group, an informa business

British Library Cataloguing in Publication Data
A catalogue record for this book is available from the British Library

Library of Congress Cataloging-in-Publication Data
Bhattacharya, Dru.
  Global health disputes and disparities : a critical appraisal of international law and population health / Dru Bhattacharya.
    p. ; cm. – (Routledge studies in public health)
  I. Title. II. Series: Routledge studies in public health.
  [DNLM: 1. World Health. 2. Health Policy. 3. Health Status Disparities. 4. Human Rights. 5. Internationality–legislation & jurisprudence. WA 530.1]
  616.85'82–dc23   2012025037

ISBN 13: 978-1-138-10846-2 (pbk)
ISBN 13: 978-0-415-67380-8 (hbk)

Typeset in Sabon by
Swales & Willis Ltd, Exeter, Devon

Contents

Illustrations

Figures

Tables

Boxes

Acknowledgements

I must thank the wonderful editorial team at Routledge/Taylor & Francis, including Grace McInnes, James Watson, Alanna Donaldson, Tamsin Ballard, Thomas Newman, and Richard Willis for their patience, diligence, and professionalism. My scholarship was concededly a patchwork of multiple ideas and disparate thoughts. After I delivered eight presentations at the 2009 annual conference of the American Public Health Association, it was Grace who recognized an underlying theme to those ideas: an honest critique of the challenges and an identification of the opportunities of international law to promote public health, with a meticulous engagement with the most controversial topics of our day: the role of treaty-monitoring bodies, religion, trade, and science. I have since polished my initial musings and the end result is a testament to their hard work.

I must thank Dr. Allyn Taylor of Georgetown University Law Center, who introduced me to the nuances of international law and its intersection with public health; and Professor Lawrence Gostin of Georgetown University Law Center, who I had the opportunity to work with while pursuing my LL.M. at Georgetown.

I must also thank Professor James Hodge of Arizona State University who offered me my first position as a public health law fellow at Johns Hopkins University, and introduced me to the nuances of domestic public health law, which was instrumental in my case study on the constitutionality of mandatory vaccination.

I would like to recognize Dr. Benjamin Mason Meier of the University of North Carolina, Dr. Lainie Rutkow of Johns Hopkins University, and Professor John Kraemer of Georgetown University. Their work sets a standard that serves as a constant reminder to improve my own research and I thank them for their ongoing support.

I must also thank my interviewees (who appear at the end of every chapter): Professor George Annas (Boston University School of Public Health), Dr. Benjamin Mason Meier (University of North Carolina), Dr. Kayhan Parsi (Loyola University Chicago), and Professor John Kraemer (Georgetown University Law Center). Their erudition illustrates the diversity of opinions and how critical engagement among individuals of different perspectives only improves our collective understanding.

I must extend my gratitude and affection to my wife, Christina Marie, and our children, Stephanie Marie and Domenico Dharmajyoti Nathan; and our extended family Dr. Indranil and Madhurima Bose, Maninder and Kamaljeet Singh, Dr. Subir, Mitali, and Rudra Narayana Sinharoy for their support. Finally, I must thank my parents, Dr. Pranab and Mrs. Indira Bhattacharya, for embodying wisdom, faith, and unconditional love. They came from humble beginnings, and it is with that spirit of humility that I proffer this treatise. All errors contained within this work are mine alone; and if there is anything of worth, I attribute it to their guidance.

1 Introduction to international law and global health

"Wisdom sets bounds even to knowledge."

– Nietzsche, Maxims and Missiles, 5
Twilight of Idols (1888) tr. Anthony M. Ludovici

What is "global health"? The term, as Dr. Koplan once remarked, is "fashionable" and, as such, has garnered significant attention in the media and in universities worldwide.[1] The field is distinct, but encompasses "international health," which was historically focused on issues in low-income and developing countries. It is also distinguishable from, but encompassing, "public health," which concerns preventive measures to secure subnational population health. It embraces "medical care," which concerns the delivery of particular health services for the benefit of an individual patient. And if we break down the terms, some have argued that "global" includes trans-national determinants (e.g., climate change, urbanization) that affect health within all countries; and others have argued that any negative "health" trends should be addressed by the international community, the cross-border threat notwithstanding.

The idea of an international body of law that could govern health-related affairs emerged from the recognition that intrastate health issues, fueled by globalization, may transcend national borders and require international efforts to mitigate the threats. But threats to what, exactly? National security? Values espoused in a myriad of international proclamations?

Ultimately, no matter what factor(s) may account for the heightened recognition of health on the international stage, we have seen a notable shift away from an exclusive biomedical paradigm that explains the onset of illness as the result of physiological changes in the body towards a broader framework that envisions health as a social construct. This is not an entirely novel proposition, as we found when the Constitution of the World Health Organization (WHO) was adopted by the International Health Conference held in 1946. The WHO Constitution states in its Preamble that "Health is a state of complete physical, mental, and social well-being and not merely the absence of disease or infirmity."[2] Public health workers would welcome these developments as an affirmation of their field, which looks at health beyond the experience of a single individual (and the walls of a healthcare system) and as a product of a social- or "population"-based phenomenon. It is unclear, however, whether the intentional omission of the term "social" is illustrative of an underlying tension in recognizing the linkages between social policies and health.

Is there a distinct body of international law that governs the practice of public health? Yes and no. Many human rights treaties are replete with health-related rights, duties, and privileges accorded the institutions and individuals responsible for securing the public's health. Numerous provisions regulate the collection and dissemination of data, the provision of services, and the disclosure of information to enhance individual decision-making and promote population health. In recent times, the year 2005 marked a landmark achievement for public health advocates with the entry into force of the Framework Convention on Tobacco Control (FCTC), which was ratified by 170 Member States of the WHO. It is undeniable that there is a burgeoning interest among countries worldwide in the role of law, and international law in particular, in shaping public health policy. This interest, in turn, has given rise to novel academic endeavors to outline the precise parameters of law on the international stage to secure population health. Professors Gostin and Taylor have conjured a term, "global health law," to elucidate this nascent field of inquiry. They define the term as follows:

> Global health law is a field that encompasses the legal norms, processes, and institutions needed to create the conditions for people throughout the world to attain the highest possible level of physical and mental health. The field seeks to facilitate health-promoting behavior among the key actors that significantly influence the public's health, including international organizations, governments, businesses, foundations, the media, and civil society. The mechanisms of global health law should stimulate investment in research and development, mobilize resources, set priorities, coordinate activities, monitor progress, create incentives, and enforce standards.[3]

Their definition draws from formal sources of public international law, for example treaties, and formal subjects of international law, for example state, international organizations; and has five distinctive features: (1) mission, that is ensure condition for public's health; (2) key participants, for example state/international organizations; (3) sources, that is public international law; (4) structure (methods for global health governance); and (5) moral foundation, that is social justice. Based on these elements, they identify four grand challenges facing the international health community, including: (i) State-centricity in the international legal system (inability to incorporate non-state actors into governance; state sovereignty results in weak treaty commitments); (ii) skewed-priority setting (limited legal framework for national action; limited international cooperation; poverty a principal obstacle to disease prevention and health promotion); (iii) flawed implementation and compliance (no dispute settlement body for global health law issues, no incentives or options to encourage State compliance); and (iv) fragmentation, duplication, and lack of coordination (proliferation of actors and institutions with health agendas, recommend that the WHO take a stronger leadership role in this regard).

While I am intrigued by the breadth of this description, I do not find the term "global health law" or the four grand challenges, above, particularly persuasive. First, State-centricity is still necessary to address (1) the nature and context of health problems and (2) the political realities of international relations. Health problems may be described in the aggregate, but often have relative causality depending on numerous determinants of health. While poverty is an obstacle, it does not absolutely absolve States or individuals of the contribution of individual behaviors on societal outcomes, laws restricting educational and economic opportunities, and existent policies and practices allowing structural violence to sustain. For women, the combination of these behaviors, laws, and practices have been associated with enhanced risk for physical and mental abuse, sexual violence, and attendant health risks, including sexually transmissible infections and diseases and chronic reproductive health problems. State-centricity simply ought not to be regarded as a scapegoat for the threats posed by complacency as relates to these social and individual factors.

In fact, State-centricity is the reality of international relations, and health rarely trumps other equally (if not more) pressing prerogatives, such as trade and national security. The explicit purpose of the revised International Health Regulations is to prevent the spread of international disease and "avoid unnecessary interference with international traffic or trade"—not for members to ameliorate, and help others ameliorate, subnational disease threats that preclude everyone's enjoyment of the highest attainable standard of health. Also, consider the dismissal by the International Court of Justice of the 1996 World Health Organization's request for an advisory opinion to determine whether "in view of health and environmental effects, the use of nuclear weapons by a State in war or other armed conflict [would] be a breach of its obligations under international law including the WHO Constitution." The ICJ found the request to arise outside the scope of the WHO's activities, and tantamount to disregarding the principle of specialty.

Second, as far as dispute settlement is concerned, consultative and (quasi) adjudicative bodies exist, but they ought to be thoroughly scrutinized. Treaty monitoring bodies provide consultative services by reviewing country reports, but provide inadequate criteria for evaluation of progress and growth. Optional Protocols (ICCPR, CEDAW, and ICESCR) also create an avenue to reflect on the application of broader principles to actual disputes; inevitably shape the development of norms, practices, and international jurisprudence; and, upon taking steps based on the Committee's recommendations, also directly affect national legislation and policymaking as well as international relations. Finally, incentives already exist but they may take different forms, which affect the degree of cooperation: political, economic, and social. Some States find being a Party an end in and of itself; others look to future bi- and multi-lateral agreements; some look to adoption to formulate national policy; while others to advocate for reform extraterritorially.

So while there is no consensus on what global health or global health law is, for that matter, it is clear that international law can affect health outcomes by providing normative standards (treaties) for specific State Party measures to reduce the perceived burden of health threats. At the very least, it provides oversight and review of efforts to promote population health vis-à-vis the reporting mechanisms, which facilitate monitoring and surveillance. More recently, international law has accommodated the role of non-traditional subjects, including individual victims and quasi-adjudicative bodies (treaty-monitoring Committees) vis-à-vis the Optional Protocols to evaluate State laws, policies, and interventions—although these avenues have not been adequately scrutinized.

Together, these developments suggest that the field of international law holds much promise for promoting population health worldwide, but there is much work to be done, and a critical appraisal of the field as relates to specific areas of inquiry is long overdue. This work does not add to the compendium of studies on international trade law, the general intersection of health and gender, or public health in particular. Rather, I adopt a critical approach that examines the challenges that are unique to each of these areas, and provide alternative frameworks to understand the potential and limitations of international law as it relates to (1) treaty interpretation and adjudication of health-related disputes, (2) human rights and religion, which often shapes prevalent social norms, (3) trade and access to preventive and therapeutics measures, and (4) epidemiology and social determinants of health.

These are controversial topics and a successful resolution of the issues that are involved stretch well beyond the scope of this book. It is my intent, however, that by engaging them in a manner that goes beyond the traditional legal analyses that are often employed, students and future health advocates will appreciate the complexity of the health burden as a function of legal processes, social norms shaped within a defined historical context, existent policies and priorities, and assumptions underlying our own scientific methodologies and characterization of public health problems.

Since I am the first to acknowledge the need to recognize different view-points, I am honored to include excerpts from personal interviews with renowned scholars and practitioners in the field, which the reader will find interspersed throughout. Among the participants include Professor George Annas (Boston University School of Public Health), Professor Benjamin Mason Meier (University of North Carolina), Professor Kayhan Parsi (Loyola University Chicago), and Professor John Kraemer (Georgetown University Law Center). I hope readers will find the diversity of opinions and insights helpful in their studies, research, and advocacy.

2 A critical assessment of treaty-monitoring bodies

A case study of CEDAW's Optional Protocol

"A decision which is the product of reasoned argument must be prepared itself to meet the test of reason."

– Lon L. Fuller[1]

Introduction

The thirtieth anniversary of the Convention on the Elimination of All Forms of Discrimination Against Women (CEDAW) should be met with ambivalence. Since its adoption in 1979, the treaty has engendered transnational dialogue for 185 States Parties to address discrimination against women. Its breadth is laudable and its depth evinced by provisions addressing discrimination in all walks of life, including employment, healthcare, family relations, and civic participation. CEDAW also occupies a unique position among other international instruments by recognizing an inextricable linkage between social determinants and health outcomes. In doing so, it bridges the ominous divide between economic, social, and cultural rights with civil and political rights. As the only treaty that specifically addresses women's health, however, CEDAW is a victim of its own success.

Despite mandatory State reports that account for progress made over the years, implementation of health-related measures has proven particularly troublesome. For example, mandating States to modify culture and ensure that families adopt a "proper" view of maternity raises legitimate questions about government interference with individual liberty interests.[2] Though discrimination may threaten the physical and social well-being of all women, inter-State disparities in health, wealth, and education may compel governments to adopt different policies for meeting the immediate needs of their populations. While socio-economic status undoubtedly affects health outcomes, there is simply no consensus on what model allocates resources in the most equitable fashion.

In some developing nations, prescribed notions of social inferiority and limited access to education and healthcare contribute to high rates of illiteracy and maternal mortality. Every year, over 500,000 women die because of pregnancy-related causes, even though the majority of these deaths are preventable.[3] Discrimination contributes to these trends by precluding access to health information on family planning, and quality medical care. The latter is exemplified in patriarchal societies where access is predicated upon, inter alia, spousal consent, or the availability of a female physician. Less obvious (but equally detrimental) examples include expectations of motherhood whereby high rates of fertility heighten the risk of complications and, coupled with inadequate healthcare systems, result in increased maternal deaths.

In wealthier States, discrimination takes on even more subtle forms, and raises complex medicolegal issues. CEDAW requires, for example, that governments promote non-discriminatory policies that enable access to "services . . . related to" family planning or "in connection with" pregnancy. Is emergency contraception "related to" family planning? Are both abortion and fertility treatment "in connection with" pregnancy? Has an insurance provider who covers varicocele ligation for men but refuses to pay for surgical impregnation for women engaged in a *discriminatory* practice? Absent express directives, interpretation is the quintessential means of demarcating the nature and scope of the provision.

The CEDAW Committee ("Committee") is the only body authorized to provide guidance on how governments should translate their treaty obligations into precise policy directives. The Optional Protocol to CEDAW ("Protocol") empowers the Committee to review individual claims, assess their veracity, and issue recommendations in response thereto. To be sure, the Committee is not a tribunal, but submitting a claim to its independent review has a unique adjudicative flavor with far-reaching implications. Recognizing the Committee's jurisdiction to pass judgment on State acts (or omissions) has political consequences to the extent that governments are perceived as complying with their international treaty obligations. On the domestic front, requiring a formal response by the State Party delineating steps taken to remedy a violation may have significant economic and social effects. Governments may be asked to provide direct remuneration to a claimant, amend existing laws, and even develop new programs. Consequently, the claims procedure not only serves as a potential avenue of individual recourse, but also implicates inter- and intra-State relations.

To date, individuals have not been reluctant to use the Protocol to address health-related issues. In fact, half of the claims submitted thus far are unique to women's health, such as forced sterilization and incidents of domestic violence. Given the profound reach of each decision, the Committee's rationale will be scrutinized for the reasons employed. Professor Fuller's general admonition is worth remembering, for "[e]ven if there is no statement by the tribunal of the reasons for its decision, some reason will be perceived or guessed at and the parties will tend to govern their conduct accordingly."[4] In the universe of international relations, treaty interpretation simply cannot afford an unseemly presentation in form or substance.

Submitting to the Committee's judgment not only concedes a modicum of competence, but lends legitimacy to the heightened rationality that inheres in the process of a quasi-judicial review. Though a State may reject the Committee's decision, it would be unscrupulous in the face of decisions founded upon a sound consideration of all the material facts and circumstances. Consistent refusal in the wake of well-reasoned decisions would also raise suspicions as to whether a State was acting in good faith to adhere to its legal obligations. The initial onus, however, rests with the Committee to impress upon its audience an objective and consistent approach in considering the merits of a claim.

This section presents the first comprehensive analysis of decisions rendered under the Protocol in the first decade since its inception (2000–2009). It specifically discusses how the Committee has interpreted and applied CEDAW and the implications for using the claims mechanism as an avenue to resolve pressing and emerging women's health issues.

Three key issues are of particular note. First, do CEDAW and its Optional Protocol afford more robust substantive and procedural safeguards to secure women's health than other international instruments? Second, has the Committee interpreted the treaty and substantive State obligations objectively and consistently? Finally, what challenges exist to address pressing and emerging women's health issues?

I argue that the Committee's legal analyses were unsound and compromised the integrity of the interpretive process. I propose an enhanced framework for interpretation that is rooted in sound principles of international law and consistent with the unique character of the treaty. Employing a robust methodology will enhance rather than vitiate the deliberative process and secure the health of women worldwide. A five-step process is formulated that draws on customary international law and the existent parameters laden in the treaty, the Protocol, and the Committee's rules of procedure. This fusion of central tenets ensures that the analyses are consistent, foreseeable, and legally sound.

Part I of this chapter explores the current laws governing consideration of a claim and proposes a model framework for interpretive analysis. Recent jurisprudence on women's health under other international instruments is challenged as inadequate and unpersuasive. The treaty is unique in its procedures and substance in securing individual rights. Still, its potential has been left unrealized for want of a diligent, interpretive mechanism. The enhanced framework utilizes select generally applicable interpretive means under the Vienna Convention on the Law of Treaties to bolster the individually centered prerogatives of CEDAW.

Part II examines the Protocol in practice by reviewing all ten claims brought thus far before the Committee under the proposed interpretive model. Interpretive trends are then identified and the utility of the proposed framework is assessed. The framework is then applied to an international case involving abortion to demonstrate its effectiveness over other instruments in resolving women's health issues.

In summary, this chapter illustrates the emerging issues posed by global health governance and the particular challenges for bringing individual health claims before international tribunals and related adjudicative bodies. The analysis reveals the perils of simultaneous adjudication and consultation and stresses the need for thorough legal analyses. CEDAW and its Protocol are unique instruments that, coupled with a robust interpretive lens, can promote and protect women's health. Adopting a more comprehensive deliberative approach will only enhance the Committee's influence to remedy individual violations and alter State practice to secure population health.

I. Proposed legal framework for considering a communication

There has been scant attention given to the decisional framework of international adjudicative bodies enabling women to raise health-related claims. The general right to health appears in a myriad of international instruments, including the International Covenant on Economic, Social, and Cultural Rights (ICESCR) and the Social Charter of the European Union (EU).[5] Even so, these instruments do not provide individuals an opportunity to bring claims in an international forum against States. The ICESCR has no attendant claims mechanism and the Optional Protocol to the EU Social Charter compels reliance on third-party institutions to initiate claims, regardless of merit.[6] Also, many EU Member States are not parties to the Optional Protocol, thereby rendering many potential claims inadmissible *de jure*.

The Protocol to CEDAW affords individuals an opportunity to challenge State conduct. Furthermore, States that are willing to be scrutinized for how they interpret the treaty are, at the very least, open to second opinions. Still, it is the Committee that bears the burden of construing treaty obligations in a consistent, objective, and well-reasoned fashion. Failure on any of these counts would yield precarious decisions and vitiate the *process* that should be as equally robust as the substantive law in securing a just outcome.

The pressing issue is not whether a Committee's decision is legally binding (it's not) but rather, what course of action a State should take pursuant to well-reasoned deliberations that illustrate the precise legal wrongs committed. A working framework to analyze the process of review can be developed by first parsing the conception of available remedies illustrating the unique character of the treaty and Protocol (subpart A, below) and incorporating the substantive elements of the Vienna Convention on the Law of Treaties alongside the procedural rules governing Committee review (subpart B). Subpart C briefly explores the nature and scope of general recommendations (which have become a focal point of Committee review) and are discussed at length in Part II, which examines each decision in greater detail. The result is a legal framework that may be used as a lens to gauge the breadth, depth, and validity of the Committee's analyses.

A. Parsing individual and structural conceptions of remedies

Adjudicating a health issue at an international level requires a determination of State violation(s) and an accounting of available remedies. The Protocol grants the Committee heightened evaluative powers to secure individual redress. Compared to other international instruments, the charge is not overtly rebellious. The International Covenant on Civil and Political Rights (ICCPR) also requires "effective" remedies for any person whose rights or freedoms are violated.[7] This approach neither undermines international legal theory nor proves impractical so long as the Committee parses individual and structural conceptions of remedies. As a practical matter, however, no international tribunal has the capacity to serve as a makeshift trial court and contemplate the adequacy of every remedy in every conceivable legal dispute.

The Protocol strikes a delicate balance between effective and efficient decision-making by affording more robust procedural safeguards than the ICCPR. While the ICCPR has been used to address reproductive rights (as discussed below), its structural deficiencies include no regard for imminent threats and an open timeframe for substantive redress.

The ICCPR protocol provides that the Human Rights Committee (HRC) will only consider communications by an individual who "has exhausted all available domestic remedies" except where "the application of the remedies is unreasonably prolonged."[8] Here, the HRC can only opine on the availability of remedies when a State delays application. In drafting the protocol, the Secretary-General confirmed the intent underlying this procedural safeguard by noting that the basic idea was "to prevent undue interference by an international authority before domestic parties."[9] Of course, the potential contradiction posed by the treaty's demand for effective remedies against the passive review under the protocol was not lost on its drafters. Evaluating the effectiveness of a remedy was not meant to be an exercise in judicial lawmaking. Notably, "national remedies would not necessarily be bypassed . . . because consideration by the Committee of such cases might result in the application of domestic remedies."[10]

The exhaustion provision of the CEDAW Protocol is distinguishable in content and scope. The CEDAW Committee may bypass the exhaustion requirement where the application of remedies "is unreasonably prolonged *or unlikely to bring effective relief.*"[11] In addition to contemplating potential delays in applying available remedies, the Protocol charges the Committee to ascertain their adequacy in securing redress for the individual victim. Determining the effectiveness of relief requires nothing short of evaluating the nature of the remedy as relates to the particular claimant. Since either exception (i.e., prolonged proceedings "or" inadequate remedies) may be invoked, the Committee retains discretion in deferring to State courts and legislative pronouncements.

Apart from a substantive remedial determination, the Protocol also recognizes that some threats to a woman's health may require immediate attention, the official review notwithstanding. The Protocol thus provides "interim measures" to avoid irreparable damage to the victim of the alleged violation.[12] Moreover, unlike the ICCPR, the Protocol requires States to submit a written response—within six months—enunciating any action taken in light of the views and recommendations of the Committee.[13]

International courts and tribunals, like the HRC, have taken pains to weave through a patchwork of laws and principles to render decisions that supposedly ameliorate individual harms. As illustrated in the case of *Karen Noelia Llantoy Huamán v. Peru* ("*K.L. v. Peru*"), the ICCPR, along with its Optional Protocol, are inadequate in fulfilling this role.[14] The deficiencies in procedural safeguards and standards of evaluative redress reveal how the Protocol to CEDAW presents a more promising, albeit imperfect, model for resolving disputes.

The ruling in *K.L. v. Peru* is particularly important because it was heralded as a landmark decision for reproductive rights "by asserting State responsibility to ensure access to legal abortion services."[15] The suit was brought by a 17-year-old female whose doctors refused to perform an abortion after she presented carrying an anencephalic fetus. Anencephaly is the most severe of fetal neural tube defects that leaves the brain partly developed, with stillbirth the most common outcome, and survival usually measured by hours rather than days.[16] The author delivered the fetus and was compelled to breastfeed it before it died a few days later. The woman also suffered vulvitis and subsequently entered a severe state of depression. Peruvian law provided for a therapeutic exception, but also imposed criminal liability on physicians who performed abortions. It was unclear whether reluctance was motivated by ideology or fear of prosecution.

The woman brought a claim before the HRC against the Peruvian government for violations under the ICCPR. Specific allegations included violating her right to: (1) *an effective remedy* after failing to secure her access to a therapeutic abortion,[17] (2) *equality* by subjecting her to sex-based discrimination,[18] (3) *life* by impeding access to reproductive services,[19] (4) *freedom from cruel and inhuman treatment* by obliging her to carry her pregnancy to term, and causing mental suffering,[20] (5) *freedom from interference with her privacy*, which encompasses decisions affecting her body and life,[21] (6) *special protective measures* on account of being an adolescent,[22] and (7) *equal protection* after the officials left her in an unprotected state.[23]

At first glance, the charges reflect traditional notions of positive and negative duties. Providing an effective remedy, special protective measures, and equal protection reflect affirmative (i.e., positive) steps to fulfill an individual's realization of her rights. Ensuring the right to privacy is a negative obligation precluding interference with individual spheres of conduct and behavior. The State, for example, had allegedly overstepped its bounds by "taking on her behalf a decision relating to her life and reproductive health."[24] Fulfilling the right to privacy allegedly required refrain from taking affirmative measures that interfere with individual decision-making.

The case was unique, however, in challenging the characteristic perceptions of positive and negative duties to secure a woman's reproductive health. The plaintiff claimed that ensuring the right to life, and freedom from inhuman treatment, entailed positive duties. Protecting the right to life, she argued, requires "positive steps, including . . . access for women to reproductive health services, including abortion . . ."[25] In particular, fulfilling the right to life encompassed measures to protect her physical and mental health. By refusing to provide an abortion service, the government had left her with only two options, namely, resort to a clandestine abortion service, or carry the pregnancy to term. Since both options "posed an equal risk to her health and safety," her physical health was endangered and, consequently, her right to life had been violated.[26] Similarly, a policy that mandated giving birth, and causing mental pain (after witnessing her daughter's "marked deformities," and knowing of her impending mortality), amounted to cruel and inhuman treatment.[27]

The HRC found violations of the author's right to freedom from cruel and inhuman treatment, privacy, and protective measures. Not enabling the author to benefit from a therapeutic abortion caused her mental suffering, which amounted to cruel and inhuman treatment.[28] The State also noted that one physician had confirmed that her pregnancy may pose a threat to her life. So by refusing to "act in accordance with the author's decision to terminate her pregnancy," the State had violated her right to privacy.[29] Finally, the HRC concluded that the government had failed to provide special protective measures on account of the author's status as a minor. Specifically, it had failed to deliver the "medical and psychological support necessary in the specific circumstances of her case."[30]

The HRC's rationale for violations—and non-violations—illustrates the equivocal nature of the ICCPR in resolving reproductive health issues. The finding of cruel and inhuman treatment rested on a single premise that the government must conduct an abortion on a woman who presents with anencephaly. Still, the clinical manifestations were only psychological in nature. Instead of claiming that mental anguish could be life-threatening— a clinically debatable proposition—the Committee relied on its General Comment No. 20, which provided that cruel and inhuman treatment precluded physical and mental suffering.

Equating the refusal to conduct an abortion with cruel and inhuman treatment is inconsistent with the object and purpose of the provision. The express language of the clause is to refrain from torture or cruel, inhuman, or degrading treatment or punishment. The General Comment interprets this provision to preclude *acts* related to the treatment of detainees or individuals subject to potentially invasive measures (such as patients within a medical setting). In context, as indicated in the second part of the clause, a primary purpose was to preclude involuntary submission to medical or scientific experimentation. There is nothing in the treaty nor its General Comment that posits an affirmative duty on States to conduct a medically invasive service—

patient consent notwithstanding—to be in compliance with its legal obligations. Furthermore, the clause (standing alone) would unlikely subsume a broader, affirmative duty of the State to protect the health and safety of its constituents. The latter is by and large a population-wide obligation that cannot be invoked to meet individual needs unless they affect a fundamental right. Here, the HRC did not proclaim that every woman has a right to an abortion. It simply attempted to justify access to abortions by recognizing detrimental health effects after carrying a child to term.

The criticism of invoking the "freedom from cruelty" clause is not meant to belittle the tragic unfolding of events, but to illustrate the legal ambiguities that inhere in a subsequent analysis. Compelling a clinically depressed minor to breastfeed a deformed fetus prior to its inevitable death is arguably sufficient to meet a test of cruelty. It does not necessarily follow, however, that such cruelty would include the refusal to conduct the abortion.

The Committee did not address whether it was the State's refusal to perform the abortion and/or the circumstances surrounding the birth and care of the fetus that amounted to cruel or inhuman treatment. The mental anguish was arguably foreseeable because she had to endure the distress of seeing the fetal deformities and breastfeed the child. The author's plight could surely have been avoided had she been able "to benefit from a therapeutic abortion."[31] Indeed, if the fetus had not been born, the author would have never seen its deformities nor been compelled to breastfeed it. But if she had not been compelled to breastfeed it, would the delivery—in and of itself—amount to cruel treatment because she knew of its likely death? The HRC did not say and the General Comment provides no guidance.

It is unclear (and improbable) that a woman could charge a State with cruelty for refusing to conduct an abortion because she may suffer mental anguish from carrying a child to term. Even the medical prognosis that carrying an anencephalic child to term would be life-threatening to the mother was not clearly articulated by either the facts or the analysis. After citing one physician's "life-threatening" characterization of the pregnancy, the Committee quickly reverted its attention to the author's mental suffering. The anguish, however, arguably stemmed not from carrying the child to term, but the circumstances immediately thereafter. Professor Cook has argued that the ethical issues surrounding abortion are overcome in cases involving anencephaly because the fetus is unviable.[32] Even so, the medically indicated facts relevant to the *woman's* health status remain unchanged. From a medical perspective, a health—as opposed to a life—exception is a more accurate characterization of the relevant reasons employed for seeking an abortion in like scenarios. Nonetheless, the ICCPR (which makes no such provisions for health considerations) becomes an awkward crutch to support this proposition. Notably, the HRC did "not consider it necessary in the circumstances to ma[k]e a finding on" the right to life claim.[33] As indicated above, it would have been a tenuous proposition nonetheless.

Though the HRC had proffered some criteria to assess a claim asserting freedom from cruelty, no such accommodation was made for finding a violation of privacy. The Committee simply noted that the physician informed the author that she could continue with the pregnancy or terminate it. Citing the legality of seeking a therapeutic abortion, the Health Ministry was found to have violated her right to privacy by refusing to perform the abortion. It is unclear how refusal to perform an abortion is a violation of an individual's broad right to privacy. The express language of the treaty posits that no one "shall be subjected to arbitrary or unlawful interference with his privacy, family, home or correspondence, nor to unlawful attacks on his honour or reputation."[34] On its face, the text does not implicate State omissions. Also, the HRC did not define the nature and scope of the right in the context of seeking medical care or services. A stronger argument could have defined privacy as encompassing medically indicated decisions as relates to the health and well-being of a woman. In that same vein, a woman could be afforded discretion as relates to the control of decisions affecting her body. Until a State interest is lawfully implicated, her discretion in such matters may remain firmly entrenched within the ambit of the provision. The HRC, however, remained silent on each of these issues. Furthermore, none of the proffered assertions resolves the issue of whether a woman's right to privacy requires the State, acting through its officials, to conduct the abortion. What if State officials were unwilling to conduct an abortion because it violated their moral convictions? Without further elaboration, the express right to privacy does not appropriate State omissions to terminate a non-life-threatening pregnancy.

Finally, rendering protective measures related to the author's medical and psychological needs does not resolve the issue concerning access to an abortion. Considering her status as a minor, the case against the State for failing to provide adequate psychological care and support is compelling. Forcing any woman to breastfeed a deformed fetus shortly before its imminent death would likely affect her mental health. When the woman is a minor, the severity and impact is not only foreseeable, but arguably inevitable. The author's diagnosis of severe depression only validates this assertion. Protective measures, however, do not speak to the issue of whether access to an abortion is a right or whether the State must conduct the procedure in the absence of a willing provider. If anencephaly posed a greater risk to a minor's health or life, an argument could be made that access to an abortion fell within the gamut of special protective measures. Indeed, the provision would reasonably embrace interventions that take account of the heightened risks associated with a minor's diminished physical and mental capacities. Again, the HRC remained silent on all of these issues.

While the association between the alleged violations and the State's duty to perform an abortion are inconclusive (at best), the non-violations are equally demonstrative of the treaty's futility in securing women's health. A critical element of the author's complaint was her claim to sex-discrimination owing to a woman's exclusive reproductive capacity. Notably, access to an abortion "is applicable only to women."[35] Additionally, she claimed that the State's refusal was a product of social attitudes and prejudices that precluded women from receiving treatment "on an equal footing with men."[36] The HRC dismissed this claim because the author "had not placed . . . any evidence relating to the *events* which might confirm any type of discrimination under the article in question."[37] By requiring an "event" or incident evincing discrimination, the HRC dismissed a woman's exclusive reproductive status insofar as precluding access to an abortion could be indicative of sex-discrimination. Moreover, it put the onus on women to demonstrate how State acts or omissions preclude their realization of equal access, notwithstanding a man's inability to reproduce. This interpretation suggests that equal access only applies in situations where men are afforded a positive benefit that has been denied women. In practice, this was consistent with the HRC's previous case law on sex-discrimination.[38] While Professor Cook characterized the decision as "the standard by which to measure other responses to prenatal diagnosis of anencephaly," her position was likely motivated by the outcome rather than the processes of the case.[39]

We shall return to the case of *K.L. v. Peru* in Part II, but suffice it to say that the ICCPR and its protocol are insufficient in securing the reproductive health and well-being of women. Having first proposed and demonstrated the utility of employing a robust legal framework to interpret CEDAW, we shall then explore its efficacy for addressing health-related claims using the Peruvian case as an example. CEDAW provides a better standard to review women's health claims and, through the proposed framework, an opportunity to balance the legitimate interests of individuals and State governments.

B. Form and substance of Committee review and deliberations

The overarching purpose of the Committee is to monitor the progress made in the implementation of the treaty.[40] It is thereby charged with periodic reviews of State Party reports, and submission of an annual report to the U.N. Economic and Social Council on its activities.[41] States are required to submit reports to the Committee within one year after the entry into force for the State concerned; at least once every four years thereafter; or whenever the Committee so requests.[42] The Committee also retains the discretion to make suggestions and general recommendations to the States Parties.[43] In the event that the Committee issues any recommendations, they must be included within the annual report submitted to the Economic and Social Council.[44]

Though the treaty is silent on its interpretation, the Compilation of Rules of Procedure Adopted by the Human Rights Treaty Bodies ("Rules") provides an operative framework.[45] Under the Rules, the function of the Committee is essentially threefold: to examine State Party reports, make recommendations, and review claims brought under the Protocol. A common theme throughout the deliberative process is the importance placed on participation of all interested parties.

The Committee neither holds itself out as the sole expert on women's issues nor presumes a State to be incompetent. A concerted effort is made to draw on expertise in the international arena and encourage States to be actively involved in the deliberative process. Specialized agencies are, in fact, entitled to be represented at the consideration of implementation of provisions as fall within the scope of their activities.[46] State reports are expected to indicate factors and difficulties affecting the degree of fulfillment of obligations.[47]

The Committee is comprised of 23 "experts of high moral standing and competence" that serve two distinct functions as a consultative entity (when reviewing State Party reports), and as a de facto adjudicative body (when assessing violations under the Protocol). Though interpretation of CEDAW falls squarely within the exclusive jurisdiction of the Committee, the Rules foster an inclusive framework that stresses participation of all parties to achieve a suitable resolution.

The role of specialized agencies,[48] intergovernmental organizations and U.N. bodies,[49] and non-governmental agencies[50] may be helpful in clarifying issues falling within their areas of expertise. As an internationally recognized agency specializing in health affairs, the World Health Organization (WHO) may serve as a useful resource by providing data on the prevalence of existing trends and behaviors. The WHO has conducted numerous studies unique to women, including a multi-country study on the impact of domestic violence on women's health.[51]

The Commission on the Status of Women may also be invited as an intergovernmental organization and U.N. body to provide documentation relevant to the issue at bar. The Commission is expressly entitled to receive the Committee's annual reports[52] and has issued reports before the Economic and Social Council recommending draft resolutions for adoption by the General Assembly.[53] In the past, health-related resolutions have included requests to provide maternal and essential obstetric care, the enactment of laws denouncing sexual violence, and elimination of stigmatization and social exclusion surrounding infectious diseases.[54] Additional measures were directed at the promotion and protection of sexual and reproductive health including, among others, universal access to health services to reduce maternal mortality, hypertension during pregnancy, unsafe abortions, and post-partum hemorrhage.[55]

The Population Council may serve as a non-governmental organization whose representatives are invited to make oral or written statements relevant to the Committee's review or to its pre-sessional working group. Historically, the Council has reported on regional trends throughout the world including, for example, the practice of unsafe abortions in Latin America.[56]

Since the treaty and Rules are silent on interpretive guidance, the Committee is accorded substantial discretion in its deliberative undertakings. Even when considering a claim under the Protocol, there is no legal framework aside from mandatory compliance with grounds of admissibility.[57] These provisions are by and large procedural devices that ensure identification of the author,[58] an adjudicative right espoused under the treaty,[59] and exhaustion of domestic remedies.[60] As discussed in subpart A, the preclusion of irreparable harms with interim measures qualify the interpretive process by ensuring that the individual's safety and well-being are paramount.

As for the substantive means of interpretation, the treaty, Rules, and Protocol are silent on precise means to be employed. None of the instruments make reference to the Vienna Convention on the Law of Treaties (VCLT).[61] Notably, the VCLT, and particularly its means of interpretation, has been accorded the status of customary international law,[62] and has been recognized by numerous international tribunals, including the International Court of Justice,[63] the European Court of Human Rights,[64] and the Appellate Body of the World Trade Organization.[65] Moreover, it was ratified by nine of the ten States (with the exception of Turkey) who have thus far brought claims under the Protocol. For consultative purposes, the effect of interpretation is uncontroversial insofar as States are not obligated to undertake any specific measures. But in matters of adjudicating intrastate disputes, interpretation is of utmost importance in securing the integrity of the deliberative process and ensuring a just outcome. As demonstrated in the case of *K.L. v. Peru*, a presumably just outcome cannot mask the gaps in legal reasoning. A flawed process compromises the acceptability of the outcome. It also jeopardizes the viability of future resolutions by discouraging States from participating in the deliberative process. As will be discussed in Part II, a State that perceives itself as part of the problem rather than the solution is more likely to ignore a decision and its attendant recommendations.

Using the VCLT to enhance the integrity of the interpretive process cannot be overstated. The treaty affords procedural and substantive guideposts that contemplate the complex web of issues that inevitably arise in the event of a dispute. The general rule of interpretation is elusively straightforward, providing that a treaty "shall be interpreted in good faith in accordance with the ordinary meaning to be given to the terms of the treaty in their context and in the light of its object and purpose."[66] Context is not limited to the text of the treaty (e.g., its preamble and annexes)[67] but includes agreements (1) related to the conclusion of the treaty or (2) its interpretation, as well as (3) subsequent State practice suggesting the same. Considering each of these three elements constitutes the general means of interpretation.

The express requirement of an agreement related to the treaty "in connection with the conclusion of the treaty"[68] and the relevance of "subsequent" agreements[69] or practices[70] indicates that interpretation may not subsume prior or other agreements that are not expressly connected to the specific treaty. While international instruments may be considered mutually reinforcing, the VCLT does not allow a treaty to be molded into whatever shape may be given under the weight of another instrument.

For disputes related to a woman's health, the general means of interpretation are crucial because States may already be parties to agreements that allude to the provision of broad measures to secure women's health and well-being. The ICESCR, for example, provides no specific mention of services exclusively for women's health. The only related provision is the call for States to provide for "the reduction of the stillbirth-rate and of infant mortality ...," which would inevitably require accommodations to secure the health of pregnant women.[71] By contrast, the General Comment issued by the Committee on Economic, Social and Cultural Rights on the "right to health" under Article 12 of the ICESCR is quite expansive in its treatment of women's health issues.[72] It provides a distinct section entitled "Women and the right to health," [73] and enunciates "[s]pecific legal obligations" that flow therefrom.[74] Since the treaty already requires States to take efforts to reduce the stillbirth-rate and infant mortality rate, the mandate that States enable women to go safely through pregnancy and childbirth is of little consequence.[75] Further elaboration that achieving this requires access to "pre- and post-natal care, [and] emergency obstetric services" is also reasonable.[76] Having cited CEDAW in an earlier paragraph, the cross-reference simply reinforces what is expressly stated in the other instrument.[77]

Where the General Comment becomes legally problematic is when it attempts to commingle distinct spheres into a single rubric. The ICESCR makes no mention of family planning, which could include access to contraceptives and like services, such as abortion. The committee asserts that reducing the infant mortality rate and allowing for the healthy development of the child includes access to family planning services.[78] When such services encompass pre- and post-natal care, as suggested elsewhere in the Comment, [79] it remains consistent with the purpose of the provision to further "the healthy development of the child." Still, the committee goes on to claim that States "should refrain from limiting access to contraceptives ..." Though the term "should" may appear to nullify the suggestion of a mandate, the committee classifies its assertion under a list of "[s]pecific legal obligations."[80] To be sure, the Comment never implies that abortion is a legitimate means of family planning. The term "family planning" is universally recognized to encompass sexual education and birth control. But in many countries, abortion—perhaps less frequently, but more controversially—is precisely used for such purposes. Moreover, the characterization of unfettered access to contraceptives as a legal obligation pursuant to a provision that is meant to reduce infant mortality *and* foster the healthy development of a child is tenuous, at best. The Comment has arguably traversed the reasonable parameters of the object and purpose of the provision.

The authority to make general comments or recommendations does not automatically create a legally enforceable duty on the part of the State to undertake them. If it chooses to do so, as suggested by an agreement or subsequent practice, then the recommendation as applied to that particular State may rise to the level of a legal obligation. The State, however, must actively trigger the re-characterization of a recommendation into an obligation. On their face, such attendant documents are not legally binding any more so than "soft" law may be considered enforceable. They cannot rise to a characterization of legality absent some indicia of formal legal recognition through an agreement or practice.

When the general means of interpretation are exhausted, a body may resort to supplementary means, including the travaux and circumstances of its conclusion.[81] Neither the travaux nor circumstances of its conclusion are regarded as exclusive means of determining the latent meaning of the text. When either means are insufficient to clarify the meaning[82] or yield a reasonable result,[83] resort to other related instruments (which the State is a party to) may proffer a suitable compromise. The Committee has, in practice, recognized the mutually reinforcing nature of international instruments. After the HRC issued its judgment in *K.L. v. Peru*, the CEDAW Committee raised concern that the government had failed to honor the decision and undertake its recommendations. The reprimand was not without significance as it relates to the Committee's oversight of State Party compliance. In the context of Peru's heightened maternal mortality rates associated with illegal abortions, the Committee had a direct interest in efforts related to promoting and protecting women's health.[84] Still, a concern is but a prefatory note that has no legal significance standing alone.

C. On the nature and scope of general recommendations

The Committee's dual functions of adjudication and consultation may become problematic when treaty interpretation is colored by non-legally binding directives. In such instances, the collective deliberative process also becomes attenuated. The legal effect of such unilateral pronouncements ignores the influence of existent international instruments (that the State may be a party to) and their impact on resolving the issue at bar. Although the Committee is authorized to make suggestions and recommendations to States Parties, they retain absolute discretion to observe them.[85]

General recommendations may become particularly controversial because they have evolved from merely structural aids to substantive legal pronouncements. The Committee's own background summary of the change is somewhat misleading. It recalls that the recommendations adopted after enactment up until 1991 "were short and modest, addressing such issues as the content of reports, reservations to the Convention and resources."[86] In 1991, it decided to issue recommendations on "cross-cutting" themes, which meant issuing "more detailed and comprehensive general recommendations which offer States [P]arties clear guidance on the application of the Convention in particular situations."[87] The characterization of "cross-cutting" themes is hyperbole; guidance cannot supplant a recognized legal obligation.

States Parties were concerned as early as 1986 (when the first recommendation was issued) of their proper nature and scope. During the fifth session, two opposing views emerged concerning the basis, substance and scope of applicability. The issue was "whether, [1] exclusively, the contents of reports should be used to prepare suggestions or general recommendations, or [2] other suggestions or general recommendations could also be made."[88] A statement was issued by a representative of the Office of Legal Affairs of the U.N. Secretariat, which stated that "since the travaux preparatoires did not provide additional guidance on the interpretation of [A]rticle 21, it had been necessary to look to the plain and ordinary meaning" of the terms used in that article.[89] He referred to the background leading to the Convention against Racial Discrimination, which sought to "place some limitation on the competence of the Committee to make recommendations which are more formal and which had to be general in nature and scope."[90] He also felt that Article 46 of the Rules of Procedure (concerning invitation of the opinions of international organizations) were "of a technical nature and more limited in scope than the provisions of [A]rticle 21 . . ."[91] The general character of recommendations, coupled with the technical nature of third-party advisory opinions, mollify concerns that a legally binding obligation has been created as applied to a particular State. The Committee, however, forged ahead and did not put much weight on the perceived legality that may attach to its proclamations.

The initial concerns raised in 1986 were reiterated almost a decade later, and illustrate the inevitable conflict in parsing form and substance in treaty obligations. In the 13th Session, the Committee observed that:

> the nature of the Committee's activities had changed in the wake of the World Conference on Human Rights and that its sphere of activity now *extended beyond merely reviewing reports*. The function of providing commentaries on articles of the Convention through general recommendations and contributions to significant United Nations conferences and events *had expanded*.[92]

World conferences do not, of themselves, alter the legal obligations that inhere in a treaty. The extent to which the Committee perceived its functions as extending and expanding should be scrutinized beyond that as defined in the treaty and the reasonable interpretation of the U.N. legal advisor.

Another concern was the haste with which the recommendations were being issued. The Committee recalled that Member States pointed out that the effort to provide general recommendations "had perhaps proceeded too rapidly, and the Committee should consider slowing the pace in order to ensure that the quality of the final recommendations would meet the highest professional standards."[93] Speed not only compromises the Committee's own ability to produce a quality product, but also detracts from the participation of all interested Parties. A recommendation of general applicability cannot be characterized as universally applicable if State concerns are not adequately raised and addressed. Moreover, the burden is not on the States Parties but the Committee to do so insofar as failure to adhere to the recommendations can be legally enforced. The treaty, not the recommendations, binds the States

Parties. Unless the Committee can demonstrate State concordance through an agreement or subsequent practice, the recommendations should not be invoked in lieu of express treaty obligations.

But must a State expressly reject the Committee's recommendation to relieve it of an otherwise authoritative interpretation of a legally binding provision? Certainly not. The treaty neither grants the Committee perpetual law-making authority nor obligates State Parties to speak up or forever hold their peace. It is presumptuous to claim that a State is wedded to such unilateral decision-making without some indication of consent. It may be argued that the process affords an opportunity to dissent; but this presumes that authority inheres in the Committee at the outset by laying forth potentially binding measures. If so, the process is not a deliberation but a promulgation of obligations that were simply non-existent at the formation of the treaty. Furthermore, the treaty expressly provides that while the Committee must submit its recommendations to the Economic and Social Council, States Parties are not required to submit any comments therewith. Their observations, "if any," must also be included, but since their comments or concerns are not required, it does not necessarily follow that a recommendation would alter the effect of their existent legal obligations.[94]

The restrictive legality of a recommendation should not devalue its contribution to enhancing the context for interpretation. As illustrated in General Comment 14 to the ICESCR, a reasonable interpretation can embolden the substantive terms by recognizing how implementation demands measures that adequately address a provision's constituent parts. For example, the provision of pregnancy-related services to facilitate childbirth should logically encompass pre-natal and post-natal care. Where a recommendation becomes suspect is when it injects measures that are inconsistent with the express purpose of the provision. In such instances, the recommendation is nothing more than an amendment to which a State must give its express approval.

The legal framework that emerges from a systematic assessment of the treaty, its Protocol, the Rules, and the general recommendations provides a delicate lens to examine the decisions issued thus far. By embedding the general and supplementary means of interpretation under the VCLT, a simple—yet robust—methodology emerges with procedural and substantive safeguards that reflect the unique character of the treaty. The five-step framework consists of a two-part consideration on the facts and merits to determine admissibility and potential violations, respectively:

Five-step interpretive framework for CEDAW

ADMISSIBILITY CONSIDERATION ON THE FACTS

1) Did the author exhaust domestic remedies? If not, proceed to step (2). If so, proceed to step (3).

2) Do the facts indicate an imminent threat to the author's health or safety that demand interim measures to prevent irreparable harm? Has the State provided any assurances that the perceived delay has been reasonable or that the available remedies are, on their face, ineffective? Exhaustion should not exclude a determination of irreparable harm.

3) Are the issues among those raised in prior State Party Reports? Request the expertise of specialized agencies, intergovernmental organizations, or non-governmental agencies to provide insight on the progress made and the issue(s) in dispute. Address the case against a backdrop of qualitative and quantitative data from the field. Mention the General Recommendations for informational purposes—if, however, a State has undertaken any acts or obligations indicating compliance therewith, include a reference to them in consideration on the merits (steps 4–5).

SUBSTANTIVE CONSIDERATION ON THE MERITS

4) Employ the general means of interpretation under the VCLT in response to the precise provision(s) that have allegedly been violated. The provision(s) "shall be interpreted in good faith in accordance with the ordinary meaning to be given to the terms of the treaty in their context and in the light of its object and purpose."[95] Context is not limited to the text of the treaty (e.g., its preamble, annexes) but includes (1) agreements related to the conclusion of the treaty or its interpretation, and (2) subsequent State practice suggesting the same.[96]

5) If the general means of interpretation do not resolve the issue, recourse may be had to the supplementary means of interpretation. This includes the travaux and circumstances of its conclusion, when the meaning would otherwise be (1) ambiguous or (2) absurd.

II. Examining the Optional Protocol in practice

Though the Committee may employ a structured approach vis-à-vis the proposed framework or promulgate an innovative method of its own choosing, consistency is vital. Facts will change and circumstances will differ, but the analysis and application of substantive provisions should be universally applicable. Absent some modicum of continuity, the reasoning becomes vitiated and the judgment suspect. When a suit is brought, the Committee must remove its consultative hat and execute its role as an adjudicatory body. Predictability aside, most States have ratified the VCLT (including nine of the ten States implicated in the decisions thus far) and it has also been accorded the status of customary international law.[97] By adopting the proposed framework, the Committee can enhance the participatory nature of States by recognizing their existent legal obligations and also deflect the inevitable criticism that is afforded an exclusive grant of decision-making authority. When deviation occurs, the burden rests with the Committee to demonstrate that the integrity of the process and the viability of the outcome are not compromised. For when international tribunals cease to be courts of principle—and become courts of power—the impetus for States to be reasonable is nothing short of wishful thinking.

As of 2008, the Committee has issued ten decisions under the Protocol in response to a myriad of allegations. A cursory review is hardly revealing. Allegations included four claims against a State's definition of discrimination,[98] two citing employment discrimination,[99] one claim about rights under nationality,[100] and another concerning the scope of legal capacity.[101] All of these counts were summarily dismissed. Of six charges alleging a failure or absence of adequate policies or legal measures, three violations were found.[102] Two out of three suits found a deprivation of basic freedoms.[103] Only one government out of four had allegedly failed to modify social and cultural patterns of behavior to promote non-discrimination.[104] The same government was found to be lacking in its promotion of education of gender relations, and limited access to healthcare services.[105] Finally, two violations were found against a government that inadequately addressed equality of women as relates to marriage and family planning.[106]

Upon closer review, certain trends begin to emerge that suggest that the Protocol may be well-equipped to address women's health issues. Four violations were found based on incidents of domestic violence, which has undeniable physical and mental health consequences. Another suit charged a State with complicity in its failure to remedy a private act of coerced sterilization.

Subpart A reviews each claim under the proposed framework to determine the sufficiency of the Committee's legal analysis commensurate with a sustainable process that heightens the likelihood of State compliance. Subpart B goes on to identify interpretive trends and reiterate the utility of employing the proposed framework.

A. Review of the allegations, violations, and reasons employed

The discussion below explores the reasoning employed in each decision in the context of the legal framework outlined in Part I. Will the aggrieved party suffer irreparable damage requiring interim measures? If the author has not exhausted domestic remedies, has the State provided adequate assurances to warrant a perceived delay in resolving the dispute? Does resolution of the dispute require expertise of specialized agencies, or other relevant organizations? To what extent does the Committee's approach conform to, or deviate from, the general and supplementary means of interpretation? A sound and legally permissible interpretation is dispositive in addressing the efficacy of the Protocol.

1. B.J. v. Germany *(2005), claim preclusion, and the exhaustion of domestic remedies*

In *B.J. v. Germany*, the claimant charged that State laws concerning the consequences of divorce (e.g., equalization of pensions, spousal maintenance) were discriminatory for not recognizing a non-working woman's unremunerated labor.[107] The Committee found that the disputed facts concerning the equalization of assets occurred prior to the Protocol's entry into force and thereby precluded consideration. Also, since national proceedings concerning spousal maintenance and the distribution of accrued gains were still ongoing, the author did not exhaust all domestic remedies prior to submitting her claim.

The decision has cited sound legal principles, but has conflated the distinct doctrines of claim preclusion and exhaustion of domestic remedies. Claim preclusion is a universally recognized legal principle that dismisses suits based on issues arising prior to the Protocol's entry into force. Historically, it was a means to prevent retroactive liability. The requirement to exhaust domestic remedies is equally reasonable since it allows States an opportunity to issue a ruling indicative of current policies and laws, facilitating an accurate international assessment of State positions.

Since the issue of spousal maintenance was not resolved as of the filing, it could not be subsumed within the legitimate preclusion of *de novo* review of asset equalization. Exhaustion is also founded on a sense of complementariness of a State duty to provide remedies and an individual duty to exhaust them.[108] Procedural safeguards assure a satisfactory resolution that is inevitably compromised in the event of separate, ongoing proceedings. While State proceedings were ongoing, was exhaustion appropriately cited for dismissing the suit? Arguably not.

As the dissent noted, the Committee should have addressed whether the State court's consideration of spousal maintenance was unreasonably prolonged or unlikely to bring effective relief.[109] The initial grant of separation maintenance was made in September 1999, including an annual sum of DM 973.[110] The author's husband stopped payment in August 2002 and in April 2004, a court awarded the author a monthly sum of 280 (with retroactive effect to August 2002).[111] The author appealed the decision and there has been no resolution.

The State's failure to give assurances of timely judicial review, coupled with the author's status, may arguably have caused her irreparable harm. The State had not given any indication that the appellate court's delay in reviewing her maintenance award was reasonable. The proceedings had continued for two years after Germany's ratification of the Protocol. Moreover, no facts have been proffered suggesting that the author was, in fact, receiving any monthly sum, however miniscule. Time was not on the author's side. The author, despite being a nurse by training, was 57 years old and presumably incapable of reentering the nursing profession 33 years after becoming a housewife. These facts indicate that the author would likely suffer irreparable harm if she was left without any source of income. In this situation, the procedural hurdle is easily overcome by citing an unreasonably prolonged proceeding. Alternatively, considering the husband's failure to make payments for two years, an appellate review that merely rubber-stamps prior determinations of the author's dues will be unlikely to bring effective relief. The Committee should have employed interim measures by demanding State input to determine a reasonable timeline for appellate review.

Once a judicial ruling has been made, the Committee can interpret the financial determination in light of the substantive treaty obligations. From the author's viewpoint, the existent German laws and policies have not yielded a satisfactory resolution. The extent to which her position is tainted by personal wants relating to her inability to practice nursing is well documented.[112] Yet, her allegations of sex-discrimination may very well be tempered by the fact that she was afforded the opportunity to become a nurse. Moreover, she opted to become a housewife of her own choosing. Personal decisions, regrets notwithstanding, do not implicate a State duty to compensate unrealized professional undertakings. Her specific claim for remuneration as a nurse would likely be dismissed, but the potential inadequacy of State laws concerning spousal maintenance—which disproportionately affects women—should be scrutinized in the context of treaty obligations relating to employment and dissolution of marriage.

The accordance of unemployment benefits and property disposition inevitably arise in the event a housewife becomes divorced. Women are entitled to social security in cases of unemployment, old age, and incapacity to work.[113] Moreover, married woman are entitled to the "same rights and responsibilities during marriage and its dissolution" and in respect of the "disposition of property."[114] The author never raised the issue of unemployment benefits, but did allege a violation of her rights during the dissolution of marriage, and in relation to property disposition.[115] Whether she incurred an injury in fact or would suffer irreparable harm owing to an inadequate accounting of these provisions was unclear. The Committee should not have dismissed the suit.

2., 3., and 4. A.T. v. Hungary *(2005)*, Yildirim v. Austria *(2007)*, *and* Goekce v. Austria *(2007)*; *domestic violence, and identifying precise legal wrongs*

Given the common theme and issues raised in *A.T., Yildirim, and Goekce*, the ensuing discussion will consolidate the cases to avoid redundancy and highlight key differences or similarities, where appropriate. In *A.T. v. Hungary*, the claimant was a victim of repeated acts of domestic violence at the hands of her husband.[116] He threatened to kill and rape their children, and physically abused her as well. Over three years, there were ten documented incidents (as indicated by the issuance of ten medical certificates) that involved severe physical violence.[117] By the time of the communication, the latest incident had necessitated the woman's hospitalization.[118] The author cited violations of the State duty to enact legislation embodying the principle of gender equality, and adopt available measures (legislative, judicial, other) prohibiting discrimination.[119] Additionally, she claimed that the State had failed to modify the social and cultural patterns of conduct to eliminate prejudices against women and practices based on the idea that men are superior to women.[120] Finally, she noted the failure of the government to take steps to eliminate discrimination against women in all matters relating to marriage.[121]

In *The Vienna Intervention Centre against Domestic Violence and the Association for Women's Access to Justice v. Austria* (*Yildirim*), the claimants brought charges on behalf of descendants of the deceased victim, Fatma Yildirim, who had been fatally stabbed by her husband after repeated instances of domestic violence.[122] Repeated police interventions and interim injunctions prohibiting him from returning to the couple's apartment or her workplace ultimately were of no avail.[123] Allegations included the State laws' incompatibility with the treaty's definition of discrimination, the absence of adequate policies and legal protective measures, and a failure to modify social and cultural patterns of behavior.[124] The Committee found that the State had neither adopted laws to secure Yildirim's physical and mental integrity nor responded with due diligence to the threats posed by her husband. A second decision was issued contemporaneously against Austria stemming from repeated instances of domestic violence.[125] The victim, Sahide Goekce, like Fatima Yildirim, found herself a victim to repeated instances of physical abuse suffered at the hands of her husband. Whereas Yildirim was fatally stabbed, Goekce was killed after her husband fatally shot her in front of the couple's two daughters. The man had procured the gun despite a weapons prohibition that had been issued against him.[126] Moreover, the police had been informed that he had the gun in his possession prior to the shooting.[127] As in *Yildirim*, the Committee found that the State had failed to act with due diligence in protecting Goekce.

The Committee began its consideration of the merits in all three cases by citing its General Recommendation No. 19 on violence against women. The recommendation provided that "[t]he definition of discrimination includes gender-based violence," and that "[g]ender-based violence may breach specific provisions of the Convention, regardless of whether those provisions expressly mention violence."[128] In *A.T. v. Hungary*, having established a rule that decried violence as a form of discrimination, the Committee went on to infer that the persistent attacks against the author reflected a failure of the State to afford her due protections. Recognizing the government's prioritization of other types of cases, the Committee issued a sharp rebuke, noting that "Women's right to life and to physical and mental integrity cannot be superseded by other rights, including the right to property and the right to privacy."[129] In the absence of specific legislation, and particularly exclusionary orders, the State was held in violation of its obligations to provide laws and take adequate measures to combat domestic violence.[130]

The Committee's treatment of allegations concerning social and cultural behavioral modification and non-discrimination in marital relations also fell back on its general recommendations. Here, it buttressed the recommendation on violence against women with a subsequent recommendation on equality in marriage.[131] Noting that violence was associated with "traditional attitudes by which women are regarded as subordinate to men," the Committee pointed to "facts of the communication [that] reveal[ed] aspects of the relationships . . . recognized vis-à-vis the country as a whole."[132] Specifically, it noted how the author "felt threatened" by her husband for over four years, had "been battered" by him, and was unsuccessful, in practice and as a matter of law, to bar him from her residence.[133] Moreover, there were no shelters available for her and her children. As a whole, these facts were sufficient to satisfy a lack of legal safeguards to protect the author, and hold the State accountable for failing to eliminate discrimination in matters relating to equality in marriage.

The Committee's analyses were promising insofar as they invoked a rule proceeded by analyses with respect to the facts and issues at hand. The reasoning, however, was lacking in its failure to explain how violence against women amounted to sex-based discrimination. Even presuming that the general recommendation is legally binding (which it is not), simply equating violence with discrimination will not suffice to recreate the definition of "discrimination" enunciated within the treaty. Also, the treaty makes no mention of a State duty to secure physical or mental integrity. While the right to life is arguably paramount and trumps competing rights to property and privacy, these are all civil and political rights that cannot be invoked in lieu of express State duties. At best, they reinforce the argument. Otherwise, they become distractions and undermine the thrust of the analysis.

Given the overwhelming evidence of repeated exposure to physical and mental abuse, the issue of irreparable harm was moot. The author had suffered greatly and had offered sufficient medical documentation attesting to her plight. The available avenues of redress are aptly characterized as deficient since the Committee had apparently requested for interim measures, but to no avail.[134] That the ultimate decision would find in the author's favor was not surprising, if not expected. The legality of the outcome, however, rests on whether violence against the author—as a woman—could be equated with sex-based discrimination. Consideration on the merits thus requires a thorough interpretation of the clause under scrutiny.

Domestic violence occupies a unique category of claims arising under sex-based discrimination. On its face, violence is usually associated with torts or crimes that involve, *stricto sensu*, acts intended to impart physical harm and bodily injury. As applied to women, however, violence can take on physical, psychological, and social manifestations. Violence may affect sexual and reproductive health, and may be associated with exploitation of a relationship throughout the lifespan (e.g., child abuse and first sexual encounter, intimate partner violence). Gender-based violence thereby implicates sex-based discrimination by targeting women on account of a power deficit within an existing relationship. Lacking the means to physically protect herself or extricate herself from a relationship (e.g., owing to financial dependency), a woman often endures the physical abuse, along with its indeterminate mental health consequences.

Since CEDAW is concerned with eliminating sex-based discrimination, domestic violence can be addressed in the context of exploitation within relationships. The Committee should have cited from an abundance of literature or expert testimony that has found that most violence against women is relationship-based and culturally institutionalized.[135] In doing so, the government should be held accountable for failing to take affirmative steps to inhibit exploitation, which may result in severe physical or mental abuse. Rectifying the power imbalance between the sexes requires substantive and procedural safeguards. A specific provision that affords protection includes a government mandate to eliminate practices based on the idea of the superiority of (males) or inferiority of (women) either of the sexes.[136] Additionally, measures entailing elimination of discrimination in all matters relating to marriage conceivably includes exploitation of a wife by her husband.[137] Procedural protections may include restraining or protection orders pursuant to the enactment of legislative or judicial avenues of redress.[138] Invoking any of these provisions, however, requires an actual act or instance of violence.

As a matter of interpretation, using physical violence as a proxy to cite sex-based discrimination is more persuasive if the violations stem from negative rather than positive rights to equality. Interpreting the treaty in the context of actual instances of violence illustrates the setbacks of using a purely positive-rights approach to enforce substantive obligations. Citing a broad provision requiring a State to ensure equality in marital relations does not automatically align State acts or omissions with the object and purpose of the provision. The "equality in marriage" clause, though not exclusive, does list eight particular categories of marital rights and responsibilities.[139] Neither the author nor the State had tied the violence to any of the rights or responsibilities espoused therein—and rightly so, because none of the provisions contemplate aggressive acts within the marriage. Nonetheless, a violation begins with an injury in fact. The State duty is not to abstractly promote equality within the marriage, but to take concrete steps in response to abuse that indicates exploitation; as well as take such measures, through public education and other programs, to further its ongoing mission to curtail violence against women.

While States are obligated to promote gender-equality, there are subtle underpinnings concerning reasonable expectations that obfuscate State accountability. The negative right of a woman to be secure in her person from her husband's violent attacks is distinguishable from a positive right to physical well-being. The affirmative acts of a State are invariably deemed deficient in enforcing a positive right when any individual is injured. Here, a comprehensive public program against domestic violence was instituted, though ineffective in protecting the author. Practical considerations also abound. In some instances, an isolated incident of violence may indeed be indicative of an exploitative relationship. Still, expecting the government to police the marital relationship around the clock is simply incompatible with reasonable expectations of privacy and impractical in practice. The State must therefore issue prompt responses to instances when a woman's security is threatened and, based on the severity and circumstances, monitor the relationship in question to determine whether aggressive remedial measures are warranted (e.g., detention, arrest, or counseling and rehabilitation).

CEDAW violations stem from a negative right to be free from exploitation, and the concomitant positive duty on the part of State government to protect its citizens. In *Yildirim*, the State should have detained the husband. Persistent attacks, coupled with her adamant pleas, indicate that the violence was not an isolated incident. Similarly, in *Goekce*, the State did not arrest the assailant despite a three-year period of continuing attacks upon the author. Moreover, it failed to act upon information concerning the husband's procurement of a gun, which would have been reasonable considering the weapons ban and his history of violent behavior. The outcomes in each suit were sound, but the reasoning neither parsed the legal obligations nor the subtle underpinnings stemming from the express language of the treaty.

5. Kayhan v. Turkey *(2006), absence of sex-based discrimination, and exhaustion*

In *Kayhan v. Turkey*, the claimant was a Muslim woman who was dismissed from her teaching position for failing to observe a dress code that barred her from wearing a headscarf.[140] She brought suit alleging employment discrimination, particularly her right to work and avail herself of the same opportunities as others, including attendant benefits of job promotion, security, pension and equal treatment.[141] The communication was dismissed for failure to exhaust all domestic remedies.

On its face, the complaint raises the scepter of irreparable harm. In Turkey, women are characteristically undereducated, and underemployed. During the 1990s, over 30 percent of Turkish women, aged 15 and over, were illiterate compared to only 10 percent of Turkish men within the same age group.[142] When woman are employed, they are usually confined to menial tasks. In 1996, 73.8 percent of women were employed in agriculture and 88.3 percent of them were unpaid family workers with no social security.[143] Between 1995 and 2002, the number of female housewives had increased from 10 million to 12 million, respectively.[144] The applicant was an exemplary woman for overcoming the social hurdles to pursue her education and become a teacher. After being dismissed, she incurred lost wages; deductions directed towards her pension; her salary and income; an education grant; and her health insurance.[145] Furthermore, she cannot seek recourse in private employment as a teacher because of the disciplinary taint on her professional record. The Committee's decision was issued in January 2006, that is, six years after the author's dismissal. In addition to the years of lost remuneration and attendant benefits mentioned above, the only viable option for future earnings is most likely in menial tasks ill-suited to the author's professional qualifications. The criteria for irreparable harm were arguably met on the date of filing (2003). The Committee should have invoked interim measures to ensure her opportunity to work as a teacher (or in an equivalent capacity) until a full accounting of her financial predicament could be determined, and due consideration given the merits of her suit.

Exhaustion was inappropriately applied in the case at bar. In particular, the Committee dismissed the suit for failure to raise charges of sex-based discrimination in the domestic tribunals. Since the author "should have put forward arguments that raised the matter of discrimination based on sex in substance . . . before submitting a communication to the Committee[,] . . . it conclude[d] that domestic remedies had not been exhausted."[146] The argument is hardly persuasive. Had the Committee taken the time to hone in on the facts and circumstances, there are ample grounds for finding potential sex-based discrimination. The underlying issue here is whether a presumably neutral government-sponsored dress code that burdens a *Muslim* woman constitutes sex-based discrimination. The State had taken the position that the dress code is universally applicable and did not target particular groups based on their sex or religious proclivities.

If the author can demonstrate that precluding her religious expression was inextricably linked to her status as a woman, she has a cause of action under the treaty. Though the treaty expressly prohibits discrimination in the field of employment, an equivalent right is also enshrined in domestic legislation. The Turkish Constitution provides that "Every Turk has the right to enter the public service" and that "[n]o criteria *other than the qualifications for the office concerned* shall be taken into consideration for recruitment into public service."[147] The State has also expressly recognized the relevance of this Constitutional provision in securing every Turkish woman's right to work and avail herself of employment opportunities under the treaty.[148] In March 2003, Turkey amended its Labor Code to protect employees against all forms of discrimination, including sex and religion.[149] Moreover, the State expressly noted that "[p]ublic servants are also protected by law from pay differentials on the basis of sex . . . beliefs, religion and sect."[150] When national labor laws afford protections on the basis of sex and religious beliefs, either may serve as legitimate grounds for a treaty violation. Here, the State discriminated against the author on account of either her sex, religion, or both. But as far as the author was concerned, her preclusion was based on her status as a *Muslim woman*; her religious beliefs were inseparable from her gender-identity. The Committee simply disregarded the inextricable linkage between her sex and religion. All the more striking was its deference to a potentially discriminatory State code that irrefutably suppressed her right to work. Potential negative interference on account of the author's sex, alongside the State's positive neglect to respect her right to work, are sufficient grounds to further scrutinize the case on its merits.

The viability of the claim ultimately turns on whether the linkage between sex and religion is dispositive to bring the suit under CEDAW rather than, say, the ICCPR. On its face, the dress code is sex-neutral; but its impact may disproportionately affect most (if not all) women, who incidentally happen to be Muslims. Though Turkey is a secular state, 99 percent of its population is Muslim.

The case raises the issue of whether a generally applicable rule that disproportionately impacts women, or particular women, on the basis of their religious beliefs constitutes sex-based discrimination. Here, the demography of the female population, the State's position on Islam as indicated in its treatment of the author, and the State's complicity in prior years, together weave a mosaic of sex- and religious-based discrimination that is difficult to disentangle.

When 99 percent of the population is Muslim, a dress code that precludes women from expressing orthodox Islamic beliefs effectively discriminates on the basis of sex. In practice, only women are affected by the restrictions. It is highly unlikely that the State was unaware of the inevitable burden the code would pose on female citizens that wear the headscarf.

Even if the majority of Turkish Muslim women are non-practicing, or do not adhere to orthodox beliefs, the dress code was clearly a pretext for discriminating against a particular devout Muslim woman. By associating her religious expression with furthering "ideological and political objectives," the State essentially implied that her practice of Islam would not be recognized as a religion, but as a political viewpoint and ideology that was incompatible with free expression in the public workplace. In doing so, it compelled her to either give up her sex-based religious identity (i.e., as a Muslim woman), or be fired.

The State's complicity also raises the issue of whether the sudden about-face was used to target the author by exploiting her status as a Muslim woman. As such, the basis for sex-discrimination is all the more apparent. Her religious attire had not disqualified her from being recruited as a public servant. Moreover, she wore the headscarf for five years without incident. Upon transfer to another State school, she was subjected to disciplinary proceedings for failure to remove it. By merely wearing her headscarf, she had somehow disturbed the "peace, quiet, work, and harmony of the institution with her ideological and political objectives."[151] Upon these premises, the religious exception would not apply—a tenuous proposition, to say the least. The dress code was nothing more than a pretext to discriminate against the author by exploiting her status as a devout Muslim woman.

The State's disparaging characterization of Islam begs the question of whether the woman was in fact targeted on the basis of her sex *and* religious views, which are inseparable charges in this particular instance. The proffered interpretation is not intended to belittle the value of dress codes or suggest that they are never useful. In many instances, for example military training, uniformity in appearance is deemed an indispensable component of the individual's experience in a collective enterprise. The burden of proof, however, is significantly higher for a public educational institution, which should be open to the diversity that often makes up the body politic. Certain measures are necessary to promote the health and safety of the school environment. Rules that prohibit carrying firearms or other objects that pose a danger to oneself or others are certainly reasonable in the scope of their restrictions. Furthermore, the State has stated that individuals should not be precluded from educational or employment opportunities on the basis of religion. Given the plethora of facts and circumstances creating an inseparable claim on the basis of her sex *and* religion, there is a rebuttable presumption that the State has violated its treaty obligations. The hasty dismissal on the grounds of exhaustion was a futile exercise in legal formalities.

6. A.S. v. Hungary *(2006), coerced sterilization, and informed consent*

In *A.S. v. Hungary*, the author was an alleged victim of coerced sterilization.[152] She was a mother of three children who was pregnant at the time of the incident. After going into labor, her amniotic fluid broke and she was rushed to a hospital. She was bleeding heavily and the duration of the trip lasted one hour. When she finally arrived, the attending physician found that the fetus had died en route, and informed her that he needed to perform a cesarean-section to remove the dead fetus. The medical records indicated that she was dizzy on arrival, bleeding heavily, and in a state of shock.[153] While she was on the operating table, she was asked to sign a consent form for the c-section and a barely legible note that requested her sterilization—with the term "sterilization" written in Latin rather than Hungarian, which is the colloquial language. Seventeen minutes later, the c-section was completed and the fallopian tubes were tied (preventing further impregnation).

The author was unaware of what had transpired. Before leaving, she asked the doctor when she could have another baby. After realizing her plight, she fell into depression, for which she and her partner later received medical treatment. As a devout Catholic, her religious beliefs prohibited contraception of any kind. A second-instance court found that since the author could still conceive by artificial insemination, her reproductive capacity was not entirely eradicated (and without lasting effect). The subsequent complaint before the Committee alleged three violations stemming from a failure to ensure access to educational information and advice on family planning, access to health-care services, and secure her right to freely decide on the number and spacing of children.[154] Given the gravity of the procedure, there was no issue of avoiding irreparable harm; the damage was done. All domestic remedies were also exhausted. The sole issue for the Committee was whether the alleged violations were by and large met by a failure to received informed consent for the sterilization. Upon review, it found violations of every charge.

By its own admission, the Committee has alluded to expert opinions on informed consent for guidance that is presumably absent within the express language of the treaty. It expressly recommended the State to bring its legislation in conformity with international human rights and medical standards, including the Convention of the Council of Europe on Human Rights and Biomedicine ("the Oviedo Convention") and WHO guidelines.[155] At least one NGO had also contributed to the deliberations. An attorney for the organization that brought the suit on behalf of the author observed that "although U.N. Committees do not formally accept third-party submissions, an *amicus brief* was prepared by the New York-based Center for Reproductive Rights on informed consent standards, *which was very well received by the Committee.*"[156] Per its Rules, the Committee may not necessarily *receive* unsolicited third-party submissions, but is more than willing to *request* (and thus receive) them should the occasion so require. What is puzzling in this instance is the lack of reference to the Oviedo Convention, WHO guidelines, or insights submitted by the Center for Reproductive Rights, within the body of the analysis. Though non-binding in their effect, cross-reference to the international instruments could, at the very least, clarify any ambiguities within the text. Moreover, advising a State to comport with such instruments without clarifying how they relate to the treaty obligations reveals gaps in bringing any meaningful analysis to the actual provisions in dispute. At the very least, indicating whether a State was a party to another relevant treaty, or had undertaken particular guidelines, would lend credence to their precise legal relevance.

Each of the treaty's informational and service imperatives does not necessarily flow from the moral and legal foundations of informed consent. Whereas the law is primarily concerned with liability of healthcare professionals, moral theory prioritizes respect for patient autonomy and provider beneficence.[157] The moral and legal principles are often interwoven and demand a careful teasing to enunciate the precise wrongs committed. Legal remedies, however, cannot be imposed for mere want of moral clarity.

The Committee's treatment of the provision on educational information began with a reference to its General Recommendation 21, which broadly covers equality in marriage and family relations, and specifically repudiates non-disclosure of information that would inhibit "informed decision-making."[158] Here, the provision protected a right "to specific information on sterilization and alternative procedures for family planning . . ."[159] Considering the author's state of health and level of stress, she was found to be under "the most inappropriate conditions" to *receive* any counseling.[160] The Committee thus held the State, through the hospital personnel, in violation of providing educational information and advice on family planning.

Aside from inappropriately beginning its analysis with a reference to the general recommendation, the Committee failed to adequately interpret the provision to illustrate the depth of the violation. The object and purpose of the text is to eliminate discrimination to ensure equal "access to specific educational information . . . and advice on family planning."[161] Is educational information meant to foster shared decision-making among partners, or simply bolster separate (but equal) disclosure requirements for men and women in their individual capacities? If an individual woman is granted decision-making status on par with a man, the moral underpinnings of the clause are arguably strengthened.

By examining the context of the provision, the interpretation in favor of the individual victim is bolstered, consistent with the object and purpose of the provision.

Since the prefatory language of the article creates a distinct identity for an individual man and woman, the exclusion of any reference to a partnership (marital or otherwise) within the specific clause arguably envisioned a provider-patient rather than a provider-couple relationship. The legal imperative to disclose information may remain unaffected, but the moral imperative rooted in patient autonomy is strengthened.

The travaux also supports this patient-centered interpretation firmly rooted in moral theory. During the initial drafting of the text, there was no consensus as to purpose of the educational information. Sweden, for example, did not want to separately link women and family planning education "since this should be a shared responsibility" between men and women.[162] Similarly, the International Federation of University Women (IFUW) insisted that whatever information was provided should "respect the moral and personal attitudes of each *married couple*."[163] These suggestions were coined to strengthen the binary function of male and female partners or, per the IFUW proposition, spouses. By contrast, Austria remarked that access should be possible for both sexes.[164] This view was supported by New Zealand's position, which provided that men as well as women required educational information.[165] Consequently, the Austrian and New Zealand positions reduced the binary nature of the relationship to its constitutive parts by moving away from a provider-couple to a provider-patient structure.

The second provision ensuring that all women have "appropriate services in connection with pregnancy" also requires further scrutiny.[166] Is the grant of "appropriate" services a reference to the types of services to be provided, or a standard of care? The issue revolves around whether the term "appropriate" inherently mandates informed consent, or simply alludes to the general availability of services. Proponents may argue that whether a service is appropriate turns on whether a patient wants it in the first place; inevitably requiring consent and, *a priori*, disclosure on the part of the provider. Opponents may counter this by focusing on the object and purpose of the provision, which is not to gauge patient compliance, but ensure the availability of particular services related to specific purposes, for example pregnancy, confinement and the pre-natal period. Moreover, the impetus for availability is strengthened by the context of the words since the subsequent half of the clause provides the need to make available services to those who cannot afford it, that is "granting free services where necessary."[167] Then again, availability aside, proponents may counter that informed consent and service availability are not mutually exclusive.

If a cause of action based on informed consent necessarily requires an implicit interpretation of the text, the Committee botched the analysis from the outset. By relying on its General Recommendation 24 (entitled "Women and health"), the Committee explained that "[a]cceptable services are those that are delivered in a way that ensures that a woman gives her fully informed consent . . ."[168] The text, however, provides for "appropriate," not "acceptable," services. Moreover, the terms are not interchangeable. An acceptable service requires acceptance on the part of someone other than the provider, be it a patient or a medical board. By contrast, an appropriate service may, as indicated above, simply refer to the types of services to be made available.

Since the general interpretation leaves an ambiguous meaning, recourse may be had to the travaux. The State Parties apparently did not dwell indefinitely on the subtle problems the provision may pose. Most prior drafts made no mention of a separate article on eliminating discrimination in the field of healthcare.[169] When a provision was finally proffered, the clause required women to "[r]eceive adequate medical and health facilities, including family planning advice and services."[170] The government of India suggested rephrasing the term to ensure that women "[h]ave access to adequate health care facilities, including information, counse[l]ing and services in family planning . . ."[171] Notably, the initial provision distinguished between "advice" and "services." Also, all references to "advice," "information," and "counse[l]ing," were left out of the final text. Member States were reluctant to impose a consultative duty on States in relation to family planning. The only consensus was in making certain services available.

The provision on access to health services is not a viable basis for an informed consent action. Though the physician undoubtedly violated a fiduciary duty to respect the bodily integrity of the patient, the dispositive issue was whether the provision creates a duty to provide the patient with information. It does not. The Committee's reiteration of facts (e.g., 17-minute timeframe, the author's mental and physical status, etc.)[172] was irrelevant as to whether the provision—as a matter of law—recognized an informed consent action. The only way around this interpretation is to recognize an implicit meaning that stems from a narrow reading of the term "appropriate." This rests on a proposition that all appropriate services require consent and ignores the context of the term within the provision, and the drafting history. At the very least, the Committee should have expressly noted its evolutive interpretation in the interests of justice (or some equivalent legal principle) to validate its conclusion.

While the third clause provides a firm basis to rest an informed consent action, it raises unique issues owing to the inherent relations between spouses or family members. It mandates non-discrimination in the context of marriage and family relations to ensure the "same rights to decide freely on the number and spacing of their children and to have access to the information, education, and means to enable them to exercise these rights."[173] The discussion has thus far focused on individual rights, and the purpose of the clause is seemingly no different. The provision is meant to ensure that women have an equal role in the decision-making process in matters related to the number and spacing of their children. Since the text contemplates partnerships (marital or otherwise) with regard to "their" children, as opposed to "her" children, must consent be procured by both partners prior to rendering a service? Specifically, does the provision create a third-party cause of action in the partner for either not receiving any information, or being excluded from the decision-making process?

While a third party may theoretically bring a suit, a reasonable interpretation will find that a woman's right will not be constrained in matters relating to her body. A husband could bring a cause of action against the State for being excluded from the decision-making process. As a procedural matter, the Protocol does not restrict claims to women. A communication may be submitted by or on behalf of "individuals or groups of individuals. . . . claiming to be victims of a violation of any of the rights set forth in the Convention."[174] In the event that the woman had already been excluded, the argument holds some weight insofar as a moral prerogative has been violated. The State may argue, however, that the husband has not suffered an actual injury in fact. (In all likelihood, his claim would be dismissed for a lack of standing). However, in the event that the woman *had* authorized the sterilization, would the husband's want of information and failure to be a participant in the decision-making trump his wife's unilateral decision? Probably not.

While the provision does not expressly create exclusive rights or protections in the individual woman, the context arguably fills any fleeting gaps. In some cultures, women do not hold much negotiating power when it comes to sexual relations and even the use of contraceptives. The phrase "marriage *and* family relations" in the prefatory passage suggests that the sense of equality furthered by the clause is not meant to merely enhance female equality—only to subsequently constrain it to the subjective whims of a male partner. In fact, by coining the phrase marriage *and* family relations, the text contemplates an imbalance in power dynamics within the sexual relationship between the man and woman; as well as the social relationship between the woman and other family members (e.g., a mother-in-law, father-in-law, sister-in-law, etc.). The provision is meant to protect the woman's autonomy in matters affecting her reproductive health. By imposing explicit informational and educational requirements, the third clause is, like the first clause, a reliable provision to base an informed consent action.

The Committee found that compulsory sterilization was a form of violence against women (per its General Recommendation 19), and thereby constituted a violation of the author's right to freely decide on the number and spacing of her children. Since the provider substituted his judgment for that of the woman, the violation of the provision is self-evident. The characterization of coercive sterilization as a form of violence does not alter the cause of action under the relevant provision. To be sure, the third clause is not, in its plainest sense, a check on violence against women. The Committee explained that "[t]he sterilization surgery was performed on the author without her full consent and must be considered to have permanently deprived her of her natural reproductive capacity."[175] The analysis overlooks a vital element of the provision: service. The State must provide "information" and "education," as well as the "means" for women to effectuate their decisions.[176] In practice, the clause is overwhelmingly patient-centered and makes the State, through its hospital personnel, agents of the woman in exercising her right to reproductive health and well-being. The Committee essentially downplayed the predominantly moral foundations that make the treaty exemplary for countries, like Hungary, that dismiss the patient entirely from the decision-making process.

7. Nguyen v. the Netherlands *(2006), maternity benefits, and social considerations*

In *Nguyen v. the Netherlands*, the claimant alleged that State policies that did not extend full compensation for maternity benefits constituted sex-based discrimination.[177]

At issue is whether an anti-accumulation clause is compatible with the treaty obligation to afford "maternity leave with pay."[178] The clause prohibits individuals with multiple streams of income from receiving more than a maximum specific amount. Some individuals, like the author, are capable of retaining both salaried and unsalaried employment. The law provides that an unsalaried employee shall receive benefits under the "Invalidity Insurance Act" or *Wet arbeidsongeschiktheidsverzekering zelfstandigen* (WAZ), whereas a salaried employee shall be covered under the "Sickness Benefits Act" or *Ziektewet* (ZW). A woman who retains both types of employment shall only be entitled to salaried benefits under the ZA unless she would receive higher benefits under the WAZ—in which case she would be afforded the difference thereon. The author claims that she is entitled to the maximum benefits afforded under *each* separate act.

Having recognized exhaustion, the Committee found that the treaty does not require "full pay" or "full compensation" for loss of income and thereby leaves to States a margin of discretion to devise a system of maternity leave benefits to fulfill Convention requirements.[179] Considering that both salaried and unsalaried women were entitled to maternity benefits, the State retained the discretion to declare a specific maximum amount (irrespective of a woman's income). Though the Committee accurately cites the treaty obligation, it does not resolve the issue of whether the victim was discriminated against owing to her status as both a salaried and unsalaried employee. If she had contributed to both schemes, and was only entitled to benefits under the salaried scheme, it is plausible that she was discriminated against by paying more than another salaried woman in an equivalent income bracket.

The differences in the State-sponsored risk-reward schemes reveal the gaps in the author's claim. The compulsory ZW scheme was meant to provide maternity leave and benefits for *men and women* and was calculated based on salary. Since higher-earning individuals would be entitled to greater amounts of money, their deductions in a given year would be greater. The ZW scheme was also open to unsalaried workers but the majority did not enroll because of cost, or were unaware of its availability.[180] The compulsory WAZ scheme was then enacted to provide insurance to unsalaried women. Unlike the ZW scheme, the WAZ contributions came not from the individual woman, but her employer, and were calculated based on the profits earned. Still, if a business ran at a loss in a given year, the State would still have to provide coverage for the unsalaried woman.

Considering the claim in the context of State responsibility, the analysis turns on whether the State required an unsalaried worker to forego the opportunity cost of receiving like benefits under a salaried bracket. Simply put, was the author unduly burdened by contributing more than she would have been expected to if she was only a salaried employee? No. The State not only assumed the burden that was initially borne by her employer, but also employed a risk-adjustment model that lessened her employer's contribution as a function of the author's salary. One could argue that the State actually assumed a higher burden by lessening her employer's contributions. Of course, the author would claim that the State was only assuming what she was, in fact, providing through higher salary deductions. Regardless, as an unsalaried employee, the author was not being unduly burdened as a matter of law since the maximum benefits she would retain remained unchanged.

The Committee did not err in finding for the State, but should have assuaged the legitimate concerns raised in the dissenting opinion. The dissent questioned whether the number of working hours in both categories of work may equal or even go beyond the hours of a full-time salaried female employee.[181] This statement presumes that benefits are intrinsically tied to a measurable standard, such as hours worked. They're not. Even if the author was working more hours because she held two jobs, her contribution is only based on her salaried position; the State and her employer assume the remainder unless the business makes no profit—in which case, the States assumes the risk entirely. The risk adjustment supposedly takes her dual status into account and lessens her employer's burden. The benefits do not reflect an inherent value attached to employment type.

The suggestion that women earning income from salaried and unsalaried sources should be entitled to more benefits than a woman who holds a single job is unpersuasive. Let us assume that the contribution made by an employer is lessened by a quarter of a percent (.25 percent) for every $1,000 in increased salary. (We shall also assume a minimum base salary of $10,000 so that no deductions will be made below that amount.) Let us also assume that her unsalaried employer is making $1,000 in annual profits and, for purposes of simplicity, keep it constant. A woman's salaried deductions and unsalaried contributions would look something like the results in Table 2.1.

In this simplistic model, it should become apparent that the salaried deduction begins to look more and more like the net loss in total income (column 5). Assume that maternity benefits are based on (1) a fixed percentage of salaried income (say, 75 percent) for salaried employees, and (2) a fixed rate of $7,450 annually for unsalaried workers plus a fixed percentage of employer contributions for that given year (say, 100 percent). That way, a person who was only salaried and making a base pay of $10,000 would be in the same position as an unsalaried worker who did not have a salaried stream of income—both would be entitled to $7,500 in the same year. (Assume the State would make up the $50 difference for an unsalaried employer whose business made no profits.) Now, under normal circumstances, a salaried employee making $20,000 would be entitled to $15,000. If she also held an unsalaried position, and her employer made $1,000 in profits during the year, she would only be entitled to $7,450 plus $1,000 or $8,450 under the WAZ scheme. Since she would receive almost double the amount of money under the ZW scheme, the State would grant her $15,000. Consider, though, if the unsalaried employer made a profit of $500,000. Under our hypothetical, the contribution would be $25,000 under the WAZ. The author would then be entitled to $7,450 plus $25,000 or $34,450. Under the current law, she would receive $15,000 under the ZW scheme and an additional $24,450 under the WAZ scheme ($34,450 less $15,000) for a total of $34,450. In the suit, the author is simply claiming that she should be entitled to benefits under both schemes no matter what deductions or contributions were made. In the first example above, she is claiming $15,000

Table 2.1 Deductions and contributions under a model equivalence principle

Salary	Salaried Deduction	Unsalaried Profits	Unsalaried Contributions	Income Loss (deduction + contribution)
$10,000	$100	$1,000	$50	$150
$12,000	$120	$1,000	$45	$165
$14,000	$140	$1,000	$40	$180
$16,000	$160	$1,000	$35	$195
$18,000	$180	$1,000	$30	$210
$20,000	$200	$1,000	$25	$225

in addition to the $8,450 for a total of $24,450; in the second, she wants $34,450 plus $15,000 for a total of $49,450. Using the author's logic, an individual who splits her time between salaried and unsalaried jobs should receive more benefits than someone who only has one job—a baseless proposition, to say the least. The author has failed to demonstrate how a facially neutral program compromises the benefits that she would otherwise be entitled to. The dissent's supposition is not persuasive to grant the claimant dual compensation. The provision of a system that affords protections regardless of an employer's profit or loss is consistent with the provision of compensation under the treaty. By assuming the risk of covering unsalaried employees, even if businesses run at a loss, the State has indicated its willingness to fulfill its treaty obligations without qualification. A discriminatory charge must provide further details to warrant further scrutiny. Deference should not have been granted, however, without explaining how the equivalence principle illustrates the State's commitment to equality by ensuring that no woman will be worse off—that is, discriminated against—because she has only one stream of income.

8. Muñoz v. Spain *(2007), titles of nobility, and material consequences*

In *Muñoz-Vargas v. Spain,* the claimant alleged that the State's rules of succession to titles of nobility gave men primacy over women and thereby constituted sex-based discrimination under the treaty.[182] Under the law in effect at the time of issuance (1978), the first-born child inherited a title unless the first-born was a girl, in which case she only received the title if she had no younger brothers. Although the author was the first-born child, she had a younger brother at the time of her father's death and the date of issuance by royal decree. But for the national inheritance law, the woman would have been deemed a "Countess."[183] She specifically cited violations of a State duty to establish legal protections against any act of discrimination[184] and to modify or abolish existing laws which constitute discrimination against women.[185] The inheritance law was eventually modified in 2006 to give equal rights of succession to men and women.[186] The Committee dismissed the allegations because they were time-barred and not of a continuous nature.

Given the vast disagreements over the material facts and issues presented by the majority, concurring, and dissenting opinions, the suit demonstrates how adhering to process can swiftly resolve a seemingly complex dispute without resorting to varied interpretive whims. Since there was no indication of irreparable harm or exhaustion, a brief review of the substantive points of each opinion is provided, followed by a critical analysis.

The majority opinion, consisting of 14 Committee members, found that the succession and the effect upon the author were completed on the date of issue (October 3, 1978), which was prior to adoption of the Convention and the Protocol. The members suggested that the legal effect inhered in the issuance itself and "as such was not of a continuous nature," effectively precluding the author from staking a contemporary claim.[187] The concurring opinion was comprised of eight members who simply posited that titles of nobility do not create legally enforceable rights under the treaty. It characterized such titles as "purely symbolic and honorific [in] nature, devoid of any legal or material effect." [188] Consequently, the communication was deemed "incompatible with the provisions of the Convention," and dismissed per this procedural safeguard.[189] The dissenting opinion was filed by a single Committee member who vigorously argued that differential treatment should neither be tolerated nor condoned on the basis of culture and history.[190] This moral pronouncement was buttressed by a provision which recognized "the negative effects of conduct based on culture, custom, tradition, and the ascription of stereotypical roles that entrench the inferiority of women."[191] She reiterated that the "immediate material consequence of such patterns of behavior does not have to be demonstrated."[192] The treaty, she insisted, was to go "beyond the obvious consequences of discriminatory acts," that is— the legal effects—and recognize "the dangers of ideology and norms that underpin such acts."[193] She expressly dismisses the concurring opinion by citing the textual reading of Article 1 (which defines discrimination) and found the allegations to be consistent with the "intent and spirit of the Convention."[194] The member also disagreed with the majority opinion and found that the violation was continuous in nature because the domestic court dismissals of her suit "affirmed male primacy in the order of succession to titles of nobility."[195] Since the legislation had been amended in recent years, the member concluded by noting that prior discrimination could not justify reversing the royal decree. It was hoped that "the author will feel vindicated that she was indeed discriminated against."[196]

While the dissent was correct in pointing out a potential violation of a State duty to modify cultural patterns, the author's failure to invoke this provision effectively precluded its consideration. On that note, it is unclear why an allegation of inadequate legal protections was raised when the law was allegedly discriminatory on its face. Nonetheless, the dispositive issue concerns whether the author's discriminatory treatment was indicative of a State failure to modify or abolish a discriminatory law, custom, or practice.

The law was unambiguously discriminatory in favoring male successors and inconsistent with the treaty obligations. It provided that first-born women could only succeed to a title of nobility if they had no male siblings. In other words, a woman could lose her right to succession on the basis of her sex. The same exception did not apply for men. The concurring opinion attempts to trivialize the dispute by pointing to the non-material consequences. There was, it asserted, no legally cognizable benefit that could be ascribed to such titles. The titles, however, are granted pursuant to existing *laws*. The government of Spain, by its own admission, noted the enactment of "*legislation* pertaining to succession to titles of nobility" in its submission on admissibility.[197] Even if the title had no legal effect, the State's duty remains unaffected. The treaty expressly mandates a State to modify or abolish laws,

"customs and practices" which constitute discrimination against women.
. . ."[198] As for the majority opinion, its characterization of the violation as
non-continuous is unpersuasive. The title's vestment as of a particular time
did not disqualify its continuous nature. The "continuing" effect emanates
from its very nature as a social—as opposed to a tangible—construct. The
author had proffered ample evidence that warranted a finding of discrimination against her. The law furthered a practice or custom that discriminated
against women on account of their sex. Consequently, the majority and
concurring opinions issued unsound analyses that were not based on the
nature and scope of the treaty. The dissenting opinion, moreover, could have
been strengthened by refusing to concede any ground on the textual basis of
the claim; and keeping its analysis focused on the State mandate to modify
discriminatory customs, legislation, or practices.

9. N.S.F. v. U.K. and Northern Ireland *(2007), violence, asylum, and exhaustion*

The author was a Pakistani national that fled to the U.K. along with her two
children to escape from her ex-husband who had allegedly threatened to kill
her.[199] In February 2003, a petition seeking asylum was rejected by the
Immigration and Nationality Directorate of the Home Office. Following
subsequent appeals, the matter was submitted to the High Court of Justice,
which affirmed the decision and made it final. On January 4, 2005, she
subsequently filed for "discretionary leave" to remain in the U.K. on
humanitarian grounds with the Home Office. A year and a half later, in May
2006, the Home Office refused her request and directed her to leave the U.K.
without delay; otherwise, it "would take steps to ensure her removal to
Pakistan."[200] In her complaint before the Committee, the author did not allege
any specific violations under the treaty. It decided that the author had failed
to "avail herself of the possibility of seeking permission to apply for a judicial
review by the High Court of the refusal to grant her discretionary leave to
remain in the country on humanitarian grounds."[201] Also, the author had never
alleged sex-discrimination in her complaint before the Home Office, which
the State Party considered "relevant for consideration by the Home Office
when again considering the author's case . . ."[202] The Committee therefore
declare the communication admissible for failure to exhaust domestic remedies.

The Committee's analysis conflated the responsibility of the State with that
of the author's native land. Pakistan, not the U.K., owes the author a duty
of care pursuant to the treaty obligations. Moreover, the issue of exhaustion
was arguably misplaced. Had the author been in Pakistan, the Committee
should consider imposing interim measures to prevent irreparable harm. The
author was a victim of marital rape and subjected to persistent abuse and
harassment. She later filed for divorce and after being threatened by her ex-
husband, fled her native land for fear of her own safety and that of her
children. These facts indicate that the author's life may be in jeopardy.

If the U.K. review process is used as a marker, it is wholly inadequate to prevent an imminent threat to the woman and her children. Over three years had passed since her initial filing for asylum, and her appeals were considered by multiple review boards and tribunals. In fact, the High Court had heard her case twice—and each time, rejected her pleas. Against this backdrop, submitting another appeal for judicial review would be unlikely to bring effective relief. This determination notwithstanding, the process has arguably been unreasonably prolonged. The Committee should have cited the relevant provision of the Protocol to make an allowance for the author's plight rather than close her only avenue of redress.

10. Salgado v. U.K. and Northern Ireland *(2007), nationality, and exhaustion*

The author was a British national who was unable to pass on her nationality to her son (born on September 16, 1954 outside the U.K.) because the existent law only allowed nationality to be conferred through the father.[203] Since the father was Colombian, the boy was considered an alien. Subsequent legislation conferred nationality of British men and women upon their children under the age of 18 ("the 1981 Act"), and enabled individuals who were born to British mothers between February 7, 1961 and January 1, 1983 to register as British nationals ("the 2002 Act").[204] Even so, neither the 1981 nor the 2002 Acts allowed the author's son (who was born prior to the February 1961 cut-off date) to acquire British citizenship by virtue of her nationality. As a result, the author charged the State with failure to discharge its treaty obligation to "grant women equal rights with men with respect to the nationality of their children."[205]

The Committee claimed that the alleged discrimination, "manifested in her inability . . . to pass on her nationality to her eldest son . . . stopped on the date on which her son achieved his majority."[206] Her son then had the "*primary right* to either retain his acquired nationality or to apply for the nationality of another State, *subject to the conditions set by that State.*"[207] The Committee held that the discrimination against the author ended with the adoption of the 1981 Act.

While the Committee's conclusions were sound, its fundamental premises were flawed, and its reasoning incoherent. There was no issue of irreparable harm, so the analysis may turn to the substantive provision. (Since the Committee raised the issue of exhaustion after its substantive analysis, it shall be dealt with separately hereafter.) The treaty makes no mention of "primary" rights or "conditions set by a State" concerning the rights of adult nationals "with respect to the nationality of their children." What, then, were the precise rights that inhered in the adult national? The provision does not say. By contrast, the preceding clause specifies the specific nationality rights of a woman with respect to all men, including a potential spouse and the effect of a marriage on her rights. In particular, she retains all rights "to acquire, change or retain" her nationality and if she elects to get married, her husband's nationality shall not "automatically change" her nationality, "render her stateless" or "force upon her the nationality of her husband." Her autonomy is expressly preserved in matters relating to her citizenship.

By referring to the primary rights of the child upon reaching the age of majority, the Committee has presumably reinforced the autonomy of an adult to acquire, change, or retain his or her nationality. This begs the question: what conditions ultimately determine citizenship? Simply put: State law. The Committee alludes to this by recognizing the "conditions set by *the* State" in the event a child who reaches adulthood wishes to change his or her nationality. This observation, though, does not resolve the issue posed by the suit, which is whether the treaty grants individuals the exclusive right to automatically pass on citizenship to their children. The preceding clause concerning the rights of a woman as relates to a man does not settle the matter. Even hinting at the preservation of autonomy would be unpersuasive since parents are often granted a plethora of rights and authority over matters affecting their children.

Since the general means of interpretation (i.e., language and context) do not resolve the issue of transmitting nationality, the Committee should have resorted to supplementary means, including the travaux. The preparatory materials indicate that most nations were unwilling to grant individuals the authority to automatically transmit nationality to their children. Notably, the *initial* draft of the provision granted men and women the right "*to transmit* their nationality to their children."[208] This wording did not sit well with many States, based on moral and legal considerations. Denmark specifically noted that the "child's welfare was at stake here, not the right of the mother to transmit her nationality to her child."[209] Italy noted that the legal basis itself was "questionable" because its exercise could yield dual citizenship or none at all (if parents disagreed) and as Denmark pointed out, "should be drafted more clearly, so that it could not be construed in such a way as to give parents with different nationalities complete power of discretion over the nationality of their children . . ."[210] The drafters did not intend for the provision to grant an individual the authority to be the final arbiter in matters of citizenship.

Though it is universally recognized that nationality is governed by State law, the particular problem posed by the suit was, as the drafters foresaw, the prospect of dual citizenship for the child. The Committee erred by presuming that an adult national has the right to confer citizenship upon their children, albeit until they reach the age of majority. The dispositive issue for the members was whether the child became an adult, at which point he (or she) had the "primary" right to pursue citizenship per their own personal inclinations. This interpretation conflicts with the Committee's own recognition that nationality is conferred *by* and *subject to* conditions set by the State. A national cannot, as a matter of law, automatically transmit nationality, regardless of the age of the child.

The Committee was also mistaken in claiming that adoption of the 1981 Act ended the discrimination against the author. Neither the 1981 Act nor the 2002 Act granted rights of transmittal upon adult nationals. The 1981 Act precluded discrimination against the child to acquire British citizenship per a maternal rather than a paternal line. As applied, this act did not affect the author's son since he had already achieved the age of majority. The subsequent 2002 Act attempted to facilitate the acquisition of authority, age notwithstanding, by allowing adults who were born of British mothers to register as nationals. Even then, the author's child was unable to avail himself of the benefits because he was born prior to the cut-off birth date under the 2002 Act. More importantly, neither the 1981 Act nor the 2002 Act discriminated against the author. She simply never had the right to transmit citizenship.

The procedural grounds to dismiss the claim were valid, though the Committee's implicit assumption that the author had absolute standing per her right of conferral was flawed. The Committee claimed that the author had failed to exhaust domestic remedies because she never filed an application for registering her son as a national before he reached the age of majority.[211] Moreover, she could have appealed to the High Court by way of judicial review.[212] Both of these observations are correct, but insufficient because they do not address the issue of whose rights were being violated.

Though the author never had the exclusive right to transmit nationality, she did retain standing to challenge the national law while her son was still a child. Since conferral of nationality upon the child necessarily rests upon a determination of the parent's nationality (i.e., the father as of the time of the violation), the female national arguably retains some modicum of standing per her legally cognizable claim to British citizenship. The State arguably discriminated against her to the extent that her citizenship was considered less valuable than a British male insofar as her son could avail himself of the opportunity to become a British national by virtue of a parent's nationality. But at no point did she have a right to confer nationality; nor did her son have a right to be a British national. Ultimately, that grant rests exclusively with the State. Upon reaching majority, however, her right to bring suit on his behalf would be moot.

B. Interpretive trends and the utility of the proposed legal framework

By examining each of the decisions, a number of trends emerge (see Table 2.2).

First, there was no formal adherence to a consistent methodology of interpretation. Second, none of the decisions identified used the criteria of irreparable harm to check whether exhaustion was an appropriate ground for dismissal. In at least five claims, however, irreparable harm should have been addressed. Third, half of the decisions cited general recommendations as if they were legally binding. More disturbing, the analyses almost always

Table 2.2 Summary of trends in interpretation of claims and legal authority for CEDAW committee decisions

Claim	Interpretive methodology employed	Addressed potential irreparable harm	General Rec cited as binding	Cited expert opinions
B.J. v. Germany	No	No	N/A	N/A
A.T. v. Hungary	No	N/A	Yes	No
Kayhan v. Turkey	No	No	N/A	No
A.S. v. Hungary	No	N/A	Yes	Yes
Nguyen v. the Netherlands	No	No	N/A	No
Yildirim v. Austria	No	N/A	Yes	No
Goekce v. Austria	No	N/A	Yes	No
Muñoz v. Spain	No	No	N/A	N/A
NSF v. U.K. & N. Ireland	No	No	Yes	N/A
Salgado v. U.K. & N. Ireland	No	N/A	N/A	N/A
Totals	0	0	5	1

began "recalling" a general recommendation as if it was the authoritative rule in question, even above the express provisions of the treaty. Fourth, there was essentially no deference to expert opinions though the treaty and Rules expressly provide for it. In the one instance where expert opinions were cited, the reference appeared in the holding rather than the body of the analysis. Fifth, decisions rarely cited the relevant text of the provision. Finally, the Committee was invariably reluctant to recognize ambiguity that stemmed from application of a broad provision to a particular case; or within the provision itself. As a result, the substantive analyses inevitably suffered in breadth and depth. As a result, the reader can only surmise whether the Committee was aware of the myriad of inferences that would be drawn from such disparate approaches. One thing is certain: the lack of consistent, legally sound analyses compromised the integrity of the interpretive process and vitiated the legitimacy of the decisions.

The proposed framework suggests a promising outlook for future deliberations. A robust interpretive process will invariably yield better results and prove more effective in implementing the treaty. Employing a consistent and legally sound methodology will lead to foreseeable and justifiable decisions. The safeguards against irreparable harm reinforce the gender-sensitive elements of the treaty and allows for proactive measures to prevent imminent harms or dangers that may beset the aggrieved victim. Aside from its status as customary international law, employing the general and supplementary means of interpretation in the VCLT enhances the overall interpretive process. The synergy of individually tailored safeguards alongside the universality of the VCLT creates a powerful lens to adjudicate claims.

The proposed framework is also pragmatic. Legal processes matter. In practice, the courts—not legislatures—have been more effective in addressing women's health issues at the domestic level. Courts are often where the most controversial women's health issues are being resolved. Legislatures have proven quite ill-equipped to promote and protect women's health. In that regard, however, legal analyses should not succumb to fleeting whims or erratic impulses. The Committee has a heightened responsibility when undertaking treaty interpretation and should do so with utmost regard for legal formalities.

The discussion has heretofore demonstrated the flaws that inhere in an unstructured approach to treaty interpretation, and the utility in using the proposed interpretive framework. We shall now turn to its application as relates to a universal women's health issue that has never been resolved under the treaty—abortion.

C. Applying the framework to a health-related claim: abortion

Having proposed a generally workable framework, its utility for health-related claims must be demonstrated for traditional and non-traditional health-related claims. Informed consent and domestic violence are indisputably health-related issues, and there is little doubt that they fall within the content and scope of the treaty. Access to abortion, on the other hand, has not been given sufficient attention and there is no consensus on whether it can (or should, for that matter) be adjudicated under the health provision.

Consider the ICCPR case of *K.L. v. Peru*, which was demonstrated in Part I as being far from exemplary in its capacity to promote or protect women's health. Unlike the ICCPR, CEDAW affords express protections to secure a woman's health on account of her sex and precludes States from limiting her freedom to control decisions affecting her reproductive capacity. Overall, CEDAW may be considered an equal-protection treaty that aims to eliminate any preordained identities or roles that restrict a woman's freedom to participate in private and public arenas. A State must, for example, "modify the social and cultural patterns of conduct" to eliminate prejudices based on "the idea of the inferiority or the superiority of either of the sexes or on the stereotyped roles for men and women."[213] Throughout the treaty, the theme of gender-neutrality is pervasive in securing opportunities relating to, inter alia, civic participation, education, and employment.[214] An exception is made, however, for services related to a woman's reproductive health.

Since women are exclusively capable of reproducing, CEDAW is gender-sensitive—as opposed to gender-neutral—in affording rights and protections related to pregnancy. Under Article 12, States are required to "ensure to *women* appropriate services in connection with pregnancy, confinement and the post-natal period . . ."[215] Against this gender-sensitive backdrop, the discussion now employs the proposed framework to analyze the substantive issues of the case.

Let us assume that the author's plight was occurring in real-time. Under the Protocol, the author may have been able to avail herself of procedural safeguards unavailable under the ICCPR. Recall the structural deficiencies of the ICCPR and how its protocol makes no accommodation for imminent threats to the woman's health or safety. Here, the Committee could have acted upon affidavits submitted by the hospital physician that deemed her condition "life-threatening" and the psychiatrists who found that it had substantially contributed to her depression. The Committee did not have to qualify its decision by citing a "life" exception—and find itself in a quagmire of political issues that would likely overshadow any medicolegal discussion. Since the Protocol gives the Committee ample discretion in determining whether a condition warrants measures to preclude irreparable harm, a health-exception would arguably suffice to demand the invocation of interim measures.

Furthermore, given the limited time frame of conducting the procedure, the Committee could find that delays at the domestic level would indicate that proceedings were "unreasonably prolonged or unlikely to bring effective relief," either of which were likely when the State actively suppressed access to the service.[216] The ICCPR Protocol, by contrast, could arguably be interpreted to only speculate as to the length of the proceeding; a reluctant Committee member could simply defer to the State by saying that it was not in the Committee's expertise to meddle in logistical issues—and be squarely within the law. The CEDAW Protocol, however, expressly provides an additional layer of support by adding a determination of remedial effectiveness, coupled with the option of imposing interim measures. If there was no consensus on the issue of irreparable harm, the Committee could then analyze the provision with respect to abortion.

Employing a general means of interpretation yields conflicting accounts as to whether CEDAW condones or condemns abortions. At the outset, it should be noted that CEDAW is silent on the express provision of abortion. Still, the service is arguably "in connection with pregnancy" insofar as it relates to its termination. On the other hand, abortion might be inconsistent as a like service within the broader context of the clause, which provides for particular services (e.g., nutrition) that are meant to sustain rather than terminate the pregnancy.[217] A reference to the preceding clause provides little additional guidance. It merely mandates that the State ensure "access to health care services, including those related to family planning."[218] Although abortion has historically been used as a family planning method in some developing and underdeveloped countries, it is universally frowned upon within the healthcare and public health community. The Committee would be subject to intense pressure from every conceivable sector for venturing down that path. In all likelihood, the general means of interpretation would be deemed insufficient to resolve the issue.

The discussion would then turn to supplementary means of interpretation. The travaux suggests that the drafters were reluctant to tie pregnancy-related services explicitly to notions of motherhood. The working draft prepared by the USSR and the Philippines initially provided that States "grant women free medical care during pregnancy, confinement and the postnatal period."[219] By contrast, a subsequent amendment submitted by the United Kingdom read, "In order to safeguard the health and promote the welfare of *mothers*, State Parties shall undertake progressively to provide free medical care which shall include treatment in the ante and post natal periods and during confinement."[220] Benin and the All-African Women's Conference recommended a similar provision that reiterated the "welfare of mothers" as the overarching object and purpose of the provision.[221] In the final language, however, the theme of motherhood would be discarded. The decision was probably meant to reiterate that maternity was perceived as a social compact between men and women. Article 5, for example, provides that maternity is a "social function" that entails a "common responsibility of men and women in the upbringing and development of children . . ."[222] It also denounced the stereotype of motherhood as a woman's function. This interpretation is somewhat puzzling considering that pregnancy-related services are meant to foster the woman's inevitable experience of motherhood in the event that she becomes pregnant—unless, of course, she chooses to terminate the pregnancy. If the modification was made to extricate any appearance of female stereotypes, it would only bolster the argument that women were thereby granted some discretion or *control* over matters "in connection with" their pregnancy. To the extent that control would encompass access to abortions remains open to interpretation. The final language creatively eluded the conflict by potentially allowing women to invoke access to abortions without denigrating the treaty's unequivocal support for the upbringing and development of children.[223]

Interpreting the text alongside the travaux and the Committee's subsequent commentary in response to State Party reports provides ample support for recognizing a woman's access to abortion under the treaty. The Committee has been forthright in supporting access to abortions. During its 11th review session in 1994, the Committee inquired of Iraq's representatives as to the practice and number of abortions.[224] The Korean representatives were also asked whether abortion was legally permitted and, if so, under what circumstances.[225] Other nations that presented an update on the legality of abortions included Romania,[226] France,[227] and Nicaragua.[228] The subsequent session included reports on abortion from Guatemala,[229] Guyana,[230] Madagascar,[231] the Netherlands,[232] Zambia,[233] Australia,[234] New Zealand,[235] and the former Yugoslavia.[236] For representatives from Columbia, the Committee expressly inquired about "plans to amend the existing laws governing the voluntary termination of pregnancies . . ."[237]

As indicated above, the treaty is not pro-abortion per se, and the Committee's insistence on amending laws to facilitate access to abortions should not be interpreted as such. In most developing and under-developed countries where abortion is illegal, the rates of maternal mortality are disturbingly high. Recognizing the association of criminalizing abortions with high mortality rates, the Committee has called for medically-indicated abortions (e.g., therapeutic exceptions) to reduce maternal deaths. In these countries, the cultures are predominantly patriarchal and women have little, if any, power to negotiate their sexual relations. They are often financially dependent on their spouse or partner. Their partners may refuse to use contraceptives and, in societies where male promiscuity is high, females are at a heightened risk of contracting sexually transmitted infections (STIs) and diseases (STDs).

Consequently, reducing the treaty or its interpretation to a single ideological construct is overly simplistic. While there is no doubt that the treaty as applied allows for abortions, the mandate for State support and promotion of pregnancy-related services and care of expectant mothers reinforces the gender-neutral *and* gender-sensitive elements. As such, the treaty affords more substantive safeguards for securing the health and well-being of women than the ICCPR (and the ICESCR, as discussed in Part I, subpart B). Against this backdrop, the Committee would likely hold in favor of the author, but reiterate it within the context of high maternal mortality rates in Peru (thereby assuaging fears by the State government that its decision was not meant to disparage motherhood).

Unlike the ICCPR, the Protocol requires States to submit a written response—within six months—enunciating any action taken in light of the views and recommendations of the Committee.[238] In *K.L. v. Peru*, the HRC requested the Peruvian government to respond to its decision within 90 days.[239] Neither the ICCPR nor its protocol, however, requires a State to conform to any timeline. Finally, the Protocol attempts to strengthen political will and enhance transparency by mandating public distribution of the Committee's decision. The State must "make widely known and . . . give publicity to the Convention, . . . the [P]rotocol and . . . facilitate access to information about the views and recommendations of the Committee, in particular, on matters involving the State Party."[240]

CEDAW and its Protocol arguably provide a more robust set of substantive and procedural safeguards to provide timely and effective remedies. The Protocol's departure in content is promising in its potential implications for *State Party*—rather than Committee—involvement in constructing effective remedies and strengthening the process of reviewing communications. What is notable is a shift from passive to active determinations during the deliberative process. Enabling the Committee to opine on the depth of domestic redress implicitly heightens the initial burden of the State to justify the adequacy of existent remedies. In *K.L. v. Peru*, an overlooked fact is the Peruvian government's active disengagement from the case. The government provided no formal response to the allegations brought against it.[241] It should therefore be no surprise that in a subsequent assessment of State compliance, the CEDAW Committee would find that Peru had not complied with the ICCPR decision.[242] In practice, the Committee should be mindful of resource constraints, and the State should be receptive to providing reasonable avenues of relief for aggrieved victims. Enhancing the participation of all parties strengthens the deliberative process and lends credibility to an objective assessment of each claim.

A few remarks concerning abortion are in order. Ideologies aside, it is disingenuous to allude to CEDAW as an "abortion-neutral" instrument when it can be interpreted to recognize access to—if not a right to—the procedure. Given the Committee's persistent inquiries over the years, an interpretation on its part in favor of reading the legality of abortion into the treaty is foreseeable. As such, the Committee would be well advised to issue a general recommendation on abortion, and particularly the association of illegal or unsafe abortions with heightened maternal mortalities around the world. Transparency should dictate all deliberations under the Protocol.

III. Conclusion

Effect, not intent, is what makes the application of treaty interpretation relevant for States Parties. While it is convenient to invoke intent by virtue of ratifying a particular provision, it becomes problematic to create obligations that are not reasonably foreseeable. The implications, however, are quite foreseeable: political discord within the national sphere that balks at international decisions, reluctance to adopt even incremental measures to ameliorate existent harms, and possibly withdrawal from the treaty itself. Haphazard decision-making also undermines national efforts to further ratification in States (like the U.S.) that are signatories to the treaty, but are uncertain (or misinformed) of its domestic legal effect. To be sure, the Committee has been charged with a difficult task and its de facto jurisprudence is in a nascent stage of development. By adopting the proposed legal framework, it can employ a robust interpretive process to create consistent, foreseeable, and legally sound decisions to secure women's health.

Key international law and public health questions

1. What are the applicable treaties that are implicated by the proposed intervention? Identify both the applicable duties (on the part of states) and rights (as pertains to individuals).
2. Who are the relevant treaty-monitoring bodies or Committees charged with interpreting the law? Identify the Committee and the current scope of treaty provisions in the subject area.
3. Are there any prior legal decisions or adjudicative rulings on the subject matter? Identify the recent disputes that have actually appeared before a Committee, and determine what can be gleaned from the decisions as relates to legal tests (i.e., criteria) employed by the Committee in assessing the merits of the dispute.
4. Based on your review of pertinent treaties, general commentaries, and other related instruments, what are the broad and narrow legal issue(s)? Identify the specific issues, for example whether a national government

may require mandatory HPV vaccination for middle school children as a condition of school entry.

5. How would you interpret the law at it applies to the issue(s)? Analyze the facts under the controlling law and tests to determine the legality of the intervention and decide what course of action ought to be recommended.

3 Perspectives from the field

A conversation with George Annas, J.D., M.P.H., Chair, Health Law, Bioethics and Human Rights; William Fairfield Warren Distinguished Professor

Q.1 On human rights and the search for a common morality

Q: In Assisted Reproduction—Canada's Supreme Court and the "Global Baby," you observed the potential of disparate nationals laws that may encourage international travel on the part of persons seeking services that would otherwise be illegal (or overly expensive) in their native country, and suggested that, "Only the development of international norms, adopted and followed by the medical profession itself, is likely to ever produce uniformity in global practices." Do you think that human rights are, on some level, a fulfillment of a search for a common morality (once deemed too abstract or aspirational for any practical purposes)?

A: That's relatively pretty well put. The whole idea of human rights is that everyone should have basic rights just by virtue of being human. It's not normatively the highest level of anything, but a reasonable level. They are rights that inhere in individuals just because they are human, and I like the thought that they are birth rights. They are a common morality in the sense that everyone has exactly the same rights. That's why non-discrimination is the most fundamental principle in human rights, so that you can't treat anyone worse than anyone else; everyone should be afforded the same basic rights, whether they are economic, social, or cultural rights, or civil or politic rights— just because they are human. It seems to be less controversial to talk about civil and political rights, but nonetheless we can still see all of them as common aspirations. They are certainly moral rights, and have reached a level of soft law at the international level, and have become rhetorical to shame people or influence governments or corporations to act better towards one another.

Q.2 On science, information, and human rights in the developed countries

Q: You were recently interviewed on the ethics of new blood tests that can inform parents of the sex of their baby only seven weeks into pregnancy. You reflected on the consumer vs. patient needs based on "social" vs.

"medical" considerations. Historically, it seems that health and human rights was primarily about securing equity in health infrastructures, reducing the egregious disparities in health outcomes in the developing countries. Does the availability of this kind of technology and information present new challenges to health and human rights advocates in the developed world, where individuals have more control in accessing, and acting upon, information of this sort?

A: In the developed world, we're going to have more widely distributed access to technologies and the decisions that come along with that. But it's also true that some citizens in developing countries can travel and access those technologies when they migrate across borders. The travel is both ways now, so not only are people coming here from other countries to get access to the high tech medicine to get screenings, but even Americans here are traveling abroad to have surrogate mothers. So far there hasn't been much outrage about it. And even though in the U.S. human reproduction is the most politicized topic, the rest of the world doesn't seem to have a hard time accepting Americans going around the world and being assisted in reproduction. I think you can see a future when you can send in a blood sample from anywhere in the world to a laboratory that could give you a genetic readout of your fetus.

Q.3 On terms and terms of art

Q: The language we use in our discourse is rapidly evolving, based on our appreciation of social determinants of health, and perhaps some scholarly creativity. For all practical purposes, are the terms "right to health," "right to healthcare," and "right to public health," synonymous in framing the challenges that we face as a public health community to promote population health? Or is it important that we distinguish the terms to achieve short- or long-term objectives, either domestically or on the international level?

A: I think we can treat the right to health and public health synonymously, but no question that most people who think of the right to health mean a right to healthcare. And that right is important but it's only a part of the right to health, which is concerned with maintaining health, populations, as well as the environment. So I think that distinction is important.

Q.4 On the challenges of adjudicating international health disputes

Q: There are numerous health-related treaties, and with the advent of optional protocols, individual citizens can now bring claims against their governments for alleged violations. In your review of the Attorney General of Canada v. Attorney General of Quebec, you noted that "Justice Thomas Cromwell cast the deciding vote in this otherwise four-to-four opinion, and he split his own decision between the two in a frustratingly brief opinion." In my review of cases brought before the CEDAW committee, I have been disappointed in the brevity of the decisions, and the less-than-robust treatment of the issues. Are these kinds of opinions deemed to be more symbolic than substantive? Or should we, as a public health and legal community, expect more from courts and adjudicative committee bodies when they're dealing with such complex issues that have profound implications on population and individual health?

A: You can't expect more from them than the advocates in front of them provide them with. So to the extent that we don't think they have deeply enough considered the issues, then that's the fault of the litigators. So we can't fault the judges for that, and they can't know everything about everything. If there's an exploration that needs to be done, health lawyers have to get the briefs right. Closer to home, I'm proud of the health law community in its filing of briefs for the Supreme Court on its decision on Affordable Care Act.

Q.5 Affordable Care Act

Q: Will this decision set the tone for how the U.S. is perceived with respect to its commitment to human rights? And any predictions?

A: Certainly on our commitment to health. We're looked at as the outlier with 40 million uninsured and a system that is not national at all, and for which the government seems to take very little responsibility. So it's an absolute watershed moment for the country. In terms of the outcomes, it would be astonishing for this Court to declare this law unconstitutional, and would put us right back to the beginning of the New Deal, with the Supreme Court declaring the Congressional acts unconstitutional.

4 At the intersection of law, human rights, and religion

A case study in female autonomy in Hinduism and Islam

Introduction

In South Asia, unsafe abortions, sex-selective abortions, lack of access to contraceptives, and domestic violence are among the myriad of health-related issues that continue unabated. According to the World Health Organization (WHO), an unsafe abortion is the "terminati[on] of an unintended pregnancy by persons lacking the necessary skills or in an environment lacking the minimal medical standards, or both" (World Health Organization, 2007). Limited access to safe abortions is also associated with a high maternal mortality rate. In India, the problem is complicated by an elevated preference for male children that has also resulted in laws precluding sex-selective abortion. While access to safe abortions and regulation of sex-selective abortions may appear as distinct issues, they revolve around fleeting expressions of female autonomy. To date, however, no study has adequately explored the cultural (and specifically, religious) determinants to *promote* female empowerment.

In this chapter, I argue that legal recourse for alleged violations of women's rights at the national or international level is futile because India and Pakistan's reservations to the Convention on the Elimination of Discrimination Against Women (CEDAW) further an unconstitutional agenda in violation of the inherent dignity and liberty of their female constituency. Undefined traditional values have resulted in a hodgepodge of unconstitutional laws, unpersuasive judicial decisions, and a subtle infusion of unsettled religious doctrine whose combined effect has suppressed any notion of female integrity. Rather than recycle decades-old arguments citing "human rights" violations, however, I take a different approach that examines motifs of autonomy, equality, and empowerment within the Indian and Pakistani cultures, focusing on Hinduism and Islam, respectively. There has been ample scholarship that focuses on cultural practices and beliefs that belie legal standards of equality among the sexes. Here, I highlight opportunities for cultural engagement—rather than examples of legal derogation—to engage communities in a diaspora where the separation of church and state is hardly rigid and socio-religious dialogue can be utilized to enhance gender parity.

In Part I, I discuss trends in global and national rates of unsafe abortions and attendant health consequences. I review the prevalence and severity of unsafe abortions and the socio-cultural issues pertinent to India and Pakistan. In doing so, I identify key barriers to access and the forces that influence a woman's capacity for decision-making. In Part II, I focus on international and national legal instruments and derogation from essential human rights obligations on the part of India and Pakistan. I specifically review international conventions and whether national instruments seek to promote or stymie women's ability to control matters affecting their sexual and reproductive health. Here, I reiterate why the plethora of national and international legal safeguards have proved themselves largely ineffective in securing women's health. In Part III, I contextualize the discussion with respect to the predominant religions of India and Pakistan to identify a unified principle of female empowerment. Moral edicts were often passed along through stories and rituals rather than a strict codification of rights and responsibilities. Select examples from traditional tales of Hinduism and Islam suggest that women are not a vulnerable class in need of protection. On the contrary, elements of equality, non-discrimination, and autonomy ring true throughout these stories and portray a cultural milieu that is ripe for female empowerment. More telling is the exposure of the historical promotion, development, and preservation of a [post] colonial Hindu patriarchy by the British government. In Part IV, I proffer recommendations for policy practitioners eager to institute ethical, legal, and structural reform to promulgate a unified principle of female empowerment. In Part V, I conclude by summarizing the argument and reiterating key measures to effectuate change to secure the health of Indian and Pakistani women, which may serve as a template to promote female empowerment worldwide.

I. Trends in unsafe abortions and female decision-making capacity

The alarming trends worldwide of unsafe abortions and their attendant health consequences demand immediate attention. The impact on individual States, however, varies. Against a backdrop of global trends, a brief exploration of the public health burden and impact on Indian and Pakistani women is vital to illustrate the diminished capacity of female decision-making in matters related to reproductive health.

A. Public health burden and impact on women in India

The burden and impact of unsafe abortion on women in India exceeds that of global trends. Of over 42 million women who face an unplanned pregnancy worldwide in 2003, approximately 20 million—or 48 percent—resorted to unsafe abortions (World Health Organization, 2007). One study used data over a 15-year period and found that 60 percent of cases used primitive methods of pregnancy termination, and *all* women invariably suffered complications—one quarter of whom died (Jain, 2004). Contextualizing the data with respect to socio-economic impediments further illustrates the complexity of the overall problem.

General reports that 48 percent of women in India have no say in decisions regarding their own healthcare are not easily applicable to women seeking an abortion (Planned Parenthood, 2007). In one study, up to 88.8 percent of adult women (i.e., over 20 years of age) were the primary decision-makers in deciding whether to have an abortion (Ganatra and Hirve, 2002). The figure, however, dropped significantly to only 75.8 percent for adolescent girls (under 20 years of age). This gap was also observed in other decisions, including whether to receive their husband's permission to go to the local health center (67.5 percent of adult women compared to 81.4 percent of adolescents).

Husbands were the primary decision-makers in aborting the fetus in 8.9 percent of cases involving adult female spouses and in 10.7 percent of cases with adolescent spouses (Ganatra and Hirve, 2002). The husband's mother (female's mother-in-law) made the decision in 3.4 percent of cases involving adolescent females, and in 4.5 percent of cases the adolescent girl wanted to continue the pregnancy but yielded to family pressure. In contrast, only 0.2 percent of adult women reported a mother-in-law as a decision-maker in choosing to abort, and 1.5 percent succumbed to family pressure despite wanting to continue the pregnancy. In fact, only 74 percent of adolescents discussed matters of contraception with their husbands, compared to 85 percent of adult females. This figure is particularly disturbing where studies indicate that 48.3 percent of married women (aged 15–49) use no contraception (Bankole, 1998). While the accuracy of these statistics may vary across female populations throughout India, the data is consistent with perceptions of male control over female sexuality. The authority to engage in sexual intercourse and refuse to use contraceptives effectively curtails (if not severs) any notion of female autonomy.

B. Public health burden and impact on women in Pakistan

Data on abortion statistics in Pakistan are scarce. Official government data are simply unavailable and most studies include significant caveats (National Institute for Population Studies, 2001). The issues, in large part, stem from inadequate surveillance and reporting. Since abortion can only be legally conducted to save a woman's life, most women may be reluctant to respond directly to surveys inquiring into abortion-related decisions. Even so, a number of studies proffer ample evidence indicating that unsafe abortions are taking a significant toll on Pakistani women.

A regional study found that up to 7 per 1,000—or 197,000—women were treated in hospitals annually for complications from unsafe abortions (Singh, 2006). This figure places Pakistan in the middle spectrum of States with rates ranging from 3 per 1,000 to 15 per 1,000 across developing countries. Still, the numbers are grossly misleading. First, the number is "likely substantially underestimated since data from most private sector facilities were not available" (Singh, 2006). Additionally, abortions are generally illegal in Pakistan unless performed to save a woman's life. Considering that 890,000 induced abortions occur annually in Pakistan, the vast majority are likely unsafe (Sathar, 2007). Moreover, one study reported up to 68.5 percent of induced abortions resulting in complications, particularly heavy vaginal bleeding and fever (Saleem and Fikri, 2001).

Women cite a number of economic and social forces that influence their ability to seek an abortion. Among these factors are the cost of affording another child, the husband's role as a decision-maker, and attitudes towards contraception. At least 55 percent of women having an induced abortion had reached their desired number of children, and 54 percent could not afford another child (Population Council, 2004). Other factors (without statistical reports) include spacing of children, and, in a small number of cases, being unmarried at the time of conception. Husbands exert significant influence in deciding whether to seek an abortion, and the use of contraceptives. While some women acknowledged that pressure by the husband or another family member (e.g., mother-in-law) prevented them from seeking an abortion, there was no data on this trend. Among women who sought an abortion, only 30 percent did so entirely of their own volition with no involvement of their husbands. When husbands were involved (70 percent), the final decision was usually a joint decision by the couple (66 percent) as opposed to a unilateral decision by the husband (4 percent). It is difficult, however, to distinguish between joint and unilateral decisions by husbands where they exert significant control over their partners' sexuality.

Husbands also play a significant role in deciding whether to use con-traceptives. While 78 percent of women had used a modern contraceptive method, the husband participated in the decision 90 percent of the time. Even so, the predominant issue was not whether or not to use contraception (in many cases favored by the husband), but *when* to use it because of differences of opinion as to when the women should become pregnant and how many children she should bear (Population Council, 2004). This observation is supported by studies where grand multigravidity (i.e., at least five or more complete *or* incomplete pregnancies experienced by a female) was a "strong predictor of induced abortion suggesting that pregnancies were terminated for the purpose of birth spacing or limiting family size" (Saleem and Fikree, 2005). In response, the Population Council recommended engaging men more directly to reduce unwanted pregnancies. It is questionable, however, how effective this approach would be against a backdrop of female disem-powerment.

When women "perceive that their husbands want large families, and indeed the men . . . express the view that it is their wives' *responsibility* to continue bearing children . . .", decisions affecting women's sexual and reproductive health are invariably a function of their husband's choice (i.e., desire for sexual fulfillment and/or procreation).

II. Legal instruments and derogation from human rights obligations

Women are not getting unsafe abortions despite or purely because of existing laws. The flaw in a purely legalistic analysis is that it overlooks the role of men as decision-makers in matters affecting their partner's sexual and reproductive health; additionally, the law is overwhelmingly indifferent to constrictions on female autonomy. In fact, upon closer examination, such restrictions are reinforced by unconstitutional laws, irrational judicial decisions, and adherence to the notion that upholding female integrity necessarily entails a curtailment—if not an absence—of female autonomy.

A. Declarations and reservations to CEDAW

India ratified and Pakistan acceded to the Convention on the Elimination of All Forms of Discrimination Against Women ("CEDAW") in 1993 and 1996, respectively. An essential tenet of CEDAW was eliminating discrimination against women among government officials and other members of civil society. This position was reiterated at the United Nation's General Assembly during the Five- and Ten-Year reviews of the International Conference of Population Development (United Nations Population Fund (UNPF), 1999). In both reviews, key actions were specified, including the involvement of religious leaders to "actively promote gender equality" (UNPF, 2004). Although CEDAW was intended to "incorporate the principle of equality of men and women in their legal system," a set of declarations and reservations by India and Pakistan effectively defeat its ultimate object and purpose.

India's declarations are essentially reservations to the overriding principle of equality between men and women. Its first declaration states, in relevant part:

> With regard to articles 5(a) and 16(1) of the Convention on the Elimination of All Forms of Discrimination Against Women, the Government of the Republic of India declares that it shall abide by and ensure these provisions in conformity with its policy of *non-interference in the personal affairs of any Community without its initiative and consent.*
>
> (Government of India, 1993, emphasis added)

This declaration is an express derogation of State party obligations that consequently marginalizes women and officially condones "Community" norms that ensure replication of these norms. From India's *Initial Report* on CEDAW, it appears that the term "community" is used to broadly refer to any minority population with particular beliefs and practices (Government of India, 1999). Whereas § 5(a) of CEDAW mandates steps to eliminate discrimination arising from notions of a superior sex or stereotypical gender roles, the Indian government clearly states that such steps are not a State-sponsored obligation absent an initiative on the part of the discriminating Community. To enforce such a mandate would constitute "interference" in the Community's "personal affairs." This reading is consistent with its application to § 16(1) concerning marital relations between spouses, including determination of family spacing and so on, whereby a man's influence on women will not be questioned since it constitutes a "personal affair." If a woman, however, attempts to assert exclusive control over her body (see India's Supreme Court decision discussed in Part II, subpart B below), she may be civilly liable.

Apparently, the government has deferred to community norms both (1) at the expense of subjecting females to discrimination and (2) condoning community practices that condone discrimination as part of their cultural fabric. Since condoning express discrimination defeats the purpose of CEDAW, the only logical rationale for allowing communities to engage in such practices is owing to the community's opinion on its cultural legitimacy. This misperception will be challenged in Part III (discussed below).

Pakistan's declaration is a single statement that, on its face, appears harmless. It states, in relevant part, "The accession by [the] Government of the Islamic Republic of Pakistan to the [said Convention] is subjection to the provisions of the Constitution of the Islamic Republic of Pakistan ("Pakistan Constitution")." Nonetheless, the qualification is telling. The Pakistan Constitution provides that "all citizens are equal before law and are entitled to equal protection of law" (Islamic Republic of Pakistan, 1948). Still, it expressly reinforces sex differences that, under CEDAW, may rise to levels of potential discrimination. Women are constitutionally a class of persons (1) that are to be protected and (2) have traditional roles as wives and mothers. The equal protection clause does not "prevent the State from making any special provision for the protection of women . . ." This exception is repeated in the subsequent clause requiring non-discrimination in respect to accessing public places, whereby "nothing . . . shall prevent the State from making any special provision for women."

Social justice is an inherent prerogative of the Pakistani Constitution, but with important qualifications. The State is obligated to "make provisions . . . ensuring that . . . women are not employed in vocations unsuited to their age or sex, and for maternity benefits for women in employment." Women are expected to work in a capacity for which they are "suited"—cognizant of their role as mothers so they may receive "maternity benefits." These provisions of the Pakistan Constitution reinforce the notion of women as a vulnerable class in need of protection, and of their traditional roles as wives and mothers.

Furthermore, such roles exist within the express domain of male-dominated societal relations. The Pakistan Constitution recognizes the "dignity of man and . . . privacy of home," and considers it an "inviolable" sphere of personal conduct. Given the difficulty for women in their traditional roles to secure their sexual and reproductive health, the Pakistan Constitution essentially fails to live up to its promise by marginalizing women and protects nothing more than cultural norms couched in the "privacy" of the home.

B. Indian unconstitutional agenda furthered by conflicting laws and rulings

While the Constitution of India recognizes equal protection of its citizens irrespective of sex, federal laws and judicial rulings attach male participation—and consent— in the exercise of female autonomy in matters affecting her sexual or reproductive health (Republic of India, 1948). Against this backdrop, the rampant discrimination against women is an affront to notions of equal protection and equality.

1. Indian Medical Termination of Pregnancy Act and its failure to secure female reproductive rights

The Indian Medical Termination of Pregnancy Act (MTPA) of 1971 (amended 2001) allows a healthcare provider to conduct an abortion to save the life of the mother, to prevent grave injury to her physical or mental health (includes rape), or to prevent the birth of a child with mental or physical abnormalities (MTPA, 1971). The MTPA is unsuccessful in securing female rights because it (1) discriminates against women under the age of 18, (2) accords no active role on State governments in regulating abortions, and (3) requires reporting of non-confidential personal information. Pursuant to § 3(4) of the MTPA, a woman who is under 18 years of age must obtain written consent by her guardian—who is often, in practice, her husband. In August 2010, for example, the Delhi high court proclaimed that a "husband who is a minor can be the guardian of his minor wife." (Daily News and Analysis, 2010). The majority of marriages involving women under 18 are in rural communities where girls are particularly susceptible to further domestic exploitation. For example, one study revealed that non-consensual sex, sexual violence, and a woman's inability to refuse her husband's sexual demands "appeared to underlie the need for abortion in both younger and older women" (Ravindran and Balasubramanian, 2004). This only compounds the difficulty in securing a safe abortion, and heightens the chances (and attendant risks) of resorting to an unsafe procedure.

Due to lack of regulation, the concomitant costs of private providers are quite high and beyond the reach of many women. The constituent state governments are not leading providers of abortions (Duggal, 2004). While abortions services are readily available, they are also not easily affordable. The lack of State regulation has resulted in private providers charging upwards of Rs. 2,000 (~$44 USD), which in some areas may be more than an average worker's monthly salary. Furthermore, a government study revealed that only 28 percent of rural hospitals are equipped with health personnel certified to carry out abortions. Absent government regulation, unsafe abortions will continue to flourish in an environment of commercial exploitation. The regulatory framework, moreover, is hardly protective of a woman's best interests. The MTPA Regulations require mandatory reporting of an abortion without the consent of the woman, including disclosure of personal information, such as her name, address, and reason for termination. A separate, anonymous form is submitted that indicates the religion of persons who underwent an abortion (although reference to any surname will likely suffice to determine religious affiliation). It is also unclear why such information is even assessed. Nonetheless, the mandatory disclosure of personal information without a woman's consent is an affront to her bodily and mental integrity.

2. Judicial decisions restricting access to abortion

On March 26, 2007, the Supreme Court of India issued a judgment severely curtailing a woman's right to abortion. In the case of *Samar Ghosh v. Jaya Ghosh*, the respondent husband brought suit to terminate the marriage based on cruelty stemming from numerous incidents and patterns of behavior (Samar Ghosh v. Jaya Ghosh, 2007). Included among the alleged acts of cruelty was the appellant's refusal to have any children with the respondent. The appellant had a child from a previous marriage and made it clear that she wanted no further children. The Court ultimately held for the respondent and determined that the appellant's behavior had amounted to cruelty to warrant a divorce.

While the Court's rationale for reinstating the divorce may be reasonable, its subsequent decree on spousal consent for seeking an abortion, and liability for refusal to have children, were inappropriate and unconstitutional. First and foremost, neither issue before the Court involved a woman's right relating to matters affecting her sexual or reproductive health. Regardless, the Court decided that:

> if the wife undergoes a[n] . . . abortion without medical reason without the consent or knowledge of her husband, such an act of the spouse may lead to mental cruelty.

This ruling expands the express provisions of the MTPA, which marginalizes girls under 18 by requiring them to obtain guardian consent and by further requiring spousal consent for *any* woman, regardless of her age. The Court reiterated the inseparable ties of a husband and wife by noting that for either to exercise a "unilateral decision . . . not to have a child . . . may amount to cruelty." By implication, a woman could not unilaterally decide to have a child; however, this perception would presumably contravene the Court's central presumption that it is a woman's *duty* to bear children pursuant to her role as a wife and a man's *right* to expect as much. This rationale effectively delegates a woman's fundamental right to decisions affecting her sexual and reproductive health to her husband and society's expectation of her role as a woman, that is, as a wife and mother.

C. Pervasive problems amidst an incoherent legal framework in Pakistan

A pressing challenge in Pakistan is reconciling the criminalization of abortion with efforts to prevent further marginalization of women and healthcare providers that provide related healthcare services. Moreover, implementing key measures to promote gender equality is problematic against an ideological backdrop that specifies a particular role for women in society. The criminalization of abortion, coupled with attitudes of healthcare providers, acts as a deterrent to women to procuring safe abortions. In Pakistan, abortion is a criminal offense that may lead to imprisonment. Two exceptions apply: if a healthcare provider deems it necessary to save the life of the woman, or if the procedure is required as a matter of "necessary treatment" (Pakistan Penal Code, 1948).

The decision to terminate a pregnancy without subjecting oneself to criminal prosecution ultimately rests with the healthcare provider. Generally, healthcare providers have an unfavorable attitude towards abortion and do not support its practice. A study that attempted to gauge provider attitudes found that 67.3 percent had an unfavorable opinion of abortion, only 25 percent favored it, and 81 percent of those who wanted to change the law wanted it to be *stricter,* that is, they wanted the law to further restrict access to abortions (Rehan, 2003). Surprisingly, only 19.1 percent of providers wanted to change the abortion law. Consequently, existent laws, societal forces, and the healthcare system afford little solace to the severe burden that women must endure.

III. Reconciling human rights, religion, and social justice

Parts I and II illustrate the complexity of alleviating the public health burden and the impact of unsafe abortions against a backdrop of international and national laws. While practitioners and scholars have written extensively on the health and political determinants, they are often reluctant (if not ill equipped) to address the underlying issue of female empowerment within the cultural fabric of India and Pakistan. Simply put, any meaningful discussion of female autonomy must be addressed and analyzed within the context of culture, which is heavily influenced by religion. India is home to a plurality of religious traditions dating back over 5,000 years, and Pakistan is an Islamic state. It is naïve to ignore this social context or limit engagement to the "ills" of such traditions.

To be sure, the inadequacy of legal imperatives has not been lost on keen observers. Rogers *et al*. argued that in India, decisions to carry a child to term or seek sex-determination are "intentionally and consistently administered by a patriarchal society," effectively denying any sexual agency so that a woman "has little choice but to avoid [the decisions]" (Rogers, *et al*., 2007). Zilberberg noted that excessive restrictions or enforcement might turn harmful practices underground (Zilberberg, 2007). As such, she argued that female empowerment and elevation of women were vital, alongside bans or other regulatory safeguards, to promote wider social change.

The human rights movement has been noble but arguably disoriented in its efforts to effectively engage the South Asian diaspora in addressing these cultural determinants. In 2004, the United Nations Population Fund called on advocates to implement programs with "full respect for the various religious and ethical values and cultural backgrounds of its people and in conformity with universally recognized international human rights" (UNPF, 2004). It also called for raising awareness and enhancing communication with religious and community leaders, and "taking into account local, cultural, traditional and religious beliefs." If a prevailing worldview does not recognize a particular motif (e.g., equality), why should everyone accord "full respect" thereto? A disagreement is a testament to an ideological difference that must be made transparent—not shoved under a rug of tolerance that brings attention to some issues, but not others. In effect, this quasi-sensitive pretense of respect is a disingenuous, hypocritical, and ineffective means to ameliorate existent harms to women worldwide.

Historically, scholars have focused exclusively on fundamentalist attitudes and oppressive practices that blatantly discriminate against women. I categorically applaud and support these efforts. I differ, however, insofar as I embrace the possibility and potentiality of identifying those motifs within the culture that may counter these fundamentalist notions. While casting the negative influence of religion on curbing women's rights is well documented, I proffer an alternative approach. I suggest that recognizing the harmony among religious principles with key tenets of women's rights (e.g., equality, non-discrimination, autonomy) refutes a rigid characterization of women as a vulnerable class in need of protection. By engaging communities in the context of familiar territory—but concededly unfamiliar motifs—repressive social policies, practices, and beliefs can be challenged and effectively dismissed as quasi-cultural attempts to engage in harmful acts and violations of individual rights.

But beyond this theoretical engagement is the recognition that these so-called cultural impediments were not unique to the subcontinent, and were in fact created by British and Indian officials in the late nineteenth and early twentieth century. This realization is particularly useful because it challenges the notion that the social and cultural barriers are ingrained in the beliefs and practices of a population unfamiliar with notions of autonomy, equality, or individual empowerment. To illustrate these points, we draw attention to the life and work of Muddupalani, a female Telegu scholar whose work was relatively unknown during her time, yet achieved tremendous notoriety 150 years later when the British government banned publication of her writing after finding it "obscene." Even today, I am aware of only one translation of her work that was published in 2011, and a cursory search for her writing online will be in vain. She has, and continues to be, an exemplary figure whose life and legacy illustrate the potential for the emergence of a twenty-first-century "religious feminism."

A. *Muddupalani's* Radhika Santawanam *and [post] colonial patriarchy*

Muddupalani was a courtesan and scholar in the royal court of Maharaja Pratap Singh, who ruled Thanjavur in South India from 1730 to 1763. Her magnum opus was *Radhika Santawanam,* a medieval Telugu poem comprised of 584 verses that explored the trials and tribulations of love and betrayal between the Hindu deity Krishna and his beloved Radha, and was by and large unknown to the public for over 150 years. It was not until 1910, when the work was republished by a devadasi named Nagarathnamma, that it met with public notoriety and was labeled "obscene" by the British government following an outcry among numerous Indian male literary critics. The work was subsequently banned in 1911, and would remain banned for over 35 years until 1947, when Chief Minister Prakasam of the Madras Presidency uplifted the ban, and noted his effort to "restore a few pearls to the necklace of Telegu literature" (Muddupalani, tr. Mulchandani, 2011).

In this section, I argue that *Radhika Santawanam* is a legitimate threat to the promotion, development, and preservation of a [post] colonial Hindu patriarchy that oppresses women and suppresses their autonomous expression and decision-making (be it sexual or otherwise), because it is (1) no less explicit than prior religiously inspired works that explore human sexuality, (2) consistent with the content of foundational religious texts, which celebrate female autonomy, and (3) bridges the ancient past with the then-contemporary present through its unique authorship, potential for accessibility, and fluid interpretation of Hindu doctrine, thereby undermining a rigid system of defined social norms, expectations of gender, and expressions of human sexuality.

This contribution is timely in an era where human rights violations are often explained—and at times, justified—by religious beliefs and practice. Moreover, legal recourse at a national or even international level (vis-à-vis optional protocols) is futile because India's legal reservations to CEDAW explicitly exempt such practices, allowing them to sustain. Thus far, scholars (including myself) have arguably wasted time by arguing that these reservations amount to a furtherance of an unconstitutional agenda in violation of women's inherent dignity and liberty. Unsurprisingly, a general complacency with undefined traditional values has resulted in a hodgepodge of unconstitutional laws, unpersuasive judicial decisions, and a subtle infusion of unsettled religious doctrine whose combined effect has suppressed any notion of female integrity. I adopt a different approach. Rather than recycle decades-old arguments citing "human rights" violations, I examine motifs of autonomy, equality, and empowerment within a tradition that was ultimately abandoned, denounced, and mischaracterized to facilitate the creation of an emergent patriarchal order. Whether its roots ought to be labeled as "British," "Indian," or some combination thereof is of little consequence because the contemporary challenge for South Asian women remains a pressing issue. This article highlights an opportunity to engage communities in a diaspora where the separation of church and state is hardly rigid and socio-religious dialogue can be utilized to enhance gender parity. Towards that end, Muddupalani is exemplary in her uncanny ability to bridge the past, then-present, and contemporary societies, and whose work, perhaps unwittingly, may serve as a rallying call for the seemingly oxymoronic emergence of "Hindu feminism."

This section will provide a historical backdrop of the manuscript and a summary of its narrative content; analyze the ban against the statutory provisions that forbade public exposure to obscene material; and scrutinize the work against other religiously inspired works that explore human sexuality, and focuses specifically on Jayadeva's *Gita Govinda* (twelfth century AD). It will then be followed by an exploration of the parameters of female autonomy and sexuality in foundational texts, namely, Vyasa's epic poem, *The Mahabharata* (500 BC). Against this backdrop, this section argues in favor of attributing a unique status upon *Radhika Santawanam* as a bridge from ancient to then-contemporary, and contemporary Hinduism.

A brief account of the historical backdrop and narrative content are essential to understand and appreciate the provocative nature and scope of the work. Also, subsequent developments in law and social mores underscore the importance of censorship as a vehicle to misinterpret and mischaracterize works of literature, art, or other media to further a particular, and invariably one-sided, patriarchal agenda.

Radhika Santawanam was crafted as a Telugu poem, in a medieval dialect, comprised of 584 verses, and divided into four sections. Muddupalani (1739–1790) was its sole author and served as a courtesan and scholar in the royal court of Maharaja Pratap Singh, who ruled the kingdom of Thanjavur from 1730 to 1763. The precise date of composition is unknown, but we can infer from the historical accounts when it was most likely written. If we assume that Muddupalani was at least a young woman when she wrote the work (e.g., 18–24 years of age or circa 1757–1763) and that it was crafted while Maharaja Singh was still presiding over the royal court (i.e., 1730–1763), we can reasonably assume that the work was most likely written sometime between 1757 and 1763.

The narrative itself is divided into four distinct parts. In the first section, Radha prepares a young woman, Ila, to become Krishna's wife. The reader is informed that Radha taught Ila how to sing, dance, write, and ultimately how to conduct herself while making love to Krishna, before the chapter's culmination in their marriage. In the second section, Krishna and Ila leave town to visit her family. Radha sends a parrot as a messenger to convey her feelings to him (so long as Ila is not present). The parrot returns, unable to deliver the message because Krishna is allegedly too engrossed in his affairs with Ila. In the third section, Radha is infuriated, and laments over her plight while her maidens console her. We learn that Krishna saw Radha's parrot and became agitated, before deciding to return to his native village and see her. In the final section, Krishna returns and is repentant before Radha. Her maidens (and even her parrot!) lash out at him verbally. Radha then breaks her silence and scolds him before he falls at her feet. She then kicks him, but upon professing his eternal love for her, they reunite.

The storyline follows an apparently simple linear sequence of events that illustrate the lovers' anticipation, separation, humiliation, and reconciliation. As a literary composition, the work remained by and large obscure and ignored over the next 150 years. It was not until 1910 that literary authorities and government officials characterized it as anything but simple, and made it a target of public ridicule.

After Nagarathnamma republished the work in its entirety, the response from within the Telugu literary circle was sharp. Noted literary critic Kandukuri Veeresalingam remarked, "Several references in the book are disgraceful and inappropriate for women to hear, let alone be uttered from a woman's mouth." (Muddupalani, tr. Mulchandani, 2011). *Sasilekha*, a Telegu literary magazine, also observed: "A prostitute had composed the book and another prostitute has edited it," and that no "literate gentleman can realize God by reading that he enjoyed sex in forty different ways with an adulterous woman" (Muddupalani, tr. Mulchandani, 2011).

Nagarathnamma did not take such charges in silence and was quick to suggest an underlying hypocrisy in the allegations: "Does the question of propriety and embarrassment apply only in the case of women, not men? Is he [Veeresalingam] implying that it is not acceptable for Muddupalani to write about conjugal pleasures in minute detail and without reservation because she was a courtesan? Are the 'obscenities' in *Radhika Santawanam* any worse than the obscenities in *Vaijayantivilasam*, a book he has personally reviewed and approved for publication?" (Mulchandani, 2011).

Nagarathnamma's pleas went unanswered and in 1910, the government banned the work and prohibited any further distribution of existent copies (many of which were seized after law enforcement allegedly raided publication houses!) Although no legal record exists as to the judicial finding of "obscenity," a review of the statutory code will reveal the vague language that could facilitate such determinations. Section 292(1) of the Indian Penal Code (1860) provides, in relevant part, that:

> (1) For the purposes of sub-section (2), a book, pamphlet, paper, writing, drawing, painting representation, figure or any other object, shall be deemed to be obscene if it is lascivious or appeals to the prurient interest or if its effect, or (where it comprises two or more distinct items) the effect of any one of its items, is, if taken as a whole, such as to tend to deprave and corrupt persons who are likely, having regard to all relevant circumstances, to read, see or hear the matter contained or embodied in it.

The statute did, however, provide for a number of exceptions, so that:

(2)(e) This section does not extend to-
(a) any book, pamphlet, paper, writing, drawing, painting, representation or figure-
> (i) the publication of which is proved to be justified as being for the public good on the ground that such book, pamphlet, paper, writing, drawing, painting, representation or figure is in the interest of science, literature, art or learning or other objects of general concern, or
> (ii) which is kept or used bona fide for religious purposes;

(b) any representation sculptured, engraved, painted or otherwise represented on or in-
> (i) any ancient monument within the meaning of the Ancient Monuments and Archaeological Sites and Remains Act, 1958 (24 of 1958), or
> (ii) any temple, or on any car used for the conveyance of idols, or kept or used for any religious purpose.

The statutory provision is notable because it enables a finding of obscenity on the basis of the content and context of an object. Subsection 1, for example, prohibits the display or publication of any item that is "lascivious," a term that is undefined in the statute itself, but which the dictionary defines as "lewd" or "lustful." The term "lewd," may be further defined as "sexually unchaste" or "vulgar," and the term "lustful" is an adjective that is defined as "excited by lust," which may be narrowly defined as "unbridled sexual desire" (Merriam Webster, 2012). These terms are not particularly helpful in determining whether a particular object is lascivious merely based on its content. The depiction of a nude male body was commonplace in ancient Greece; and acts of sexual intercourse can be found decorating the Hindu temple walls in Khajuraho, India. In other words, the mere display of nudity is not a persuasive argument for a finding of obscenity. A more practical and objective standard can be found in the latter half of the statute, which speaks to the "effect" of the item, that is, whether it, "if taken as a whole," tends to "deprave or corrupt" persons who read, see, or hear it. Here, by examining how individuals respond to an item would reveal its propensity to invoke such sentiments. The problem, however, is that such determinations cannot be made *a priori* since an effect cannot be measured if it is not given an opportunity to arise. The attempt to determine an object's "tend[ency]" to create such effects is equally unpersuasive as a standard since, as we observed earlier, such efforts would require conclusions to be drawn from the inherent characteristics of the item itself. And as we have seen in the examples, above, the absence of any public outcry in response to the display of nude bodies engaged in sexual acts in religious forums suggests that such determinations must be founded on concrete and specific criteria.

The purpose here is not to establish a standard of sexual references that would satisfy a finding of obscenity; but rather to illustrate the ambiguity of the statute and the ease with which a public official could make such a finding.

Here, we examine one particular work that has enjoyed (and continues to enjoy) a heightened status as devotional literature and a source of worship within the Hindu (and particularly Vaishnava) communities: Jayadeva's *Gita Govinda*. A proponent of Jayadeva's work could arguably make a case for its bona fide use "for religious purposes," under subsection 2(ii) of the obscenity statute. But an equally persuasive argument could be made for Muddupalani's work, and both manuscripts could arguably "be justified as being for the public good on the ground that such . . . writing[s] . . . [are] in the interest of . . . literature . . ." under subsection 2(i). The more appropriate question, then, is how sexual references within *Radhika Santawanam* fare in comparison with other religiously inspired works.

Jayadeva was a twelfth century poet who crafted the *Gita Govinda*, a collection of 24 songs composed in Sanskrit that glorify the courtship of Radha by Krishna. The work has influenced devotional songs, dances, and literature, and has even been added to temple inscriptions (Jayadeva, tr. Holcombe, 2008). Unlike Muddupalani, Jayadeva's name was not lost to the archives of religious literature, but is well known in the Vaishnava and broader Hindu diaspora. Our inquiry does not seek to challenge the high regard for Jayadeva or his work, but to examine whether there are notable differences in comparison to Muddupalani's work that would explain or merit the latter's denunciation in the Hindu tradition. Scholars familiar with Hindu texts may ask why I have refrained from examining the *Kama Sutra*, authored by Vatsyayana in 400 BC, which is notorious for its sexual content. Indeed, both texts deal with human sexuality, but *Gita Govinda* is a more suitable comparison because, like *Radhika Santawanam*, it is (1) a narrative, whereas *Kama Sutra* is more of a treatise on sex; (2) similar in content, exploring the same Radha-Krishna motif; and (3) unlike *Kama Sutra*, which is by and large irrelevant in the practice of Hinduism by Hindus with respect to prayers and rituals, *Gita Govinda* has been incorporated into the bhakti (devotional) movement within the Vaishnava community, which worships the deity known as Vishnu (who Krishna is said to be an incarnate of during his worldly exploits). The select verses in our study were chosen precisely because they were made in the context of a sexual act and comparable in content—not to challenge a *prima facie* determination of which sexual references may constitute a finding of obscenity or some related charge. The purpose here was not to establish a standard of sexual references that would satisfy a finding of obscenity; but rather to illustrate how those references fare in comparison with the *Gita Govinda*, which has notably been regarded in high esteem and enjoys a heightened status as devotional literature and source of worship. The select verses appear in Table 4.1.

The initial review of the texts included an identification of verses that were explicitly sexual in content; an accounting of the particular actor who was

Table 4.1 Select verses from Jayadeva's *Gita Govinda* and Muddupalani's
Radhika Santawanam based on content and context

Gita Govinda	Radhika Santawanam
Song 2, verse 9: Madhu's killer, clasped upon the lotus-goddess's exhausted breasts, has caught her mark of saffron in his fondest loving: may you follow in his sweated drops.	**Chapter 1, verses 65–66:** O Lion among cowherds Will her tender breasts bear your scratches? . . . When your lover embraces you, Press gently holding him against your breast.
Song 6, verse 5: By all love's treatises he won his pleasure; Like the cuckoo bird I cooed in murmurs. My massy breasts he scored with nail-marks, made My hair go all ways as it dropped its flowers.	**Chapter 1, verse 82:** He teased her then Stroking her breasts As his nails scratched her, She winced in pain.
Song 10, verse 6: As was passion first accomplished, now Is Madhava withheld by river bower: Constantly in thought and chanting prayers He feels the ferment of your spilling breasts.	**Chapter 2, verse 115:** Don't press my breasts, it makes me shy, I say he playfully scratches them with his fingernails even more.
Song 18, verse 2: In essence fuller than the fan-palm fruit, Why won't you press on him those pitcher breasts?	**Chapter 3, verse 126:** 'Don't touch me, I've just bathed,' I'd say . . . she'd press against my body with her breasts seductively.
Song 22, verse 12: Like Rati Devi in her hoarded beauty So Radha in the lake where love is played: A sporting Vishnu shook those lifted breasts As geese the lotuses of Manasa.	**Chapter 4, verse 105:** Like breeze circulating, She spun him around. Like a mechanized ball, She bounced around. Like the spinning top, Giddily she played him with gusto.
Song 24, verse 1: Anoint with sandal-dewy hands my breasts and, Krishna, make them worthy with your musk to be receptacles produced in thought. In this she spoke to him while Krishna played delighting in her heart.	She posed and preened Slapping his cheeks Chiding him lovingly Kissing him incessantly Touching his organ Caressing him slowly They made love, Bala Hari and his Radhika.

the aggressor in the verse, along with specific mention of any body parts that would implicate a sexual connotation; and the devotional invocation and benefits that often appear in Hindu texts. These criteria are elaborated upon, as follows:

- **Actor.** Here, I took account of whether the actor, defined as the character that was the aggressor of an act in the verse, was male or female. This was conducted to ascertain to what extent the work may reinforce gender stereotypes of the male as the aggressor, and the woman as the passive observer or, here, object of the sexual act.
- **References to genitalia or sexually related bodily references.** Explicit references to male and female genitalia or other bodily references facilitate a comparison of the specificity and context with which the references were made.
- **References to religious invocation and salutation** (mangalacharam). The *mangalacharam* refers to prayers that salute God or a particular deity, as well as the saints, and often appears in the opening lines of a religious text.
- **References to religious benefits** (phala stuti). The *phala stuti* refers to an enumeration of the benefits or fruits ("phala") of reciting or listening to a religious text and often appears in the concluding lines.

Table 4.2 provides a summary of the criteria following a close examination of the select verses.

Based on our snapshot, we find that *Radhika Santawanam* and *Gita Govinda* share many notable characteristics. Both texts feature verses wherein the male is the predominant actor (60 percent and 80 percent, respectively), and a description of explicit female body parts (and particularly a woman's breasts) is prevalent throughout. We also find a strong devotional component to both works, which contain a *mangalacharam* and *phala stuti*.

Notwithstanding their similarities, the texts are distinguishable in telling ways insofar as their distinct features may help explain the lukewarm reception

Table 4.2 A summary of explicit sexual references with respect to body parts and the dominant actors

Texts	Gita Govinda %	Radhika Santawanam %
Male actor	83.3% (5/6)	60.0% (3/5)
Female actor	16.7% (1/6)	40.0% (2/5)
Bodily references		
Male	– (0)	20.0% (1/5)
Female	100.0% (6/6)	100.0% (6/6)
Mangalacharanam	Yes	Yes
Phala Stuti	Yes	Yes

(if not outright rejection) of *Radhika Santawanam*. We find that while Krishna remains the predominant actor in love-making, Radha is accorded a greater role (40 percent vs. 16.7 percent) in verses where she takes on a more active role. Moreover, while *Gita Govinda* makes no mention of a male body part, *Radhika Santawanam* makes an explicit reference to Krishna's "organ" and goes even further by describing how Radha caresses him as part of a graphic depiction of her handling of him during their love-making (Chap. 4, v. 105). This particular verse is thus a very potent device in that it grants Radha physical power over Krishna and makes him particularly vulnerable as a partner— and male human being—by describing her control of him down to his most vulnerable (and for a man, the defining) body part.

A reader would have to be hard pressed to characterize *Radhika Santawanam* as a more vulgar text. Though it does make one reference to a man's penis and a woman's handling of it, *Gita Govinda* is equally aggressive in its characterization of a woman's breasts and a man's handling of them. The request, for example, for Krishna "to anoint . . . my breasts and make them worthy," and a description of how he "shook [Radha's] lifted breasts as geese the lotuses of Manasa," are quite explicit and arguably more so in that the request was a directive initially put forth in the first-person, whereas *Radhika Santawanam* only describes the act in far less vigorous imagery (i.e., caressing vs. shaking) (Song 22, v. 12 and Song 24, v. 1).

This analysis begs the question of whether *Radhika Santawanam* is an outlier within the tradition because it affords a heightened sense of empowerment for Hindu women (as portrayed by Radha). In the next section, I argue that such a characterization would be misplaced based on an examination of female autonomy and sexuality in foundational Hindu texts.

B. The parameters of female autonomy and sexuality in foundational texts: The Mahabharata

A pressing challenge is articulating the balance of rights and responsibilities of stakeholders while reconciling the varied languages of religion, law, and the social sciences. This is problematic since perspectives that cannot recognize some modicum of common ground are invariably bound for disagreement. It is therefore essential to establish a framework that can identify those commonalities.

Hindu law is not codified in a single text. Its traditions, while at times relegated to written form, have been passed on orally for over 5,000 years in the form of scriptures and stories. Whereas the scriptures consist mostly of hymns, philosophical discourses, and other abstract allusions, the tradition comes alive in the personification of characters and deities in the epic poetry, particularly the *Ramayana* and *Mahabharata*. The *Ramayana* and *Mahabharata* are the foundation for understanding the laws and principles that govern a Hindu's own life (*svadharma*) and those that govern the entire society (*sanatanadharma*). The *Mahabharata* speaks of its own authority in

Hindu thought, claiming that any person who "knows the four Vedas with their branches and Upanisads, but does not know this epic, has no learning at all" (van Buitenen, 1971). The oral tradition was later accompanied by a literary tradition manifest in the *Puranas*, a compilation of 18 treatises (and 18 further sub-treatises) consisting of stories that include the characters, tales, and even novel circumstances based on the epic poems. It is a foundational text because it presents both an ideological basis and a historical relevance within the religious tradition that cannot be easily dismissed.

The *Mahabharata* is Hinduism's grand epic, comprised of 18 sections or "books," 10 times larger than the Iliad and Odyssey combined, with over 100,000 verses. It is of particular historical import because it is considered among Hindus to be *itihaasa*, which means a historical event that actually occurred. So unlike a code of laws, philosophical treatises, or other related materials, this epic, with its sister epic, the *Ramayana*, are considered as authoritative in both content and relevance to the course of Hindu history.

The central narrative explores the breakdown of a royal family that culminates in the equivalent of a world war between the warring cousins. As for its scope of religious influence, as described above, the epic proclaims itself as greater than any scripture, and that it is the repository of all truths. Its influence, moreover, is far-reaching as to its applications to contemporary Hindu beliefs and practices. Many prayers recited in Hindu temples are taken verbatim from the epic. Also, its tales, which the central narrative is only a part of, are cited for illustrating the moral dilemmas in Hindu life. Its characters are cited as personifications of human qualities (honesty, strength, courage, love, lust, greed), in scriptural interpretation, and continue to be portrayed in a positive light in contemporary media (art, cinema, religious iconography).

While we may be quick to concede the importance that is ascribed to the epic within the Hindu community, understanding how to make sense of its content as relates to feminism and female empowerment in particular presents a greater challenge. The terms "autonomy," "empowerment," and the like may not appear explicitly in ancient texts, but this does not deny their existence or importance. Nonetheless, we must be careful not to stretch our imagination beyond the text and engage in such creative enterprises so as to render our inquiry meaningless. Renowned feminist scholar and philosopher, Professor Martha Nussbaum, articulated a list of "central human functional capabilities," which I believe can be utilized to illustrate why religiously inspired tales are more useful in securing women's empowerment than mere legal instruments.

In fact, efforts to promote functional capabilities vis-à-vis religiously inspired works are arguably a powerful step to promote female empowerment because they originate from within the tradition, making the content more amenable to the cultural disposition of the affected population. Specifically, these capabilities include: (1) life; (2) bodily health; (3) bodily integrity; (4) senses, imagination, and thought; (5) emotions; (6) practical reason; (7) affiliation; (8) other species; (9) play; and (10) control over one's environment (Nussbaum, 1999). As indicated in Table 4.3, these capabilities

Table 4.3 The Intersection of human rights and functional capabilities

Nussbaum Central Functional Capability	Life	Bodily Health	Bodily Integrity	Thought, Imagination	Emotions	Practical Reason	Affiliation	Other species	Play	Respect for environment	Totals
Corresponding CEDAW Provision											
Definition of discrimination	✓	✓	✓	✓		✓	✓	–	✓	✓	8
Adopt policies for equality	✓	✓	✓	✓		✓	✓	–	✓	✓	8
Guarantee basic rights	✓	✓	✓	✓			✓	–		✓	6
Modify sociocultural acts	✓	✓	✓	✓	✓		✓	–	✓		7
Acquire, change nationality							✓	–			1
Educational opportunities				✓		✓		–			2
Employment opportunities							✓	–			1
Access to healthcare	✓	✓	✓					–			3
Legal rights (e.g., property)							✓	–		✓	2
Marriage, family planning	✓	✓	✓				✓	–			4
Totals	6	6	6	5	1	3	8	n/a	3	4	

are consistent with many themes in the international Convention on the Elimination of Discrimination Against Women (CEDAW).

The outstanding issue, therefore, is how well these functional capabilities hold up in religiously inspired works, and particularly the *Mahabharata* and its treatment of female characters. Many women with strong personalities appear in the epic, with the character Draupadi popularly cited as a precursor to Hindu feminists, but in the text, Savitri and Damayanti are cited as the examples for others to appreciate Draupadi; so while Draupadi is certainly on par with these women, they are presented as the "authoritative" lives or "legal precedent" in this Hindu worldview of what constitutes legitimate female conduct in the private and public spheres. Here, we shall focus exclusively on the tale of Savitri (see Box 4.1 for a summary of her tale) and illustrate how this story fulfills many of Nussbaum's functional capabilities, consistent with contemporary human rights as articulated in CEDAW, and serves as a legitimate precursor long before *Radhika Santawanam* in setting a foundation for female empowerment and autonomy.

Box 4.1 Excerpts from the *Mahabharata*: Savitri

King Asvapati longed for a son and offered prayers for 18 years to propitiate the goddess Savitri; at the end of the eighteenth year, the goddess appeared and asked him what he wanted. The king asked for a son, since he was "told by [society's learned men] that having many sons" is "the highest Law." To this, the goddess smiled and told him he would beget a daughter and that he was not to reply. The king happily agreed and named his daughter after the goddess, Savitri. When Savitri grew up, she was exceedingly beautiful, intelligent, and independent. Her splendor was as such that no prince dared approach her to ask her hand in marriage. Eventually, the king asked her to choose a husband "for yourself with virtues that match yours" (van Buitenen, 1971). Savitri then came upon a young hermit named Satyavan. A chance appearance of a wise seer, however, informed her that Fate had declared that Satyavan would die within one year from that day. Regardless, Savitri, having chosen him, discarded her royal attire and joined him, along with his parents; Satyavan's father was Dyumatsena, a blind king who was exiled from his kingdom and lived with his wife and son in the surrounding forest.

On the days leading up to Satyavan's "day of death," Savitri undertook penance for three days, restricting her diet, and standing day and night in prayer. The blind king told her that the vow "was too severe [for a] *daughter* of a king," and "exceedingly difficult." Nonetheless, she continued. At the break of dawn, Satyavan grabbed his axe to chop wood and Savitri expressed her desire to accompany him. At first, he refused, commenting that she looked "gaunt" and that the "path [was] difficult." Savitri replied, "I am not weak," and joined him. Deep in the forest, Satyavan began chopping wood, and soon broke into a sweat, exclaiming, "I don't have the strength to stand." He then fell into her arms, and died. A moment later, Death arrived. After praising Savitri for being "a devoted wife," and "now acquitted of all debts to your husband," Death encouraged her to return home. Savitri refused and began walking with Death deeper into the forest. After walking seven steps, Death asked her why she was following him. Savitri replied: "It is masters of their souls who practice the Law in the woods, and austerities; and knowing the Law they promulgate it—hence the strict say the Law comes first. By the Law of the one as approved by the strict we all proceed on the course he has set. I don't want a second, I don't want a third—Hence the strict say the Law comes first." Pleased with her reply, Death granted her a boon (except not Satyavan's life). She requested that her blind father-in-law be restored of his eyesight. An exchange continued as Savitri refused to let Death walk off with Satyavan's soul. Her answers were rewarded with additional boons (with which she restored her father-in-law's reign over his kingdom), until Death granted her one final wish. Savitri requested that she be a mother. Death agreed and subsequently restored Satyavan's soul. As Savitri raced back to Satyavan's corpse, he awoke to find her waiting for him. As they returned to thc forest, many seers gathered and proclaimed:

> "The king of men's dynasty was mired
> In a pool of darkness, beset by evils.
> And you, good woman, blessed by the Law,
> You, noble lady, have rescued it!"

Consider the following observations:

Capability of life

Nussbaum describes this capability as being able to live to the end of a human life of normal length; not dying prematurely or before one's life is so reduced as to be not worth living. To this I would add female valuation and an explicit rebuke of sex-selection and sex-selective abortions. Son-preference has become a scourge of Indian (and particularly Hindu) culture, and it is no longer confined to the borders of India. A recent study found that current trends suggest that Indians in the U.S. may also be engaging in prenatal diagnostic procedures to conceive male children. The tale begins with society's preference for males over females, epitomized in King Asvapati's desire to have a son, pursuant to the counsel of society's learned men and in accordance with *paro dharma,* or "highest dharma." The term *dharma* is a catchall for law, righteousness, and virtue. Unlike the overly rigid and narrow conception of law in modern society, dharma refuses to be devoid of a moral attribute, though the potential conflict of an individual sense of dharma (*svadharma*) and a universal and generally applicable sense of dharma (*sanatanadharma*) is recognized. In fact, this is a central theme of the tale. Here, the conflict concerns the issue of son-preference. Notably, the king was *not* advised to have a son. The council had advised him that *samt_nam* was in accordance with the highest dharma. In Sanskrit, *samt_nam* means "offspring" or "progeny," not "son." Thus, the king had not chosen in accordance with the *sanatanadharma,* but out of his own personal preference. The granting of a daughter in response to his request is a clear rebuke of his misperception. While Savitri herself wishes to have sons later in the tale, she does not conflate her personal wants with the common morality. Female valuation is an explicit theme throughout the tale.

Capability of bodily health and integrity

Being able to have good health, including reproductive health, is indicated by Savitri's upbringing up to the point where the people, upon seeing her, remark, "We have received a goddess" (Ganguli, 1896). There is perhaps no better characterization of adequate nourishment and shelter than a presentation that commands divine comparisons.

Capability of bodily integrity

The freedom to move freely, have opportunities for sexual satisfaction and for choice in matters of reproduction are neatly packaged in a series of events. Savitri is given absolute freedom to choose a husband according to her own wishes. She thereupon roams throughout all the kingdoms in search of a suitable partner. Savitri chose Satyavan and upon becoming his wife, attended to him by "indications of her love in private," the nature of which should not be lost on readers as an indiscriminate allusion to conjugal affairs.

Capability of senses, imagination, and thought

This capability concerns the ability to imagine, think, and reason in a human way that is informed and cultivated by education. For Savitri, this capability is illustrated in a series of acts that encompass her (1) choosing of a husband of her own accord, (2) undergoing severe physical penance, (3) confronting Death, and (4) receiving the unique praise by the seers upon completing her trials. Her choice of Satyavan is not haphazard. As her father advised, she was to find a partner that had virtues that were comparable to her own. It was upon finding Satyavan "fit to be my husband," that Savitri *chose him.* Her subsequent undertaking of penance was equally profound. Society cannot see the rationale in this—personified in the *blind* king who only sees her as a "daughter," and nothing more. Despite her newly acquired strength (as a result of her penance), her own husband observes that she looks "gaunt," although she affirms that she is not weak. Her capability to express her beliefs, though questioned and even mocked, does not preclude her from fulfilling her vow. Consequently, she is able to confront Death and withstand his attempts to dissuade her. She ignores his reference to her being a "devoted wife," and having fulfilled a pre-defined societal role, thereby "acquitting herself of debts . . ." She chooses of her own volition to bear children, and also how many she will have. In doing so, she conquers Death, and restores her husband's life and her father's eyesight—that is, she restores balance to a society by asserting her strength and independence to exercise her autonomy unfettered. She is *not* praised by the seers as a "wife," or a "daughter," but as a "good woman," and "noble lady," thereby "rescu[ing]" a society that has gone astray. Savitri was not merely capable, but exemplary in her exercise of senses, imagination, and thought.

Capability of emotions

The first instance of Savitri's capability of emotions is found when she falls in love with Satyavan and chooses him "in my heart." She later refuses to choose another husband upon hearing of his impending doom. As a seer observed, the "heart of . . . Savitri wavereth not!" Third, she engages in "honeyed speech" with him, along with "indications of her love in private." Fourth, in the "sorrow" she felt as the day of Satyavan's death was nearing, and finally, in her refusal to let Death carry him away. Recalling that her "debts" to her husband were paid, Savitri's longing stem from her intimate relationship, founded not on duties and debts, but love and friendship. She also hints at this as exemplary in all relations when, in her opening verse to Death, she calls on him as a friend to engage her in dialogue.

Capability of practical reason

Being able to form a conception of the good and engage in critical reflection is a central theme of the tale. From the outset of her dialogue with Death, Savitri is praised for speaking words "with fine reason." Her authority does not stem from citing scriptures or personal figures—she speaks with conviction based on reason that yields universal *human* truths. Though society has declared four stages of human life (e.g., study, domestication, retirement, renunciation), adhering to true dharma, according to Savitri, consists of "true knowledge," which in turn stems from people who have brought "their souls under control." Using reason to articulate the good is thereby "the foremost of all things" and speech is its vehicle. At the outset of each subsequent exchange, Death begins by remarking how he is "pleased with the words that you speak." Moreover, reasoning is not merely a reflection on the past, but an opportunity to create and develop new ideas. As Death observes, Savitri's reasoning "enhance[s] the wisdom of even the learned."

Capability of affiliation

Being able to live in affiliation with others, and also retaining self-respect and non-humiliation, should coexist without qualification. This is a central theme within the tale. On the one hand, Savitri pleases her in-laws by "her virtues and services," and looks after each of them (i.e., her father-in-law, mother-in-law, and husband) and cares for them. Her virtues are not lost on any of them, including Satyavan, who observes that she is "possessed of every accomplishment." Yet her father-in-law's initial reluctance to approve of her undertaking a vow and Satyavan's comments on her appearance thereafter are important. Her father-in-law opined that such hardships were not suitable for the "daughter of a king." Satyavan also observed that she appeared "gaunt" after completing her fast. Though their remarks were not intentionally berating, they reflect (as today) a society that is hesitant to recognize a woman's potential to achieve and succeed in whatever endeavor she so chooses to embark on. By asserting her own capabilities, she conquers Death, and notably restores her husband's life and her father's eyesight.

Capability of [being sensitive to] other species

Being able to live with concern for and in relation to animals, plants, and the world of nature is explicitly declared by Savitri during her exchange with Death. She declares that "the eternal duty of the good towards *all creatures* is never to injure them in thought, word, and deed, but to bear them love and give them their due" (Ganguli, 1896). Recalling that Savitri and Satyavan live in a forest, the sincerity of her remarks in relation to her daily interactions is unquestionable.

Capability of play

Being able to laugh, play, and enjoy recreational activities is indicated in a childhood reference to the upbringing of Satyavan. As a child, he took great delight in horses, used to make horses out of clay, and even drew pictures of them. But this allusion to his past is not merely reminiscent of childhood dalliances. The reference also hints at what distinguishes Satyavan from other men, and is vital to recognizing why Savitri describes him as "fit to be my husband." Within his character is an innocence, which is at once present and absent in his being endued with wisdom, juxtaposed with his unawareness of his impending death. Satyavan, like a child—and all persons, for that matter—never feigns to control the world around him or subjugate Savitri to comport with his view of the world. His childlike (as opposed to childish) demeanor enables him to not only win Savitri's love, but prepares her subsequent encounter with Death, who explains how Satyavan's virtues required Death (rather than his emissaries) to take his soul in person.

Capability of control over one's environment

This capability entails being able to engage in political and material choices that govern one's life vis-à-vis freedom of speech and expression; and avail oneself of the opportunities to work, hold property, and engage in meaningful relationships with others. Since the political landscape in ancient India was intertwined with a worldview of cosmic proportions, the allusions to control decisions affecting one's personal life and relationships with others will suffice. The entire tale of Savitri is a constant assessment and reassessment of human proclivities. From the outset, speech is the manner in which sound determinations can be made. It is through speech that King Asvapati recognizes his own merits in fulfilling his penance and thinks himself entitled to a son. And though the goddess told that king that "I knew before this [request] this intention of yours," she did not suppress his freedom to express his wants.

In each tale, we find numerous instances of Nussbaum's central functional capabilities, and *Radhika Santawanam* is no exception, continuing a long tradition that dates back to the *Mahabharata* and proceeds through the *Gita Govinda* into the eighteenth century, spanning a course of over 2,000 years. Thus, female empowerment and autonomy is not only an important motif in the precolonial era, but arguably arose anew in *Radhika Santawanam*, posing a unique threat to the British and Indian colonial authorities. This may appear puzzling, given its conformity with a theretofore Hindu tradition and consequently raises the question of *whose* Hinduism was, in fact, being created, developed, and promoted within the early twentieth century, and arguably onto modern times. The unique threat that the work posed is discussed, below.

Radhika Santawanam is particularly unique in structure and content, which together enable it to pose a serious threat to a patriarchal order. On the surface, the structure is particularly unique with respect to authorship, accessibility, and the capacity for interpretation. The work was composed by a woman whereas the *Mahabharata* and *Gita Govinda* were composed by men. It is also more accessible among the literate, having been composed in the vernacular (Telegu) whereas the aforesaid texts were written in Sanskrit, which was and remains a language that has become exclusive to Indologists and Brahmin priests. Finally, the work surprisingly exhibits a fluid interpretation of Hindu thought and doctrine that is uncharacteristic of written texts, but absolutely consistent with foundational texts. It is noteworthy that the epics were passed down orally for centuries, allowing novel interpretation and (re)tellings that made the works relevant to the time and place of recitation. Despite being composed upon a palm leaf manuscript, and later published in print, *Radhika Santawanam* transcends the rigid borders of print media by defying time in its retelling of the Radha-Krishna saga, situating itself linguistically within a religious and social tradition, and retaining a consistent devotional tone.

The work emerges as a recitation by a sage, Sukha, to the sage-king, Janaka. Sukha is the child of Vyasa, who was the original composer of the *Mahabharata*, and Janaka was a king who lived in the age prior to the *Mahabharata*. This results in him being up to 1 million years old, which is illogical from a biological standpoint, but of paramount importance in the context of the Hindu worldview, that accords significance to the succession of teachers (i.e., Gurus) and the continuity of divine intervention (i.e., avatars or incarnates of the Divine). Janaka is not only a king, but the father-in-law of Krishna's divine predecessor, Rama; and his dialogue with Sukha reveals

Figure 4.1 Radhika Santawanam (1972)

the continuation of a spiritual tradition vis-à-vis progeny (Sukha being Vyasa's son), and the appeasement of a woman (Radha) just as Rama had appeased Sita (Janaka's daughter) in the prior age.

The work also situates itself in a Sanskrit and Telegu lineage by citing Valmiki (author of the *Ramayana*), Vyasa, and Kalidasa, who were all Sanskrit poets, and Nannaya, Tikkana, Nachana Somana, among other notable Telegu poets. In doing so, Muddupalani elevates the vernacular and directly challenges the historical prioritization of Sanskrit and the proprietary nature of that knowledge or wisdom unique to that class of individuals (i.e., Brahmins) who were exclusively charged with the retention and interpretation of Hindu doctrine and application.

Finally, the devotional tone of the work requires further elaboration. We previously noted the presence of both the *mangalacharam* and the *phala stuti* in the text as characteristic of devotional pieces. The opening stanza includes a prayer, "To all gods and great scholars, and to the Lord God, refuge of all beings . . ." and the concluding stanzas recite the benefits of listening such that "Riches will be bestowed, and all desires fulfilled on one who reads, possesses, or listens to *Radhika Santawanam.*"

Why ban an obscure work penned in a medieval dialect by a courtesan in the remote past? At the very least, such an act would make an example of what was considered distasteful, but this was an inadequate answer given the relative obscurity of the work. A more probable proposition was that the poem created a sense of fear among a cohort of private citizens and public officials. My initial analysis suggests that such fears were not unwarranted and merit further study to understand how a unique Hindu patriarchy developed in the [post] colonial era, and continues to exert a powerful influence over the lives of Hindu women. Muddupalani's *Radhika Santawanam* was a remarkable composition with the potential to serve as a cornerstone for the further development of "Hindu feminism," a term that should be welcomed—not as a novel construct—but as a fulfillment of an ancient tradition with deep roots, and the potential to empower Hindu women.

C. The principle of awliyah and the exercise of female autonomy

Shari'a is the common term used to denote Islamic law and stems from the *Quran, Hadith, Ijma, Qiyas,* and *Ijtihad* (Ali, 2000). The Quran is Islam's equivalent of a religious Constitution, the word of God revealed through the angel Gabriel to the Prophet Mohammed (hereafter "Mohammed"), comprised of 6,666 verses, of which scholars estimate 500 retain a legal element, and 80 that deal specifically with issues relating to women's human rights. While Islamic law affords some structural semblance to modern legal jurisprudence, its dissimilarities are profound. Unlike a State constitution, the Quran cannot be amended. As the Word of an infallible Deity, complete and perfect, it is considered flawless and immutable. Still, where it is silent or provides little express guidance on a particular issue, other sources of

Islamic law may be instructive. Nonetheless, a law that expressly rejects a Quranic mandate cannot be reconciled by resorting to traditional statutory interpretation (e.g., relying upon the plain meaning of the text).

While scholars continue to debate specific Quranic verses that seemingly grant women more or less autonomy than others, the concept of "Wali" in verse 9:71 captures the spirit of female empowerment as portrayed in the Ahadith. In 9:71, "the believers, men and women, are *awliya*, one of the other" (Ali, 2000). The term "awliya" is the plural form of "wali," which in Arabic means "friend, charge, guide, and protector." This term does not suggest subservience, but collaboration in a spirit of friendship whereby men and women engage in different roles, at different times, to help, guide and protect one another.

As a secondary source of Islamic law, the Ahadith (collected sayings of Mohammed) contains numerous stories that illustrate the principle of wali as a cornerstone of female empowerment. Unlike the previous Hindu tales, these accounts should not be read as distinct stories but as parts of a single story that captures the wali between Mohammed and his wife, Aishah bint Abi Bakr. Consistent with our prior discussion, these accounts depict (1) the self-destructive nature of male abuse, (2) the necessity to exercise autonomy based upon principles of freedom, and (3) a woman's strength in enduring, withstanding, and overcoming threats to her inherent dignity.

1. Aishah bint Abi Bakr and the Mortality of Man

Box 4.2 **Aishah bint Abi Bakr and the Mortality of Man**

Aishah bint Abi Bakr ("Aishah") was considered Mohammed's favorite wife. On one particular occasion, Aishah was in charge of overseeing a prisoner who escaped while she was attending to some other affairs. Mohammed then came, and Aishah recalls the dialogue that ensued:

"I [Aishah] said, 'I was preoccupied with the women and he escaped.'

"'What is the matter with you?' exclaimed Mohammed. 'May Allah cut off your hand!'

"Then he went out and gave orders that the prisoner should be sought after and returned. After the prisoner was brought back, Mohammed came in and found me examining my hands.

"He said, 'What is the matter with you? Have you gone mad?'

"I said, 'You cursed me, so I am examining my hands, wondering which one of them will be cut off.'

"Then he praised and extolled Allah and raised his hands high, saying, 'O Allah, I am only human. I get angry like any other human. Let me atone for any believer I may have cursed.'"

(Source: Fernea and Bezirgan, 1977)

The tale begins (see Box 4.2 for a summary) with Mohammed as the leader, in charge, directing Aishah in her post to keep an eye on the prisoner (Fernea and Bezirgan, 1977). In response to an innocent mistake, Mohammed succumbs to his anger and betrays their relationship of *wali* to assume a superior role. In doing so, he attempts to exert his power by "cursing" Aishah and exclaims that her hand be severed. Aishah's reluctance to react only evokes a sense of guilt as Mohammed concedes his mortality, for "[he is] only human," and "get[s] angry like any other human." As a result, he pleads with Allah to "atone" for not only his outburst towards Aishah, but for *anyone* he may have cursed. Mohammed recognizes the self-destructive nature of his behavior and its capacity to disrupt wali between him and his wife, along with awliyah within the greater society. Aishah's ability to endure his anger and withstand any inclination to react (as he did), inevitably causes Mohammed to make amends, securing their wali and her dignity.

2. Aishah bint Abi Bakr and the Affair of the Slander

Box 4.3 Aishah bint Abi Bakr and the Affair of the Slander

During an expedition, Aishah was once accidentally left behind when she left the camp to perform her ablutions. In the meantime, a young man on a camel came along and offered to take her to Medina. She accepted and he took her back to her convoy. The incident, however, raised rumors and gossip of her alleged relations with the young man. Some of Mohammed's close allies urged him to scorn her, while others tried to convince her otherwise. Mohammed eventually confronted her and said, "Aishah, if you have been tempted to evil or done wrong, repent; for Allah accepts repentance from his servants." Aishah, however, stood her ground.

She recalled: "If I said that I had done nothing and Allah knows that I would be telling the truth, you would not believe me for you already think me guilty. If I said I were guilty and Allah knows I am not, you would say I had confessed. Thus, all I can do is cite Joseph's father: 'My course must be fitting patience, and Allah's help is to be sought for the problem you describe.'"

Mohammed then had a revelation revealing her innocence and urged Aishah to rejoice. When her parents insisted that she return to Mohammed, Aishah replied, "I shall neither go to him nor praise him nor you who believed what you heard about me and did not deny it. I shall praise Allah who revealed my innocence."

(Source: Fernea and Bezirgan, 1977)

The "affair of the slander" was a significant crisis in Aishah's life (see Box 4.3 for a summary), but she remained adamant in securing her innocence. Here, the self-destructive nature of male abuse is portrayed in accusations of Aishah's infidelity, encompassing the entire society, particularly among Mohammed's comrades who attempt to dismiss Aishah. Reflecting on this predicament, Aishah speaks directly to society's indifference to the truth, explaining how she was in a no-win situation of speaking the truth (whereby nobody would believe her) or proclaiming her guilt (a lie that would be received as a confession). She cites her own endurance—fitting patience—to withstand society's attempt to trespass on her dignity. Afterward, she holds Mohammed accountable for betraying their wali, recalling his disbelief. Still, it is Aishah's strength and endurance that alone secures her dignity.

3. Aishah bint Abi Bakr and the Verse of the Choice

The famous account of the Verse of the Choice ("Choice") alludes to Mohammed's proposal to Aishah that "If you desire the life of the world and its embellishments, then come and I will compensate you and release you honorably, but if you desire Allah and his Prophet and the life of the hereafter, then Allah will prepare for the chaste among you a great reward." Aishah replied, "I want Allah and His messenger and the hereafter. I don't need to consult my parents." Mohammed laughed upon hearing her reply.

The Choice succeeded a period when Mohammed was thought to have considered divorcing all his wives. He had "retired to be alone, to contemplate and meditate." It is unclear whether he found his worldly life a distraction or what may have propelled such thoughts. Regardless, as reflected in the Choice, he deferred to each wife the decision to stay with him—as opposed to the suspicion that he would outright reject them. Aishah, as his favorite wife, asserted her autonomy in choosing him and also negated any notion that her parents had any say in the matter. The choice reflects a departure from earlier efforts to exert control by engaging in an honest dialogue that solidified the friendship and trust of their relationship. In 632 AD, Mohammed died in Aishah's arms.

D. Utilizing religion to promote human rights and functional capabilities

These tales provide a sample from the corpus of literature within the Hindu and Islamic traditions from ancient to relatively modern times. Their capacity to inform, and arguably promote, female empowerment can be summarized in the identification of salient features that are consonant with specific rights and capabilities, summarized in Table 4.4.

Table 4.4 How religiously inspired tales fulfill human functional capabilities

Nussbaum Central Functional Capability / Tale	Life	Bodily Health	Bodily Integrity	Thought, Imagination	Emotions	Practical Reason	Affiliation	Other species	Play	Respect for environment	Totals
Savitri (Mahabharata)	✓	✓	✓	✓	✓	✓	✓	✓	✓	✓	10
Radha (Gita Govinda)	✓	✓	✓	✓	✓	✓	✓	–	✓	–	8
Radha (Radhika Sant.)	✓	✓	✓	✓	✓	✓	✓	✓	✓	–	9
Aishah, Mortality of Man	✓	✓	✓	✓	✓	✓	✓	✓	–	–	8
Aishah, Affair of Slander	✓	✓	✓	✓	✓	✓	✓	–	–	–	7
Aishah, Verse of Choice	✓	✓	✓	✓	✓	✓	✓	–	–	–	7
Totals	4	4	4	4	4	4	4	3	3	1	

IV. Recommendations for ethical, legal and structural reform

The present analysis illustrates that the cultural bases for female empowerment are fertile ground to respect, promote, and secure the sexual and reproductive health of South Asian women. Upon consideration, the following recommendations are proffered:

1. Amend declarations to CEDAW to align policies with its object and purpose

Condoning community beliefs and practices that infringe upon women's exercise of reproductive rights furthers discriminatory practices, thereby defeating CEDAW's underlying object and purpose. State and local laws become toothless if they do not stem from policies that denounce gender inequality and empower women to actively participate in matters affecting their sexual and reproductive health. Religious or cultural norms cannot deny any woman her fundamental right to assert control over her body. Nor can the law remain silent and allow such practices to remain unfettered. It is irrelevant if exercising her right is consistent with religious or cultural perspectives. Women must be the ultimate decision-makers in matters affecting their sexual and reproductive health.

2. Institute State regulation of abortions to reduce social and economic impediments to care and ensure post-complication treatment

Abortion laws in India and Pakistan do not adequately address the prevalent social hardships imposed on Indian and Pakistani women. Power differentials between husbands and wives may stymie women's access to services and the flow of information to secure their health. For example, while contraceptives may be readily available, access to and use thereof is often a function of the willingness on the part of a women's husband. Laws should be implemented that recognize women's autonomy as paramount, encourage women to seek out information on matters affecting their health and sexuality, and foster their collective health and well-being.

3. Engage community religious leaders to promote education that respects, promotes, and fulfills women's autonomy and right to self-determination

While the ICPD Five- and Ten-Year reviews encouraged the participation of religious leaders to implement key actions, the guidelines remained silent on precisely how to do so. Identification of religious principles that value women's autonomy and right to self-determination creates a bridge to engage communities in meaningful dialogue. Religious leaders may act as educators to demonstrate the consistency of government policies with underlying religious tenets. While religious leaders may not have a legal obligation to the government or society at large, they occupy a unique position in promoting communal solidarity and enunciating the roles and responsibilities of their constituency.

V. Conclusion

In this brief sketch, we find a fascination with the human quest for meaning that transcends traditional dichotomies of East and West, of man and woman, of moral and legal imperatives. The tales of Savitri and Aishah offer an opportunity to utilize religious traditions to engage communities to deliberate on contemporary issues of sex, gender, and equality. They also rebuke a contemporary awakening among unenlightened Hindu and Muslim women presumably wedded to a patriarchal worldview with no sense of dignity, value, or equality on par with men. On the contrary, these tales illustrate a seemingly perpetual struggle that was no less real a few thousand years ago than it is today. Aligning efforts in public health, law, and religion is a challenge that should be embraced to encourage female autonomy in matters affecting sexual and reproductive health. If Socrates is the Father of the Humanities, Savitri is surely its Mother. While no less a renowned scholar as Dr. Leon Kass would describe Socrates and Plato among the "world's first and greatest humanists," I find the absence of any mention of their female, non-Western counterparts quite tragic.

Suggested further reading

Desan, Philippe (1977) *Engaging the Humanities at the University of Chicago.* Chicago, IL: University of Chicago Press, 9.

Grimes, David G. (2006) Reducing the Complications of Unsafe Abortion: The Role of Medical Technology, *Lancet*; 368: 1908–19, appearing in Warriner I.K. and Shah I.H. (eds) *Preventing Unsafe Abortion and Its Consequences: Priorities for Research and Action.* The Guttmacher Institute, New York (2006): 73–91.

Howland, Courtney (1999) *Religious Fundamentalisms and the Human Rights of Women.* New York: St. Martin's Press.

Kapur, Ratna (1999) The Two Faces of Secularism and Women's Rights in India, in *Religious Fundamentalisms and the Human Rights of Women.* New York: St. Martin's Press, 149.

Kapur, Ratna (2005) *Erotic Justice: Law and Politics and the New Politics of Postcolonialism.* Permanent Black, Delhi; distributed by Orient Longman, Bangalore.

Khan, Sadaf (2005) Abortion: A Major Contributor to Maternal Ill Health. *Journal of Pakistan Medical Association* 55;7: 269.

Menski, Werner F. (2003) *Hindu Law: Beyond Tradition and Modernity.* Oxford University Press, New Delhi; New York.

Pandit, M.P. (1982) *Introducing Savitri.* Cennai, India: Rajsri Printers.

Rao, V.N. and Shulman, D. (2002) *Classical Telegu Poetry: An Anthology*. Oxford: Oxford University Press.

Rodwell, J.M. (1994) *The Koran*. Oxford: Oxford University Press.

Sedgh, Gilda (2007) Induced Abortion: Estimated Rates and Trends Worldwide. *The Lancet 370: 1338.*

Shah, Iqbal and Ahman, Elisabeth (2004) Age Patterns in Unsafe Abortions. *Reproductive Health Matters* 24: 9.

Tharu, S. and Lalita, K. (1993) Empire, Nation and the Literary Text, in *Women Writing in India*. New York: Feminist Press, 199–219.

5 Perspectives from the field

A conversation with Benjamin Meier, Ph.D., J.D., LL.M., Assistant Professor of Global Health Policy at the University of North Carolina-Chapel Hill

Q.1 On human rights and the search for a common morality

Q: Are human rights the fulfillment of a search for a common morality?

A: I think we have to go back at least to the HIV/AIDS pandemic. The idea that human rights takes off in public health and the idea that human rights and health is inextricably linked. So what is good for human rights is also good for health. And similarly, when public health respects human rights, it would aid its results. So in this context, Jonathan Mann through his introductory book on health and human rights stated that while public health is providing breathtaking practical results, it's missing something. And it's losing its full potential because it lacks a sense of values—why we care about global health. So human rights fills this void, Mann believes, because it provides these values, and specifically values that are necessary to frame policies. So I would see human rights as a particular way to frame ethical norms about global health. And while we're talking about ethical issues, social justice, and ethics, the way we frame these ethical norms for the purpose of structuring global health policy is through the language of human rights, and concrete and discreet legal obligations that have been developed by the United Nations over the last 65 years.

Q.2 On complementary, but distinct, norms based on philanthropy or religion

Q: Do you believe that articulation complements private charitable interests or missionary groups that are driven by similar, but distinct, norms stemming from personal motivation or even religious faiths? Are these complementary?

A: I think they work in concert with one another. You mentioned earlier how individuals often invoke the language of human rights rhetorically. But I would say that human rights takes these social justice norms, whether it be equity, and the duty to protect, and links these ethical norms with concrete legal obligations that create policies that are realized out of a sense of obligation. One of my concerns with philanthropic work is that it's fleeting, and that there's no sustainability. Human rights provides a stable normative framework that can be used to create obligations on the international community and individual actors that are necessary for global health. So I like to think that many of these norms that exist in other realms, whether they be religious, ethical, or other in nature, they can become translated into the language and obligation of human rights, which is I believe the way that most current global health policies are being structured.

Q.3 On terms and terms of art

Q: For all practical purposes, are the terms "right to health," "right to health-care," and "right to public health," synonymous? Or is it important that we distinguish the terms to achieve short- or long-term objectives?

A: I think it's important to distinguish them. In a different time, people talked about a right to healthcare, and in the public health community, we understand that healthcare is a small part of what influences health. As the World Health Organization states, health is a state of complete physical, mental, and social well-being, and not merely the physical absence of disease or infirmity. So as we're thinking through this more complete understanding of health, we understand that human rights are not static concepts because they were created by individuals sitting around the table representing States at the end of the Second World War. Since then, our understanding of human dignity has changed, our understanding of what is necessary to create health has changed. There was a belief then that healthcare was all that was necessary to realize health. And yet even countries like Great Britain came to appreciate that even with equal healthcare, there is still a social gradient with respect to health outcomes. So as we come to understand these underlying social, economic, and political determinants of health, the right to healthcare has transmuted into a right to health, a larger concept of what is necessary to protect people's physical, mental, and social well-being. And as that happened, we have moved to a more encompassing view as to what governmental obligations exist to realize health for all individuals.

Q.4 On the challenges of adjudicating international health disputes

Q: General Comments are not legally binding but they have become quite elaborate in expounding upon the obligations of states parties. Critics believe that this approach affords too much discretion to treaty monitoring committees to create novel interpretations (and thus, obligations). How has this played out in actuality?

A: There's something here with the concerns but whether it's entirely valid is debatable. Let's step back for a moment and consider a country that has ratified the ICESCR; the Committee comes along and interprets the treaty and the nation disagrees with the interpretation and no longer wants to be bound by it. This is one reason why clarification is necessary because it's simply not always self-evident with respect to articulating the policies that would implement those treaty provisions.

Q.5 When States disengage themselves from the deliberative process Affordable Care Act

Q: In the landmark reproductive rights case of *K.L. v. Peru* (2005), the Committee on the ICCPR found that Peru had violated the rights of a young woman who was not afforded an opportunity to have a therapeutic abortion after she was diagnosed with anencephaly, and was forced to give birth to a deformed fetus that was expected to die (and did) within hours after the delivery. An overseen aspect of the case is that the Peruvian government did not submit any materials to the ICCPR Committee when this claim arose, and effectively ignored the process of addressing this issue—notwithstanding the fact that it had ratified the optional protocol to the ICCPR. Should states that ratify a treaty and refuse to engage the processes and protections afforded to potential victims be automatically excluded from membership?

A: We have to look at it from the other side. If you nullify ratification, we have one less country. The international human rights standards are created by States, but are created by States that in particular moments may be to their disadvantage. So a tension exists because we want every country to participate and to deny a country membership would certainly cease any future dialogue on that matter. It's a challenging predicament.

Q.6 On prioritizing interventions

Q: These General Comments speak to a lot of different health interventions, and begs the question of how best to allocate resources. Have these challenges arisen in your work?

A: That, in fact, is one of the reasons for drafting General Comments, in how nations think through priorities when considering the progressive realization of human rights so that States can come to understand how their own obligations are evolving over time based upon their own national resources. The General Comments will have a minimum core that all nations are bound by, but at the same time recognize certain priorities within the Member State as relate to its own health burdens. We begin by saying that at the minimum, you need a national health plan; and from there, start to prioritize some underlying determinants of health that are either most closely associated with human dignity or are more cost-effective. With respect to human dignity, we may refer to a list of, for example, essential medicines as prescribed by the WHO that are so crucial for human dignity that they fall near or at the core of governmental obligations. Secondly, we can look to something such as clean water, which also provides significant benefits and addresses health in a widespread manner with minimal financial expenditure. There are also priorities that are placed in the General Comments on issues such as sustainability, equity, interconnectedness of rights. So these comments exist to provide normative frameworks for countries to think through how to set national health policies to ensure realization of health as a human right.

Q.7 On substantive interpretation

Q: Do you agree with how Committees generally interpret the provisions?

A: There will always be an issue of whether the Committees have exceeded their mandates because in some ways, they are somewhat broad and are being clarified in substantially more detail. So if we look at human rights as a dynamic process, and understand that these treaties are living documents, then one can say that although the General Comments, even if they are not perfect, Reflect an evolving notion of what is required to realize specific rights.

Q.8 On the effectiveness of General Comments

Q: So for you, it is not so much the rigid textual reading that could be undertaken, but the dialogue that is created by these instruments that are vital for their effectiveness?

A: Yes, and I would say that these General Comments are only one way that these treaty provisions are being interpreted and implemented. We also look at a number of different accountability frameworks, indicators, national reports to treaty-monitoring bodies, academics seeking to clarify what these provisions mean, as well as international conferences that bring together national policymakers to ask how best can we realize specific rights.

Q.9 On the potential incoherence of related instruments

Q: With all these diverse instruments, could you foresee a situation where a diverse interpretation could present a problem? Or is this too theoretical to address at this point?

A: At a certain point, States have agreed to be bound by these and there is no enforcement to ensure that States actually follow through. So working with treaty-monitoring bodies, and States is ultimately a dialogue with national governments trying in one form or another to impress upon them that it is an obligation that they have themselves assumed. So if it's not a conversation or a dialogue, and is too restrictive, then we'll see cases like

K.L. v. Peru, where countries will simply back away from the process because there is no enforcement that prevents them from walking away from the table.

Q.10 On the nature of the relationship between Committees and States

Q: So should this relationship between the treaty monitoring-bodies and States be looked at as a partnership rather than a process that requires states to renounce their sovereignty, which is often cited as a common rhetorical device in political circles?

A: Well, States are on both sides of this issue. It's not as if at the end of the day, in *K.L. v. Peru* for example, that Peru walked away from the United Nations, which would be the worst possible situation. What we have here is a continual negotiation with other countries as to what the rule of law will be, and the universal ethical norms will be, for the rest of the world. And when countries feel that the international consensus is getting ahead of them, they back away from the conversation. So it's not so much a partnership because the sovereign is on both sides of the partnership! So it's the individual State versus the community of States, which is what the Optional Protocols seek to represent.

Q.11 On Optional Protocols

Q: Shouldn't States be afforded more robust decisions when these Committees adjudicate claims vis-à-vis the Optional Protocols?

A: I think this is the difference you see between the ICESCR and CEDAW, where the former has General Comments whereas CEDAW has General Recommendations. And there's a legal distinction between the two. The distinction is that in the aftermath of creating the ICESCR, the community of States was worried that if they had such an inflexible system on gender, countries would back away. And the goal at the end of the day with human rights is to keep as many countries as possible at the table and continue the dialogue. That's why when treaty-monitoring bodies engage countries who submit national reports, the recommendations reflects a dialogue upon review of the report, rather than a prescriptive, concluding, demand.

Q.12 On the thoroughness of Committee decisions on claims brought before them via Optional Protocols

Q: Doesn't it fuel the criticism when Committees request countries to submit hundreds of pages of documents in reports, and fail to reciprocate that effort in the robustness of decisions rendered?

A: Yes, but at the end of the day, it is a State-driven process, and I think as you reflect on it in the 65 years following the creation of the United Nations, it has been a smashing success because it has brought everyone to the table. There have been compromises along the way, ambiguities along the way, but it has never been so onerous on the States to compel them to walk away. Even when rights are violated and States are reluctant to ratify, for example, an Optional Protocol, they still remain engaged with the international community through their membership.

6 Trade and health

Emergent paradigms and case studies in infectious diseases

Introduction

The intersection of trade and health is often discussed as a function of core economic principles, including efficiency, scarcity, and social welfare. These elements, in turn, constitute the popular framework to analyze the availability of resources and services to secure health at the individual or population levels. Efficiency, for example, refers to the optimal utilization of land, labor, and capital given the scarcity of available resources. The net gains that flow from this utilization are an indication of social welfare, or the satisfaction from consumption of goods or services. Here, we do not rehash an economic framework or summarize the major themes and methods of analysis (cost-benefit, cost-effectiveness, cost-utility, etc.) because at the global level, the implication of health as a human right elevates the attention to non-economic themes that may (or ought) to be equally pressing in consideration of the effects of trade upon health, and the role of States in fulfilling their obligations in a web of interrelated, albeit distinct, health-related treaties.

Global health as it is commonly understood is driven by the forces of globalization, which has become synonymous with the rapid pace of travel, information-sharing, and the heightened potential for cross-border threats. It is hardly surprising, therefore, when nations preclude the importation of contaminated food products, or instill quarantine or isolation measures for airline passengers suspected of carrying an infectious pathogen. A more difficult challenge arises when states attempt to restrict the travel of individual healthcare providers, or establish uniform standards of care at the international level. And perhaps the most daunting task is how, as an international community, we can muster the resources and political will to build the healthcare and public health infrastructure (i.e., capacity) of nations disproportionately affected by morbidity and mortality as relates to a pressing health threat, or simply lack the resources owing to their general status as a developing or undeveloped nation.

Legal analysis on the intersection of trade and health often contemplates the reconciliation of mutually competing rights and duties, such as the right for an individual to travel freely and pursue employment where she so chooses against a state interest in precluding "brain drain" and ensuring an adequate and competent healthcare workforce.

The World Health Assembly adopted resolution WHA 57.19, which requested the Director-General of the World Health Organization to consult with Member States to develop a code of practice on the global recruitment of health personnel. On May 21, 2010, the WHA adopted the WHO Global Code of Practice on the International Recruitment of Health Personnel. The code emerges against a backdrop of the urgent need of some countries to seek qualified healthcare personnel (e.g., nurse shortage in the U.S.). The code is voluntary, and encourages employers and recruiters to be aware and consider the outstanding legal responsibility of health personnel to the health system of their own country (Art. 4.2), and promotes the development and retention of qualified health personnel in every country (Art 5.4). Though cross-border training is supported, Member States "should encourage and support health personnel to utilize work experience gained abroad for the benefit of their home country" (Art. 5.3). The non-emergent restriction of healthcare personnel appears to be a clear violation of a right to leave one's country under Art. 12(2) of the International Covenant on Civil and Political Rights (ICCPR), which states, "Everyone shall be free to leave any country, including his own." But the loss of qualified healthcare personnel—many of whom are trained free of charge by their home countries—is only exacerbating the health disparities among and within countries worldwide. At a fundamental level, what this tension reveals is that the right to health, and the provision of health services, is contingent upon the utilization of healthcare providers who, incidentally, also have rights that implicate a complex matrix of legal decision-making that must be resolved on a case-by-case basis.

It remains unclear whether the international health community will embrace attempts to quantify, standardize, and regulate the conduct of health personnel by restricting individual rights to travel, seek employment, and practice pursuant to one's free will. What is readily apparent is that such codes and attendant policies will affect trade in health services, and challenges the predominant framework that examines health through a lens of trade (e.g., GAT, TRIPS, etc.). Rather, this debate is beginning to examine the parameters of trade through a lens of health. Unfortunately, however, we are far from establishing a uniform policy on global health as applies to every nation.

This section builds on this emerging paradigm shift by exposing the disparities that exist at the interface of trade and health as it relates to the international control of infectious diseases, and the national and subnational access to medicines, particularly in vulnerable populations using a central case study of Indonesia's reluctance to share samples of the H1N1 virus with the WHO in 2007, and other instances of outbreaks (SARS) and human rights violations (South Africa, U.S.).

I. Indonesia's withdrawal of H1N1 viral samples

In 2007, H5N1 avian influenza had reportedly claimed the lives of 186 persons worldwide, 77 of whom resided in Indonesia.[1] On February 7, 2007, the government of Indonesia announced that it would withhold strains of H5N1 avian influenza virus from the World Health Organization (WHO). On the same day, Indonesia signed a memorandum of agreement with Baxter Healthcare, a United States-based company, to purchase samples and presumably ensure access to subsequent vaccines at a discount.

In the past, the WHO received samples from afflicted nations and then provided them to vaccine manufacturers. Among the manufacturers was Australia's largest pharmaceutical company, CSL, which announced a week prior that it had developed the world's first vaccine against avian influenza. Initial trials suggested promising results, and the company claimed that it could manufacture sufficient quantities to protect the entire Australian population within six months. In response, Indonesian Health Minister Siti Failah Supari vowed that Indonesia would not share future virus samples "without a change in rules" to preclude poorer countries from becoming "commercial target[s]."[2] Indonesia's requests included a legally binding agreement that would prevent the WHO from sharing viral samples without the donor country's consent and limited use for public health risk assessment purposes.

The WHO claimed that withholding samples would prevent essential monitoring of the virus's potential evolution and oversight of key diagnostic capabilities of individual laboratories. The result was a stalemate in which WHO officials pleaded with Indonesia to resume sharing its viral samples. The decision to withhold samples came amidst fears of the pathogen evolving into a human-to-human transmissible agent and potentially causing a pandemic. On May 30, 2007, the World Health Assembly adopted a stopgap resolution[3] among its 193 Member States (including Indonesia) to share viral strains and thereby encourage global surveillance and monitoring of intra-State diagnostic capacities. A WHO official reported that failure to do so would "put the whole world at risk."[4] Nonetheless, many questions remain unanswered. What are the legal bases to preclude States from claiming viral ownership to secure future access to medicines? Although international viral sharing has resumed, what particular avenues exist to promote intra-State capacity building? Is the current international legal landscape amenable to foster inter-State collaborations to secure global health? These issues remain important for a myriad of reasons. Indonesia is currently lacking the developmental capacity to produce a vaccine (hence, its agreement with Baxter), and "cannot afford to buy" vaccines produced by other countries (e.g., Australia).[5] While the revised International Health Regulations (effective June 15, 2007) adds legal pressure for States to comply with the new resolution, the WHO has yet to identify any specific pathways to secure global health by promoting intra-State capacity building. By capacity, I mean an adequate balance of population and individually tailored interventions to protect public health, which specifically includes the use of non-pharmaceutical interventions (e.g., isolation and quarantine, health promotion) and available treatment options (e.g., provision of vaccines, health services). A failure to recognize the appropriate balance of both initiatives leaves a gaping hole in global public health preparedness.

Under the WHO resolution, States agree to provide "fair and equitable distribution of pandemic-influenza vaccines at affordable prices," but their progressive realization is undermined by failure to appreciate the underlying public health crises existent in developing and least developed States.[6]

In this chapter, I argue that existent health and trade agreements are necessary to control infectious diseases, but insufficient to secure global health. I focus specifically on the Agreement on Trade-Related Aspects of Intellectual Property Rights (TRIPS) and the Revision of the International Health Regulations (IHR). While the agreements must be read in concert to ensure an effective response to disease outbreaks, they disproportionately favor post-event treatment options. This is problematic where a particular State has an unstable health infrastructure, thereby undermining global cooperation to minimize cross-border public health threats.

The analysis first explores conceptual and temporal fallacies that permeate the current international legal landscape. The conceptual fallacy is the presumption of stable health infrastructures—the most stable nation status—without which the provision of health and public health-related services are ineffective. The temporal fallacy is that infectious disease control strategies are invoked only during circumstances that cause unstable States to remain in states of perpetual emergencies.

Against this backdrop of conceptual and temporal fallacies, I proceed to focus on State obligations to advance epidemic control and property interests in the use of biological materials (e.g., viral strains). Discordant views of express legal obligations obfuscate a State's role and responsibilities in protecting sovereign interests without jeopardizing global health. By resolving these issues, international health advocates can encourage collaboration among States to control infectious disease outbreaks and promote global public health preparedness.

Finally, recommendations are proffered, including the following: (1) adoption of intra-State laws facilitating implementation of non-pharmaceutical interventions; (2) incorporation of minimum protections and additional rights to protect individual liberty interests; and (3) the construction of suretyship arrangements to secure political accountability and support public health capacity building.

A. Conceptual fallacy of the most stable nation status

Developing and least developed States bear a disproportionate burden of dealing with potential infectious disease outbreaks. For example, Christopher

Murray *et al.* estimated that an influenza pandemic mimicking the 1918–1919 pandemic would claim 62 million lives, with 96 percent of deaths occurring in developing countries such as Indonesia.[7] Of the 186 deaths caused by H5N1 influenza over the past four years, 41 percent have occurred in Indonesia.[8] Inadequate resources and tenuous health systems make developing countries ill-equipped to respond to imminent outbreaks of infectious diseases. Also, Indonesia's decentralized health system empowers local governments as the focal point for the provision of health care services;[9] this may result in regional disparities that deter efficient public health responses to disease outbreaks in the absence of statewide surveillance and policies.

Effective national capacity to meet local threats and prevent their escalation into a statewide incident is vital. Consequently, international agreements that attempt to protect international public health should address the disproportionate impact on certain States by identifying viable avenues to strengthen intra-State health infrastructures.

Non-pharmaceutical interventions (NPIs) are an important component of State capacity in responding to the potential spread of disease in developed and developing or least developed nations. Although treatment of infected persons is essential, there will most likely be an inadequate supply of vaccines during the initial stages of a pandemic. In the United States, for example, the Centers for Disease Control and Prevention (CDC) estimates that neither well-matched vaccines nor sufficient quantities of antiviral medications will be available at the onset of pandemic flu.[10] It is reasonable to assume a similar predicament during the onset of an H5N1 pandemic. The CDC proposes numerous NPIs to curb the spread of disease, including isolation of infected persons, voluntary quarantine of exposed individuals, school closure, and the use of other social distancing measures to reduce human-to-human contact.[11]

B. An overview of the Declaration on the TRIPS Agreement and the IHR

TRIPS (including its subsequent amendments) does not adequately address the use and limitations of NPIs. TRIPS was initially enacted to compel Member States to adhere to minimum standards of intellectual property protection, which includes conferring rights and duties to the holders of patents for pharmaceutical products and medicines. Amidst criticism concerning the disproportionate impact on developing States, an exception was carved to allow for compulsory licenses in the wake of an emergency (the "Doha Declaration," discussed below).

The Doha Declaration on the TRIPS Agreement and Public Health (Doha Declaration) was adopted by the World Trade Organization (WTO) in November 2001 to address the gravity of communicable diseases and other epidemics. Its purpose is to protect public health and "in particular, to promote access to medicines for all."[12] States may access medicines by granting compulsory licenses only when that particular State determines a national emergency or circumstance of extreme urgency exists.[13]

The Doha Declaration focuses solely on the emergency containment of a disease and fails to address existent public health preparedness, including the role of NPIs. This approach undermines event preparedness and continues to ignore the disproportionate impact of infectious diseases on developing and least developed nations. Further, it conflates State and global interests without recognizing existent disparities across health infrastructures. Still, no identifiable legal or economic avenues foster inter-State collaborations that promote intra-State preparedness.

The revised IHR was adopted in May 2005 to provide a global instrument for protection against the international spread of disease. The IHR complements TRIPS by recognizing the importance of NPIs in controlling the spread of infectious diseases. Its recommendations include quarantine, isolation, and treatment of persons infected or exposed to communicable disease threats.[14]

Moreover, the IHR urges Member States to "collaborate actively" to ensure an effective implementation of the proposed measures.[15] Nonetheless, it is unclear how such collaborations can be successful where development of intra-State capacity is lacking. While the IHR urges States to take all appropriate measures to ensure public health capacities are well equipped to respond to potential outbreaks, it is silent on precisely how Member States should collaborate to meet this challenge.

The IHR does not provide any substantial guidance on individual State capacity building. Access to medicines and the implementation of NPIs is predicated on inter-State collaborations and adequate health infrastructures. From a public health perspective, such collaborations are vital to mount an effective response to disease outbreaks. For example, the global response to the SARS outbreak of 2003 illustrated the importance of collaboration among Member States to curb the spread of a communicable disease.

The recommended use of NPIs (specifically isolation and quarantine) resulted in significant post-event outbreaks. Even so, provisions enabling capacity building to implement these containment measures are simply non-existent in the agreement. While TRIPS protects pre-event intellectual property interests and supports post-event disease containment, it does not facilitate development of stable intra-State health infrastructures. Even the IHR, despite its support of strengthening and maintaining public health capacities, "does not generate fresh financial resources to support capacity-building."[16]

II. Securing global health interests cannot be traced to the Doha Declaration or the IHR

Securing global health by identifying specific avenues of State capacity building cannot be traced to the Doha Declaration or subsequent decisions by the Council for TRIPS (Council). The Doha Declaration affords a public health exception to grant compulsory licenses, but may have a limited impact without fostering capacity building and reducing inter-State dependency.[17]

Compulsory licensing allows for the production of a patented product or process without the patent owner's consent. Parallel importation concerns the importation of a product into a country without the approval of the patent owner. This is implicated where a patent owner may have a drug patented in multiple countries, and another company purchases the drug (presumably at a lower cost in one country) and subsequently imports it into another country where it sells it for less. The patent holder's rights are said to be "exhausted" upon its initial sale. TRIPS and the Doha Declaration allow Member States to "choose to deal with the exhaustion in a way that best fits their domestic policy objectives."[18]

For countries, such as Indonesia, a lack of adequate domestic research and development capacity precludes production of pharmaceutical products. This is precisely why they are dependent on other States for medicines in the event of an outbreak. Although compulsory licensing and parallel importation are useful measures, they only address one aspect of State capacity building, that is, securing viable treatment options. Even so, as discussed earlier, acquiring a supply of medicines for everyone is not likely during an outbreak.

Subsequent decisions by the Council waived the obligations of least developed States to apply provisions of TRIPS until 2016,[19] and detailed conditions upon which compulsory licenses should be granted.[20]

While recognizing "insufficient or no manufacturing capacity" within afflicted States, the decisions simply reiterate the goal of cooperating to promote "the transfer of technology and capacity building in the pharmaceutical sector."[21] Where medicines under the Doha Declaration are market commodities, their availability in response to public health threats has a limited effect on State capacity building. Moreover, facilitating access to medicines may be premised on human rights obligations; the outcome, however, amounts to nothing more than a charitable exception if it continues to foster inter-State *reliance*—as opposed to *collaboration*—to secure public health preparedness. The Doha Declaration essentially shields developed States from inter-State threats and encourages afflicted States to rely on inter-State aid to contain diseases within their own borders. The South African experience illustrates the conceptual fallacy and its impact on securing access to essential medicines in response to public health threats (see Box 6.1).

A. HIV/AIDS and access to treatments: The South African experience

In 2001, a lawsuit brought on behalf of 39 pharmaceutical companies against the South African government to prohibit importation of generic HIV/AIDS anti-retrovirals revealed early attempts to prevent developing countries from bypassing economic hurdles to secure population health (see Box 6.1). A subsequent suit brought by affected individuals afflicted with HIV/AIDS sought a reduction of allegedly overpriced medications under South Africa's

Box 6.1 HIV/AIDS and access to treatments: The South African experience

Reducing access barriers fails to stymie infections amidst fragmented systems

In 1997, the South African government passed Section 33 of the Medicines and Related Substances Control Amendment Act, No. 90 of 1997 (Act) that enabled importation of low-cost generic versions of HIV/AIDS drugs. Upon enactment, thirty-nine pharmaceutical companies brought suit challenging the constitutionality of the Act.

The complaint alleged, *inter alia*, that the Minister of Health was granted excessive authority, had sole power to determine when patent rights apply, and that patent owners would be deprived of their property interest without any provision for compensation.[22]

The cost of the drugs was estimated at $12,000–$15,000 per year for patients in the U.S. While some companies offered to sell the drugs at these costs, rival manufacturers in India offered generic versions at significantly lower prices.[23]

While a spokeswoman for the companies insisted that the "industry requires patents," she failed to contextualize the Act with respect to the ongoing public health crisis. Approximately five million people in South Africa are HIV positive, amounting to 11 percent of the country's total population.[24] Yet by mid-2005, at least 85 percent of South Africans who needed antiretroviral drugs—900,000 people—were not receiving them.[25]

Amidst international political pressure, the lawsuit was eventually dropped. Even so, the problem persists and is attributable to factors beyond legal impediments to secure essential medicines. The WHO reports that where HIV prevention programs are not sustainable, infection rates are staying the same or increasing.[26] What is needed is a combination of treatment programs and more aggressive "life-saving prevention efforts"[27]—that is, public health capacity building to ensure focused and sustainable prevention programs.

Activists and afflicted persons encourage pharmaceutical capacity building

In 2002, AIDS activists represented by the Treatment Action Campaign (TAC) and others, along with persons afflicted with HIV and health care workers, brought a complaint against GlaxoSmithKline (GSK) and Boehringer Ingelheim (BI) before the Competition Commission (Commission) alleging excessive prices on four patented antiretroviral medicines. The Commission is an independent body that investigates allegations of unfair competition under the Competition Act 89 of 1998. Upon review, it may refer the complaint to the Competition Tribunal, which formally adjudicates the charge.

The complaint specifically alleged that the prices were significantly excessive of generic prices available worldwide.[28] It also took into account estimated costs of research and development, profits, licensing fees, and the incentive to develop additional drugs.[29] The parties later entered into a settlement agreement, revealing obligations geared towards capacity building.

Among GSK's obligations was an extension of a voluntary license to Aspen Pharmacare Holdings Ltd—Africa's largest pharmaceutical manufacturer—"in respect of the public sector to include the private sector" and permission for it to export anti-retrovirals to sub-Saharan countries.[30] Particular focus on capacity building was reinforced under Section 2.2.5, which provided that licenses be strongly encouraged to manufacture drugs "in the interests of developing local pharmaceutical manufacturing capacity and job creation."

By implementing WHO's recommendations to strengthen prevention programs, a comprehensive strategy will eventually supplement these initiatives. It is unclear, however, whether the parties' obligations will offset access issues if infection rates continue to increase.

Competition Act. The quintessential element of both lawsuits was the absence of a public health capacity that adequately balances population and individually tailored interventions to reduce rates of infection and disease transmission. Yet, despite the 2001 Doha Declaration, reliance on inter-State aid continues to be the norm for afflicted States with little guidance on capacity building. In the meantime, the incidence of HIV/AIDS continues to increase.

The IHR, like TRIPS, is silent on specific avenues to promote capacity building and simply reiterates inter-State cooperation to foster global surveillance and intra-State efforts to contain public health threats. In doing so, the IHR strengthens inter-State collaborations on a premise that States can adequately deal with localized threats. The regulations do not expressly compel States to share viral samples, but require ongoing surveillance and notification of disease outbreaks and related information. After an event[31]— the manifestation of disease or an occurrence that creates a potential for disease—States may implement quarantine, isolation, and restrictions on persons from infected areas.[32] The effect of containment strategies, however, is limited without a legal framework that balances the use of NPIs and available treatment options.

The conceptual fallacy is an impediment to securing global health, but withholding viral strains only exacerbates the problem by requiring all States to resort to NPIs as a primary containment strategy. This will only strain existing State resources and threaten health at the individual and population levels. It may also discourage States from engaging in future collaborative efforts to share goods and services—threats to population health and safety are seldom welcome as invitations to cooperate in mutually beneficial ventures.

Temporal fallacy of perpetual public health emergencies

The temporal fallacy stems from when TRIPS and the IHR may be triggered in response to threats of infectious diseases. These agreements may only be invoked when threats amount to an emergency. While this may facilitate post-event containment, it undermines pre-event preparedness and a sustainable intra-State public health capacity to meet localized threats. Consequently, States must resort to NPIs as a primary containment strategy, which is not a long-term solution to contain infectious diseases.

B. The Doha Declaration and public health emergencies

Whereas Article 31(b) of TRIPS allows for use of the subject matter of a patent without the authorization of the right holder during emergencies, the Doha Declaration expressly addresses public health emergencies and recognizes Members' rights to protect public health and promote access to medicines for all.[33]

Allowing States to define what constitutes a public health emergency is hardly conciliatory for developing and least developed nations. Faced with insufficient resources, many States (such as Indonesia) cannot take advantage of compulsory licenses by merely declaring a public health emergency. Moreover, the Doha Declaration is reactionary and affords flexibility in trade only after a disease has become prevalent.

This approach undermines State capacity building and compels afflicted States to rely on other States to provide necessary aid. The Doha Declaration thereby fosters continued dependency on inter-State aid under the pretense of responsible State action to protect public health. However, reliance on inter-State aid is unproductive where there are limited supplies of essential medicines. Also, NPIs are most effective during the early stages of a pandemic. Since States are in the best position to conduct intra-State surveillance, a State-wide policy allowing for an efficient implementation of NPIs is essential. State control of public health maximizes the likelihood of containing a disease outbreak before it evolves into a potential inter-State threat. Empowering States to optimize their capacity to contain potential outbreaks strengthens inter-State collaborations by decreasing the likelihood of cross-border threats and thereby reducing the need to rely on inter-State aid.

The current language allows developing and least developed States to remain in perpetual states of public health emergencies. Under the Doha

Declaration, a public health emergency or circumstance of extreme urgency exists whenever a State determines that the general health or safety of the population may be compromised.[34]

This is a low threshold for States that lack stable infrastructures, potentially allowing any threat to expand and be duly characterized as a situation of extreme urgency. Whether the threat stems from the diagnosis of a single case, or a local outbreak, States are given broad discretion in initiating a declaration of public health emergency. Without viable treatment options and sustainable public health programs, States must resort to the aggressive implementation of NPIs—a short-term solution that is only effective in early stages of a pandemic (discussed below).

C. NPIs are not a long-term solution to contain infectious diseases

NPIs are limited in their effect because they are optimal during the initial stages of an outbreak. However, after disease prevalence has been established, NPIs will be unable to thwart its incidence and hence be rendered ineffective. A highly lethal and easily transmissible pathogen will implicate nothing short of extreme measures to protect the population. As illustrated in the worldwide response to SARS and XDR-TB, aggressive implementation of NPIs may compound health problems and threaten fundamental civil liberties (see Box 6.2).

Box 6.2 SARS and XDR-TB: Aggressive implementation of NPIs may compound health problems and threaten fundamental human rights

Global response to 2003 SARS outbreak reveals challenges of aggressive quarantine

In March 2003, the WHO issued a global alert after numerous cases of severe, acute respiratory syndrome (SARS) arose. Recommendations were made to isolate individuals diagnosed with SARS or persons who exhibited similar symptoms.[35] After the announcement, no country where outbreaks had occurred experienced the same magnitude of outbreaks as prior to the alert.[36]

While the recommendation was apparently successful, a review of global efforts to implement quarantine had potentially deleterious health effects. One study observed symptoms of posttraumatic stress disorder (PTSD) in 28.9 percent of 129 persons who were quarantined following the SARS outbreak in Toronto, Canada.[37] Thirty-one percent of respondents also exhibited symptoms of depression. A report by Rothstein *et al.* for the Centers for Disease Control and Prevention

(CDC) reported that aggressive use of quarantine in Taiwan contributed to public panic and was counter-productive. They also found incidents of violation of quarantine in every country.[38]

It is imperative that States enact local laws and protocols that ensure civil liberties, cultural sensitivities, basic needs, and communication for populations isolated or quarantined during a disease outbreak. Reluctance to establish uniform procedures continues a tradition dating back to the late nineteenth century when Eastern European Jews were singled out for quarantine upon entering New York City ports to curb the spread of cholera.[39] A century later, lack of progress continues to stifle global preparedness for future pandemics.

U.S. handling of person with XDR-TB reveals limitations of isolation

In August 2006, Robert Daniels, a 27-year-old Russian immigrant, was isolated in Phoenix, Arizona, after being diagnosed with extremely drug-resistant tuberculosis (XDR-TB). The disease is considered highly lethal and untreatable. Upon his alleged failure to comply with doctor's orders to wear a mask in public, Daniels was jailed in a local prison cell, where he currently resides indefinitely.

Although details are scarce, Daniels's claims of alleged mistreatment raises concerns as to whether local governments are capable of handling a large-scale quarantine without violating fundamental civil liberties. In an interview, Daniels claims that he was never informed of how XDR-TB was transmitted; that he is not allowed to shower, but cleans himself with wet wipes; and that he has no means of communication with others.[40]

His allegations raise issues of due process and the provision of basic needs and services. The lack of uniformity in U.S. quarantine laws reiterates the need to re-examine state laws. Given the highly lethal and easily transmissible nature of XDR-TB, the case also illustrates the limitations of implementing NPIs to contain disease outbreaks. Daniels's predicament is reminiscent of that suffered by Mary Mallon, a cook and healthy carrier of typhoid fever, who was isolated in 1909 for a total of 26 years.[41] While Mallon knowingly violated orders to refrain from cooking, an action which led her to infect others, Daniels claims he was unaware of how the disease is transmitted. Effective communication between health officials and the public is vital in ensuring cooperation and protecting the public's health. Nonetheless, indefinite isolation is not a long-term solution to combat infectious diseases.

D. SARS and XDR-TB: Aggressive implementation of NPIs may compound health problems and threaten fundamental human rights

Isolation and quarantine laws were traditionally targeted at maritime vessels and may not afford comprehensive civil liberty protections to persons or populations. Even developed nations (e.g., the United States) have antiquated quarantine laws that are neither comprehensive nor uniform. Without available medicines or vaccines, NPIs are, at best, short-term solutions. Having the capacity to develop and distribute medicines will not obviate the need for NPIs. It will, however, reduce the likelihood of the *aggressive* use of NPIs and the potential legal and ethical challenges that will inevitably stem from their implementation. Thus, reliance on NPIs as a primary containment strategy is not feasible to secure population health. Schools and businesses may be closed, and interference with trade may limit the availability of many essential goods and services.

While a goal of the IHR is to broadly harmonize the legality of NPIs, the legal obstacles to implement them within sub-State regions (e.g., states, counties, localities) in a timely manner may compromise a public health response. A study by the Centers for Law and the Public's Health at Johns Hopkins and Georgetown Universities on the legal bases for school closure as an NPI during pandemic influenza revealed a lack of uniformity among U.S. jurisdictions. Multiple agencies were authorized to close schools for different reasons; multiple levels of government were vested with the authority to act; and few intrastate pandemic influenza plans cited express legal authority to implement closure.[42] Reliance on NPIs to curb disease outbreaks is unproven and may be stymied by a myriad of legal impediments.

III. State epidemic control and use of biological materials

States optimize available resources to protect population health. In the absence of sufficient resources, States may be tempted to use whatever means necessary to acquire essential products, disregarding global public health objectives. While Indonesia's reluctance to share its viral samples invited worldwide criticism, there was little explanation as to why its claim was legally unsubstantiated. This section explores (1) whether withholding viral strains is in contravention to State obligations to advance epidemic control under the IHR and (2) the relationship between State control of biological materials and global public health imperatives.

A. Withholding viral strains is in potential contravention to a State's obligations under the IHR in taking measures to control epidemics

If epidemic control is a global public good, then States would certainly collaborate to protect the health and safety of their citizenry. Although there is no consensus on a precise definition, David Woodward and Richard Smith define a global public good as a good which it is rational, from the perspective of a group of nations collectively, to produce for universal consumption, and for which it is irrational to exclude an individual nation from its consumption, irrespective of whether that nation contributes to its financing.[43] Under this definition, epidemic control may be broadly characterized as a global public good owing to its collective benefits and the inability to eliminate the threat by excluding an individual nation from implementing measures to curb its spread. Still, the specific legal obligations must be enunciated in the context of international law and agreements.

Under the IHR, epidemic control at a national level is an integral obligation of Member States. In 2003, Johan Giesecke explained how national infection control consists of an alert function (i.e., notification to other countries when an outbreak has been discovered) and control measures to contain its spread;[44] these roles are consistent with State obligations under the revised IHR (discussed earlier). The emerging issue is then whether withholding viral strains amounts to State action that threatens epidemic control.

On its face, withholding viral strains is not per se a violation of epidemic control. Epidemic control requires an actual outbreak and failure to take measures to control its spread. In the absence of an outbreak, State action in contravention of epidemic control becomes legally impossible. Even so, this is based on a premise that withholding viral strains is immaterial to the factors that give rise to an outbreak or measures to control it. This premise, however, is debatable.

In some instances, the efficient development of control measures should not be considered too remote from the actual measures themselves. Since States are aware that the H5N1 virus evolves and that constant surveillance is necessary to develop the appropriate vaccines, withholding viral strains may jeopardize an optimal response. Waiting until an actual outbreak occurs will delay development and risk the health and lives of affected persons until a vaccine is made available.

This predicament illustrates that legal impossibility is outweighed by factual possibility. While withholding strains may not be correlated to an actual outbreak, it will be associated with an inevitable delay in developing a vaccine (should an outbreak occur).

Thus, withholding viral strains precludes taking efficient control measures (including vaccine development) and may be in contravention to a State's obligations under the IHR in controlling epidemics.

B. State control of biological materials is an invalid proxy for individual rights and is superseded by public health imperatives

Indonesia never explicitly denied its obligation under the IHR in taking control measures to prevent the spread of an epidemic. Its primary argument in withholding samples rested on its exclusive possession and control of biological materials. This approach is flawed because, as discussed above, a State's property interest is superseded by a global public health imperative, that is, infectious disease control. Additionally, Indonesia's claim is nothing more than a proxy for asserting an individual right that would not withstand scrutiny at the national level, and, by implication, would obviate a subsequent claim on behalf of the sovereign State to take a similar stance to preclude an overriding global interest.

While it is widely held that public health imperatives (e.g., infectious disease control) supersede property rights, Indonesia has distinguished its sovereign interest from an individual's claim to biological materials on questionable grounds. The policy rationale to preclude an individual from asserting a claim in her own biological materials against public policy was aptly summarized in the United States' case of *Moore v. Regents of the University of California*.[45] In *Moore*, the California State Supreme Court addressed the issue of whether biological materials can be equated to personal property. The court found that granting Moore an interest in his biological materials was inappropriate on two levels. First, it broadly noted that state law governing the disposal of biological materials was within the exclusive purview of the state health department. Second, Moore's particular cells constituted a potential bio-hazardous threat, which required the state health department to dispose of the materials pursuant to its duty to protect the public's health. Indonesia's argument is similar to Moore's claim, but cannot be distinguished to warrant a dissimilar outcome. Since Indonesia gave its viral samples of its own volition to the WHO, its disclosure obligations are not in question. Indonesia was aware of what the samples would be used for, yet it simply claims exclusive rights to ownership and the terms upon which the samples—and any products derived thereof—may be used.

The nature and lethality of the H5N1 viral strains pose a grave threat to public health and safety. Among those infected with avian flu virus, the H5N1 strain has caused the largest number of detected cases of severe disease and death in humans.[46] Moreover, more than half of all individuals diagnosed with the virus have died.[47] Its lethality would clearly qualify it as a biologically hazardous agent subject to control by a state health agency. Additionally, if H5N1 gains the capacity to spread easily from person to person, its transmission may trigger an influenza pandemic.

Regulation of viral strains should not be subject to political and economic considerations in lieu of public health objectives that affect population health on a local, national, or global scale. An exception to this narrow rule may grant control and usage of biological materials as a function of their lethality and scope of transmission. For example, an individual may reasonably exert ownership and control over biological materials that do not pose a threat to another's health or safety. On the other hand, if the materials pose a threat to the health of another person, then the state government may exercise its control over the materials pursuant to its duty to protect the public's health. Nonetheless, Indonesia's claim is nothing more than a proxy for an individual property interest that is superseded by overriding global public health impertives to control the spread of infectious disease. Efforts to preclude essential monitoring and diagnoses on economic grounds would belie these overriding public health considerations.

Recommendations

A developing country's fear of being "left behind" and not having access to future medicines is a legitimate concern, particularly during a state of public health emergency. This fear is compounded against a fragile legal backdrop that fails to address intra-State public health capacity building as an integral component of protecting global health.

An effective public health response to potential disease outbreaks requires a legal environment that recognizes the limitations of available resources, facilitates the implementation of NPIs (e.g., isolation and quarantine, social distancing measures), and is also amenable to affected persons and populations. These requirements are not mutually exclusive; rather, successful interventions should apply sound public health measures while securing, to the extent possible, fundamental rights and respect for human dignity.

Adoption of intra-State laws facilitating implementation of NPIs

Since it is likely that there will be insufficient vaccines available for all individuals at the outset of a pandemic—even in developed States—the implementation of NPIs is vital to protect population health. Even so, worldwide response to the SARS outbreak and inconsistent State laws reveal a lack of uniformity in legal provisions relating to isolation and quarantine or social distancing measures. Given different political regimes and legal systems, a single inter-State treaty may be ill-equipped to address State-specific challenges.

Research on intra-State laws across all States is required to identify barriers in implementing NPIs in a timely and efficient manner. Specifically, laws should identify key officials at the local, state, and national (or federal) levels that are authorized to implement NPIs and the circumstances under which such authority may be exercised. Such provisions should complement the IHR and serve as practice-based regulations that facilitate timely and effective responses. This will alleviate the conceptual fallacy by complementing the availability of treatment options with pragmatic NPIs to protect population health.

Incorporation of IHR Article 32 minimum protections and additional rights into existent state laws

The implementation of NPIs must also be coupled with efforts to secure the basic needs and fundamental rights of affected populations. During the 2003

SARS outbreak, aggressive implementation of NPIs may have compounded health problems and contributed to public panic (see Box 6.2). Timely and effective implementation of NPIs relies on garnering public

support and cooperation. Communication is vital and should also be accompanied by reassurances that minimize societal disruptions (e.g., work-from-home options for parents taking leave to care for ill children, distance learning for displaced students).

The protections afforded under Article 32 of the IHR are necessary, but not sufficient to secure each individual's fundamental civil liberties and basic needs because many States often submit reservations or declarations that do not recognize the legally binding character of the treaty on particular constituencies (e.g., India and CEDAW) or based on potential conflicts with national law (e.g., U.S. and federalism).

Article 32 affords minimum protections to individuals who have been isolated, quarantined, or subject to other procedures for public health purposes. Basic protections include treating travelers with courtesy and respect; taking into consideration the gender, socio-cultural, ethnic, or religious concerns of travelers; arranging for adequate food and water; accommodation and clothing; protection for baggage and other possessions; appropriate medical treatment; and necessary communication in a language they can understand.[48]

Additional protections should include the following: (1) a right to procedural due process (notice and a hearing within a reasonable period); (2) specific scientific criteria (e.g., incubation period) to determine the appropriate length of detainment; (3) means of communication with family members; (4) privacy protections for the acquisition and use of health information; and (5) clarity as to who bears the cost of examinations and other health-related procedures.

The lack of uniformity in most States as it relates to protections afforded affected populations risks multiple human rights violations. This would create a scenario reminiscent of the treatment of Eastern European Jewish immigrants in the late nineteenth century at the port harbors of New York City[49] to combat cholera, and of vulnerable populations such as individuals afflicted with HIV/AIDS in the mid-1980s continuing into the present day. Aggressive implementation of NPIs must be accompanied by assurances to secure the fundamental rights and basic needs of affected populations. These assurances will alleviate the burden of the conceptual fallacy by providing a check on implementing NPIs within parameters respecting fundamental individual rights; they will also alleviate the temporal fallacy by securing fundamental rights irrespective of whether an emergency has been declared, but all the more so when coercive measures are taken in deprivation of individual interests.

Suretyship arrangements to secure political accountability and
support public health capacity building

The lack of political accountability stifles inter-State cooperation and must be addressed in concert with efforts to secure global health. Indonesia's reluctance to share H5N1 samples drew attention to a fragmented global health system. Threats of non-cooperation, however, do not pose a sound model for global health policy and will only stymie future collaborations. Prospective reform should identify avenues of support for capacity building in developing and least developed States, and hold States accountable for their obligations pursuant to the IHR. Trade in particular goods and services should remain unhindered, but highly lethal and easily transmittable infectious diseases pose a unique threat that compels State action and involvement. In 2000, the U.S. National Intelligence Council (NIC) issued a report discussing the impact of global infectious diseases on national security.[50] The report highlighted potential social fragmentation, economic decay, political polarization in the hardest hit regions, and worldwide disruptions in trade and commerce. No State is immune from the impact of a pandemic, and an effective response entails global cooperation.

Regulating intra-State research on highly lethal and easily transmittable infectious diseases to foster inter-State capacity building is essential to secure global health. Funds should be allocated to promote public health capacity building of States disproportionately burdened by potential disease threats. Effective collaborations will require arrangements that recognize horizontal and vertical privity among States and corporations researching highly lethal and easily transmissible infectious diseases.

Suretyships provide an apt model to secure compliance and cooperation. A surety is a person who is primarily liable for the payment of another's debt or the performance of another's obligation. Against the backdrop of States' duties to secure the health of their populations and inter-State efforts to secure global health, States should be politically and, to the extent possible, economically accountable to inter-State efforts to protect global health.

Under a suretyship model, States' governments would be a surety for an intra-State corporation's "debt" to inter-State efforts to advance global health. The debt stems from the two-fold recognition that Member States are bound by international law to promote epidemic control and that regulation of intra-State activities may (and should) entail an allocation of risk among key participants. Moreover, given the inevitable global impact of highly lethal and easily transmissible infectious diseases, such contributions would be a wise investment to minimize disruptions of global trade relations. By taking steps to develop effective control measures, corporations would be fulfilling an otherwise State function. Consequently, they may potentially avail themselves of the rights and benefits afforded State agents (e.g., limited liability protections). Potential arrangements may entail (1) direct taxation of corporations engaged in research and development who profit from the procurement of samples from affected states and their constituents; (2) matching funds by the State(s) to support intra-State research and development; or (3) a combination thereof. Arrangements must also take into account multinational corporations that have multiple bases in different countries.

While this model is not legally enforceable pursuant to any existent international agreements, it may be incorporated within the existing framework by complementing State efforts to promote epidemic control. Although the IHR does not expressly generate financial resources for capacity building, it does encourage intra-State regulation and inter-State collaboration. The suretyship model streamlines public- and private-sector contributions to harmonize public health objectives, and ensures minimal capacities to meet the threat of highly lethal and easily transmissible infectious diseases. It also fills a gap owing to the conceptual fallacy by reducing disparities across Member States' capacities to meet localized threats. This would also alleviate the temporal fallacy by reducing the likelihood of emergencies stemming, in large part, from a lack of minimal capacity and provision of basic healthcare services. Finally, it solidifies State governance of public health and enables communication and sharing of data or funds, thereby promoting global health surveillance.

IV. Conclusion

The international legal landscape is fraught with loopholes that impede optimal inter-State cooperation to secure global health. While the conceptual fallacy reveals an absence of adequate efforts to secure intra-State public health capacity building, the temporal fallacy potentially leaves developing and least developed countries in perpetual states of public health emergencies.

Drawing attention away from these fallacies to protect sovereign interests at the expense of global health objectives is equally inappropriate. Highly lethal and easily transmissible infectious diseases implicate health and safety issues affecting all States. Inter-State collaborations should ensure minimal public health capacity in developing and least developed States. This objective can be accomplished by (1) a legal framework that allows for timely implementation of NPIs, which would include (2) uniform adoption of minimum protections afforded affected populations and (3) suretyship arrangements to secure political accountability and contribute to intra-State capacity building.

The appropriate roles of public- and private-sector actors are often blurred in the free market where inter-State trade acts independently of political objectives. Responding to infectious disease threats is every State's prerogative, and inter-State collaborations—with a particular focus on capacity building—are essential to secure global public health preparedness.

7 Perspectives from the field

A conversation with Kayhan Parsi, Ph.D., J.D., Associate Professor of Bioethics and Health Policy, Loyola University Chicago

Q.1 On morality and rights

Q: It appears that the terms "human rights" and "ethics" have become synonymous in their practical application in the global health arena. In your recent article featured in the Hastings Report, 'The Dread Disease: Cancer in the Developing World,' you argue that "global cancer disparities illustrate a collective failure to actualize the universal human right to access an adequate standard of health, and these disparities in cancer care and mortality demonstrate some of the most glaring social inequalities in health." Do you think that human rights are, on some level, a fulfillment of a search for a common morality (once deemed too abstract or aspirational for any practical purposes)? Or could ethicists who expound on "global health" issues be inclined to carve out a distinct niche for themselves, that is, outside of the rights-based frameworks?

A: I can speak to this issue from a bioethics perspective. So take for instance Beauchamp and Childress' popular principles that are based on a common morality that all morally committed people share regardless of culture, geography, or time. So they've looked at numerous theories, including Kantianism, Communitarianism, Virtue Ethics, Libertarinism, etc., and they mentioned the power of rights-theory to advance ethical goals in healthcare in medicine. Rights have an incredibly hortatory kind of power insofar as people pay attention when they are invoked. If you look at the Universal Declaration of Human Rights, it's all in rights language. Rights talk now is quite secularized, but it arguably emerges from the belief that everyone has the same ethical value; and values the same things, such as free speech, assembly, the things we see formalized in our own bill of rights; and the Universal Declaration speaks to other rights, as well, though they include positive rights that are more difficult to quantify and fulfill. So with regards to rights, it's interesting because in bioethics, we don't talk about rights per se in the literature here in the U.S. Some may say there is a right to autonomy or beneficence but it is typically viewed as individuals retaining the capacity to make health-related decisions, which then empowers one to make such decisions. I think most people agree that a civilized society ought to offer some kind of safety net for its population. I'm not sure it's necessarily a rights kind of discourse, or a deliberation on what a civilized society ought to look like.

So going back to your question, it is highly contextual with respect to your audience. For an American bioethicist, we do not speak of rights in the fashion that people speak of it in traditional philosophical circles or even among public health scholars. But if we look at how bioethics has evolved, the principles have played a large role in how we conceptualize ethical obligations. Justice has been the most challenging to define; and there you could perhaps smuggle in this notion of rights. If people all aspire for a just society, then how do we articulate that? One way is saying that people have a right to a basic minimum amount of healthcare.

Q.2 On conceptualizing the ethical dilemmas

Q: The issue of justice seems to always arise at the extremes, that is, when someone immediately needs the care. It seems to suggest that there is an ethical theory that can embrace a modicum of care, plus room for the industry of healthcare to flourish. Can both coexist?

A: When we talk to a right to healthcare, people often think about it as an acute situation. So here in the U.S., we have the Emergency Medical Treatment and Active Labor Act (EMTALA), a federal law which requires that individuals who present to an emergency room be screened and stabilized before transfer. So hospitals can't just dump the patients, which was a problem back in the 1980s. And on some level, we can label that a right to healthcare, but it's an unfunded mandate. Another way to look at this is asking whether people have a right to preventive services that may alleviate morbidity and mortality. So the question then is: is there a right to this kind of preventive care? And who has the obligation to fulfill that? Also, what is the individual's responsibility? So the hope is that people won't wait until problems are acute owing to complications and costs; but we are always drawing lines as to who ought to be included.

Q.3 On vulnerable populations

Q: Could you give an example of vulnerable populations and how we draw lines?

A: One topic that I've become interested in is undocumented patients. So patients may present who are undocumented and get treated, screened, and stabilized. The care may be paid for through a charity coffer. When it comes time for them to become discharged, and these are complex discharges because they no longer need care from an acute care setting, but a long-term facility.

The challenge then becomes identifying a facility that will take them because of their undocumented status and lack of resources. Because of their legal status, they are precluded from being covered under any public assistance, such as Medicaid. So this is an example of how we draw lines, where we say that if you lack legal status, you will not be able to avail yourself of this assistance. So where do we transfer these individuals? Long-term care facilities have no legal obligations, and if there are no family members who can take up their care, what do we do? Some argue that only individuals who legally reside here may take advantage of this assistance. Others argue that these are individuals who are contributing through other means to our society through payment of taxes and are de facto members of the community, transcending the formality of the legal argument; implicating, as a community, a moral obligation to render such services to meet their needs. So it becomes a very interesting rights-based conversation.

Q.4 On ethical theories and population health

Q: There are numerous theories that we can employ to address the ethics of population health, domestically or at the international level. Is utilitarianism the logical fit for a population-health perspective, or is it simply convenient as a definition because it aims to maximize the good as it applies to the maximum number of people, consistent with definitions of public health that speak to benefits accruing for the population at large rather than a particular individual?

A: One way of looking at population ethics is through our commitment to the public or community writ large, i.e. community, state, nation, etc. If that is our obligation—to improve health outcomes of big populations—then what we're really interested in, under a utilitarian framework, is promoting the greater good for the greater number. But what is it that we value? Health outcomes? Reduction of morbidity or mortality? We employ some kind of calculus to determine based on what we estimate to be the benefits and costs of an intervention so that the individual burden is relatively low. Consider seat belt mandates or vaccine mandates. What's interesting about these kinds of debates is that we always find an opt-out provision, so it essentially becomes a soft mandate. Now the downside is that if too few people do so, herd immunity is compromised. So to get to your question more directly, you are trying to make more compatible the consequentialist argument to establish the greater good while trying to protect some individual rights.

A communiatarian approach would look at a community's values and see how they are expressed and upheld. And it's not necessarily about individual rights. A good example of this would be the recent Patient Protection and Affordable Care Act. One could argue that act is an example of communitarian thinking because of the individual mandate. The communitarian may argue that we have a large number of free riders, which may be due in large part to being uninsured, and so when they become sick, everyone else must finance that. This is morally problematic for many people, and is an issue that does not seem to arise in the broader political discussion, and ironically reflects broader American values because we will all get sick at some point in our lives, so why not take such measures to protect against your own inevitable predicament and the concomitant effects on the system and others? So this may seem to be a subversion of rights in the sense that the government is requiring purchase of something that someone does not want. So if you are a libertarian or even a liberal theorist, you could argue against that requirement. But the communitarian would argue that if we as a community or nation value health, then we ought to take those measures to secure that for everyone in the community, and hopefully reduce the overall costs and burdens that it places on the system and individuals at large. Another good

communitarian argument would be the approached advanced by Dr. Ezekiel Immanuel. Before he got involved with the Obama Administration, he promoted the idea of a voucher program whereby we individually spend roughly $7000 to $8000 per year, and instead of having individuals purchase insurance through the employer, you provide this voucher so individuals can go out and secure health insurance and fulfill the goals of everyone; maintaining the private health industry and strive for universal coverage at the same time. So in one sense, the Affordable Care Act is an instantiation of a communitarian ethos.

8 Epidemiology and the challenge of regulating social determinants of health

Introduction

As the preeminent science of public health, epidemiology is the basis for advocating for, or against, an intervention. For example, the ineffectiveness of abstinence-only educational programs in curbing rates of sexual intercourse among adolescents was heralded as the reason to promote safe sex educational initiatives. Although refraining from sexual intercourse will unquestionably prevent infection with sexually transmissible illnesses, the role of epidemiology as a science to determine the effectiveness of a particular intervention is a related, but independent, endeavor. Here, the epidemiologist is not positing that engaging in (or refraining from) sexual relations is ethically sound, but rather, whether particular educational programs have been proven to reduce the rates of such practices. Therefore, advocates must be cautious in citing epidemiological findings as "evidence" or "proof" without recognizing the context in which such determinations are made.

Why this matters in our discussion of law and health stems from two problems in our contemporary discourse. First, our epidemiological findings are based on our predetermined emphasis on particular loci of intervention. Programs may be geared towards a particular demographic, engaged in the provision of particular services, or evaluated based on particular criteria. In each instance, we have assumed that such targets are inherently warranted based on what we deem important in the characterization of illness. In doing so, our attempt to regulate conduct or promote activities that would ameliorate the attendant rates of morbidity or mortality is invariably restricted to those particular elements. Secondly, in practice, we find that such predetermined targets, services, and criteria are generally devoid of the social context of disease. Health is a social construct, which is a generally accepted principle within the public health community, and is in sharp contrast to the emphasis on a biomedical paradigm. Not that the latter is not relevant; on the contrary, it is indispensable to our identification and treatment of illness. But public health practitioners undertake efforts to address the manifestation of illness longitudinally across the lifespan while emphasizing access to information that may be utilized to promote the prevention—and not merely the treatment—of disease. Consequently, advocates ought to be aware that promoting (or opposing) particular interventions reveal more than the obvious support for a "proven" intervention; but a concession to the underlying prioritization of the particular target, service, and criteria of evaluation. This can result in the misallocation of resources to effectively ameliorate a public health problem. In this chapter, we will examine the issues surrounding the availability of the vaccine for the human papilloma virus (HPV) to illustrate these points.

Let us begin our case study with a seemingly simple legal issue, namely, whether a government should mandate HPV vaccination as a condition of entry for school-age adolescent females. We will begin our analysis at the national level by examining the issue against a backdrop of existent U.S. laws and disease trends. The first section shall present an argument in favor of mandatory vaccination, followed by an opposing argument.

I. Argument in favor of mandatory vaccination

Sexually transmitted diseases (STDs), such as genital human papillomavirus (HPV) infection, pose significant national public health challenges. Over 20 million people in the United States are currently infected with HPV, and an estimated six million Americans will acquire a new genital HPV infection annually.[1] In some cases, HPV infection may also lead to the development of cervical cancer.[2] The prevalence and incidence of HPV infection, especially among adolescents, is concerning. A recent study estimates that HPV prevalence may be as high as 24.5 percent among females aged between 15 and 19.[3]

Conventional methods to prevent and treat HPV infection are limited. Like most STDs, the surest way to prevent HPV infection is to abstain from any sexual contact with another individual. Vaccination is another effective strategy to prevent infection. On June 8, 2006, the Food and Drug Administration (FDA) approved Gardasil, a vaccine to prevent HPV and cervical cancer.[4] While initial clinical trials among females aged between 16 and 26 were promising, the efficacy of the vaccine among other age groups remains unclear. At present, there is also no cure for HPV infection, but the virus usually goes away on its own within two years after infection.[5]

Current federal guidelines concerning HPV vaccination are based on the recommendations of the Advisory Committee on Immunization Practices (ACIP), which supports vaccination of females, aged between 11 and 12 years, and as low as 9 years of age.[6] While the clinical trials were based on a sample population of females aged between 16 and 26, the ACIP noted that the vaccine should be "administered before sexual debut" since there is a "high probability of HPV acquisition" once a female becomes sexually active.[7] The ACIP, however, neither addressed the legal issues that may potentially preclude vaccination nor how state governments could ensure maximum uptake among their female constituencies.

In response, state legislatures have struggled in gaining consensus as to how, and under what circumstances, the vaccine should be delivered. As of December 2007, bills requiring, funding, or educating the public of the HPV vaccine were introduced in 41 states and the District of Columbia.[8] In 24 states, the legislation specifically mandates HPV vaccination for entry into school (usually sixth- or seventh-grades).[9] Only one state (Virginia[10]) has enacted a law conditioning enrollment upon vaccination.

We have done an inadequate job in exploring the intersection of public health, sexuality, and the role of state governments in vaccinating adolescent females against HPV. Missing from the current debate is an analysis of the interplay of law and public health in protecting *and* promoting population health. Effective public health interventions ought to serve as both a social safety net and an instrument of growth. Whereas the safety net is formed by efforts that protect the community (e.g., curbing the spread of disease), the collective health of a population is improved by interventions that promote healthy decisions and lifestyles (e.g., education campaigns). Against this backdrop, current initiatives to secure the health and rights of females appear grossly inadequate.

I argue in support of one-time mandatory HPV vaccination programs of 11-year-old females that are accompanied by comprehensive sexual education campaigns that address existent trends in adolescent sexual activity, knowledge of HPV infection, and its corresponding public health burden and impact.

We begin by discussing trends in national rates of adolescent sexual behavior, and knowledge of HPV along with its attendant health consequences. It provides an evidence-based approach to understand the public health burden and impact on adolescent females. In doing so, key issues are contextualized within existent patterns of disease awareness and behavior among the adolescent population.

Thereafter, we can explore the legal basis of mandatory vaccination and the insufficiency of the current framework to *protect* and *promote* adolescent health. The discussion first focuses on the role of state governments in protecting population health and affirms the constitutional basis for imposing mandatory vaccination programs. It then provides additional support for a mandatory schedule by arguing that existent HPV trends may constitute a public health emergency. Still, the characterization of a threat as either a matter of public health *concern* or as an *emergency* is not dispositive. State governments should move beyond a narrow perspective of protection and embrace efforts to *promote* adoption of healthy lifestyles. A review of legislative bills supporting HPV educational campaigns illustrates the shortcomings of state governments and health educators in empowering individuals with information to make healthy decisions to curb the spread of HPV infection.

The argument is for a one-time mandatory HPV vaccination, but reiterates that a sustainable and effective public health program may be futile absent comprehensive education campaigns.

A. Trends in national rates of adolescent sexual behavior, knowledge of HPV, and its attendant health consequences

National rates of adolescent sexual behavior and attendant public health consequences are continuing at an alarming rate. A 2007 study by Dunne *et al.* reported that the prevalence of HPV infection was approximately 40 percent among sexually active adolescent females, aged between 14 and 19.[11] Clearly, there is a high likelihood of infection among individuals who are sexually active. Even so, the public health impact stems not only from the probability of infection, but its prevalence within the entire adolescent population.

An assessment of the scope of sexual activity among adolescents is vital in explaining the public health impact of HPV infection. Moreover, a determination of current knowledge of HPV and its attendant health consequences may suggest the future incidence of infection if current trends in knowledge and behavior continue unabated. Finally, rates of sexual knowledge and activity must be addressed against a backdrop of potential societal influences. The dichotomy of voluntary and non-voluntary sexual behavior offers additional considerations when determining the potential advantages and disadvantages of vaccination as a prophylactic measure.

1. Sexual activity among adolescents

The public health burden of HPV infection cannot be determined by relying solely on the percentage of infection among sexually active adolescents. The public health implications stem from a population perspective and consequently require a comprehensive assessment of trends in sexual knowledge and behavior, along with knowledge of HPV and its attendant health consequences. As discussed below, current patterns in sexual activity and knowledge suggest the necessity of a comprehensive approach to curb rates of STD infection.

2. Ages and rates of sexual activity

Trends in national rates of adolescent sexual activity have been consistent over the past decade. In 1998, studies reported that 52 percent of females and 56 percent of males aged between 15 and 19 had engaged in sexual intercourse.[12] In 2003, the Kaiser Family Foundation (Kaiser) conducted a survey that expanded the notion of sexual activity to include sexual contact, but not necessarily intercourse. The Kaiser study found that 56 percent of adolescents aged between 15 and 17 had been with someone in an intimate or sexual way.[13] Since HPV can be transmitted by any sexual contact (i.e., not limited to intercourse), approximately half of adolescents are at risk of becoming infected. Moreover, this risk increases significantly considering that 39 percent of adolescents reported having between two and five sexual partners.[14] The national Youth Risk Behavior Survey (YRBS) reported similar results, finding that 33.9 percent of adolescents in grades 9 to 12 had up to three sexual partners within the past month.[15]

Data for sexual activity, not including intercourse, among other adolescent age groups was unavailable. The Kaiser study did, however, report on the age at first intercourse as: 11 percent for adolescents aged between 12 and 13 (6.2 percent reported by the YRBS study based on 2005 data); 44 percent for adolescents aged between 14 and 15, and 37 percent for adolescents aged between 16 and 17.[16] Thus, there is a likely risk of contracting HPV across all age groups and 50 percent of adolescents will potentially become infected with HPV between the ages of 15 and 17.

3. Narrowing of gender disparities as relates to sexual activity

While males constitute the majority of sexually active adolescents, the gender gap lessens with increasing age. The Kaiser study reports that overall, 66 percent of males aged between 15 and 17 had been with someone in an intimate or sexual way (including, but not limited to intercourse), compared to 47 percent of females.[17] Also, 30 percent of males reported having their first sexual intercourse between the ages of 14 and 15, and 42 percent by aged 16 and 17; whereas 25 percent of females reported their first intercourse by ages 14 and 15, and 39 percent by ages 16 and 17.[18] Whereas males are at a high risk of HPV infection across different age groups, females evidently become particularly susceptible with increasing age.

Recent data suggesting an overall decrease in sexual activity among adolescents reflect a lessening in gender gaps, as opposed to a relative reduction of sexual activity within the male and female populations. The YRBS study, which focuses solely on adolescents in grades 9 to 12, illustrates the lessening gap among the older age groups. In 2005, the YRBS reported that 46.8 percent of adolescents had engaged in sexual intercourse, compared to 54.1 percent in 1991.[19] This was accompanied, however, by relative decreases and increases within the male and female populations, respectively. Male sexual activity decreased from 57.4 percent in 1991 to 47.9 percent in 1991.[20] By contrast, female sexual activity had increased from 45.7 percent in 1991 to 50.8 percent in 2005.[21] While overall trends in sexual activity among adolescents may be decreasing, more females are becoming sexually active. As a result, absent vaccination, the incidence of HPV infection among females is likely to increase.

4. Voluntary and non-voluntary engagement in sexual activity

While early exposure to sexual activity among adolescents is a risk factor for numerous health complications, the decision to engage in sexual activity cannot be wholly attributed to female adolescents.[22] Forced sexual activity is a "considerable public health problem among young adolescent women in the United States."[23] In 2004, a study by Raghavan *et al.* found 7 percent of adolescent females in grades 7 to 12 (ages 12–14, 15–17, and over 18) reported having been forced into sexual intercourse.[24] Of these cases, 8 percent of females were revictimized in the following year.[25] Also, 2.4 percent of females, aged between 12 and 14 reported being forced into intercourse; among 15- to 17-year-old females, the percentage had risen to 8.8 percent.[26] Another study by Abma *et al.*, reported that 25 percent of females, aged 13 or younger, who had engaged in sexual intercourse claimed that the experience was non-voluntary (compared to 10 percent of females, aged 19–24).[27] A third study by Luster and Small found that 10 percent of adolescent females in grades 7 to 12 had been sexually abused by an adult or someone older than themselves.[28] Notwithstanding the discrepancies in the estimated rates, sexual abuse experienced by adolescent females is a significant public health problem. Although vaccination cannot prevent sexual abuse, it can lessen the inevitable risk of exposure to STDs and other negative health outcomes in situations where a female's autonomy is compromised.

B. Knowledge of HPV and its attendant health consequences

Public awareness of STDs is essential to inform individuals of the risks involved when they engage in sexual activity. Health departments, hospitals, clinics, and schools serve as potential forums to educate the public and specific populations (e.g., adolescents). Knowledge of HPV within the general public and the adolescent community is central to encourage measures that would minimize risk of exposure. As discussed below, however, neither the average individual nor adolescents in particular are sufficiently aware of HPV infection and cervical cancer.

1. General public awareness of HPV and cervical cancer

Despite one study that found 69 percent of clinicians routinely provided education about HPV infection to adult and adolescent patients, awareness among the general public remains low.[29] Thirty-five focus groups among individuals aged between 25 and 45 conducted under the auspices of the CDC "rarely listed [HPV] as an STD about which they were concerned or aware."[30] Upon learning of HPV's association with cervical cancer, many participants "expressed concern that they had not been previously informed of the disease and did not have the important information they needed to address their concerns."[31] The dearth of public information was consistent with a study of 111 news media reports related to HPV and cervical cancer that found inadequate descriptions of HPV, its symptoms and transmission.[32] Only 50 percent of the stories reported that HPV was common, and 30 percent mentioned wrong, uncertain, or unnecessary test results.[33] Based on these findings, it is evident that the public remains generally unaware of HPV infections and essential measures to reduce exposure to the virus.

2. Adolescent knowledge of HPV and cervical cancer

Consistent with general public unawareness of HPV infections, most adolescents are uninformed of HPV and its association with cervical cancer. One qualitative study employed 11 focus groups with 78 females, ages 12–17,and reported that "participants overwhelmingly lacked knowledge about [cervical] cancer."[34] Quantitative studies have thus far focused on older age groups, but have consistently reported low levels of knowledge. A study by Baer et al., for example, found that while over 87 percent of male and female university students looked to health education classes for information about STDs, only 4.2 percent of males and 11.6 percent of females knew that HPV caused genital warts.[35] A separate study of 500 university students reported that only 37 percent of respondents had ever heard of HPV, and knew the least about it compared to six other STDs.[36] Respondents also indicated that HPV had received the least educational effort on behalf of health educators.[37] Indeed, individuals across all age groups, including teenagers and young adults, are not receiving sufficient information about HPV infections.

C. Legal basis for a mandate and insufficient efforts to protect adolescent health

In the United States, the rate of vaccination among school-age children exceeds 95 percent, and is higher than most developed countries.[38] The success rate, in large part, can be attributed to mandatory state vaccination laws that require immunization against a variety of infectious diseases including, inter alia, measles, mumps, and rubella. We first review state governments' authority to protect the population against communicable diseases by requiring mandatory vaccination. Next, we argue that existent HPV trends may constitute a public health emergency, providing additional support for a mandatory vaccination schedule. We can then distinguish the legal authority to impose vaccination requirements from the perspective of individual- and population-based interventions. We conclude by addressing whether current legislative efforts to encourage HPV vaccination fulfill state governments' prerogative to protect the public's health. As discussed below, imposing mandatory vaccination under the present legal framework is necessary but insufficient to secure the health of adolescent females.

1. Constitutional basis for states to protect against communicable diseases

Vaccination falls within the ambit of a state's police powers, which include those measures reasonably related to the promotion and maintenance of the health, safety, and morals of the public. The police powers are an inherent attribute of state sovereignty preserved under the 10th Amendment of the U.S.

Constitution that reserves those rights not expressly delegated to the federal government.[39] When the police powers are exercised to protect population health, they should be rooted in scientifically sound principles and, to the extent possible, be restrained by constitutional safeguards respecting individual interests (e.g., autonomy, liberty, association).

The Supreme Court has consistently upheld mandatory vaccination in response to public health threats and as a condition of school entrance. In the seminal public health case of *Jacobson v. Massachusetts*, the Court ruled that a state government could control an individual where the latter's refusal to be vaccinated against smallpox would threaten the health and safety of the public.[40] The Court found that the government's intrusion into an individual's sphere of liberty was warranted insofar as it was deemed *reasonable* to secure the public's health.[41] In *Zucht v. King*, the Court upheld a Texas ordinance prohibiting a child from attending school without having first presented a certificate of vaccination.[42] The Court reiterated the ruling in *Jacobson v. Massachusetts* that it is within the police power of a state to provide for compulsory vaccination.[43] It then held that an ordinance requiring proof of vaccination as a condition for school entrance fell squarely within a "broad discretion required for the protection of the public's health."[44]

Despite the expansion of the scope and nature of public health laws over the past century, compulsory vaccination is still a legitimate exercise of state police powers. As discussed in subsection (1) below, the distinction between conditions of public health importance and public health emergencies do not restrain state governments from requiring mandatory vaccination. Moreover, as illustrated in subsection (2), compulsory vaccination is not dependent on a determination as to whether a disease is sexually or nonsexually transmitted. As such, the constitutional basis for vaccination programs is still intact and would likely overcome any future judicial scrutiny.

2. Compulsory HPV vaccination is not restrained by distinctions between conditions of public health importance and emergencies

Since the late 1980s, state governments began updating their public health statutes and regulations. Initial efforts were largely in response to a call for public health statutory reform by the Institute of Medicine (IOM) in its 1988 report on the future of public health.[45] Specific recommendations included revisions that fulfilled two objectives, namely, a clear delineation of basic authority and responsibility entrusted to public health agencies, and support for modern disease control measures that address contemporary health problems (e.g., AIDS, cancer, heart disease).[46] Despite this initial request, there was minimal reform during the 1990s, and the IOM reiterated its request in its 2002 report *The Future of the Public's Health in the 21st Century*. The report noted that "[p]ublic health law at the federal, state, and local levels is often outdated and internally inconsistent."[47] This would lead to inefficiency and a lack of coordination, and even pose a danger in situations requiring an immediate and effective public health response.[48]

In its 2002 request for statutory reform, the IOM cited the *Turning Point Model State Public Health Act* (Turning Point Act) as a primary source for a national commission appointed by the Secretary of the Department of Health and Human Services (DHHS) to develop a framework and recommendations for state public health law reform.[49] As of August 2007, at least 33 states have passed legislative bills or resolutions based upon the act's model language.[50] One important contribution of the Turning Point Act has been its standardization of common public health terms and phrases. Relevant to the present discussion are the act's definition of "a condition of public health importance" and "a public health emergency."[51] Under these definitions, HPV infection may be inappropriately characterized as simply a condition of public health importance. As a result, the impetus to mandate vaccination may be diminished, jeopardizing the health and well-being of the adolescent population. As applied to HPV infection, the distinction between a condition of public health importance and an emergency becomes tenuous. In fact, against the backdrop of Supreme Court precedent, a plausible argument can be made for characterizing the spread of HPV as a public health emergency.

The significant distinction between a condition of public health importance and a public health emergency rests on the appropriate response of state governments. A condition of public health importance refers to "a disease . . . or other threat to health that is identifiable on an individual or community level and can reasonably be expected to lead to adverse health effects in the community."[52] Requiring vaccination as a condition for school entrance, for example, is based on a legitimate condition of public health importance, that is, a potential outbreak that may lead to adverse health effects in children who, but for immunization, would be susceptible to contracting the disease. Many states allow individuals to opt out of vaccination schedules pursuant to moral, religious, or philosophical exemptions.[53] From a public health perspective, the 95 percent vaccination rate within the U.S. reinforces the *herd immunity* of the population, that is, the resistance of the population to invasion and spread of an infectious agent based on the resistance to infection of a high proportion of its members.[54]

At first glance, it would appear that individuals who opt out of vaccination are merely free riders that benefit from the collective efforts of the majority. Indeed, if most people chose not to become vaccinated, an outbreak may potentially give rise to a potential population-wide emergency. In 1916, for example, polio claimed 6,000 American lives and paralyzed 26,000 more.[55] While a case of polio has not been identified in the U.S. for over 25 years, the CDC explains how its presence in other parts of the globe requires continued vaccination because it would take only one case to trigger a potential outbreak.[56]

In other instances, the potential disease may be infectious, but relatively less severe. Mumps, for example, is an acute viral illness that usually results in fever, headache, fatigue, loss of appetite and swelling of salivary glands.[57] Severe complications, however, are rare.[58] In December 2007, an outbreak of mumps in Maine prompted officials at the University of Southern Maine to require 426 of its students to get vaccinated following a single confirmed case.[59] Still, the situation did not raise national concern owing to widespread immunity and containment. Ultimately, the absence of disease, coupled with widespread immunity, secures the well-being of populations, and protects against the emergence of a public health emergency.

Although a situation entailing either a condition of public health importance or an emergency would warrant mandatory vaccination, a public health emergency would require state governments to take additional measures (e.g., quarantine, isolation) against individuals who refuse vaccination. A "public health emergency" is:

> an occurrence or imminent threat of an illness or health condition that poses a high probability of any of the following harms: (i) a large number of deaths in the affected population; (ii) a large number of serious or long-term disabilities in the affected population; or (iii) widespread exposure to an infectious or toxic agent that poses a significant risk of substantial future harm to a large number of people in the affected population.[60]

The distinctive features of a public health emergency are (1) the *imminent* nature of the threat and (2) the *magnitude* of its resultant harm, manifest in a "large number" of deaths, disabilities, or widespread exposure to an infectious agent.

A pandemic influenza epidemic, for example, would rise to the level of a public health emergency. The imminence of the threat would stem from its rapid transmission and high lethality. In the U.S., initial estimates suggest that a category 5 epidemic could claim 1.8 million lives.[61] To be sure, HPV infection can be distinguished from pandemic influenza on numerous grounds. HPV infection is not air-borne and consequently would be less easily transmissible. Also, HPV infection is not extremely lethal. Nonetheless, HPV infection may still constitute a public health emergency.

Against a backdrop of Supreme Court precedent, as applied to HPV, the distinction between a condition of public health importance and an emergency become tenuous. Moreover, sufficient evidence exists to characterize the spread of HPV as a public health emergency. Notwithstanding the Turning Point Act definitions, the Court in *Jacobson v. Massachusetts* described the smallpox epidemic as an "emergency" but did not define it so narrowly to restrict a state's exercise of its police powers. Instead, it left such determinations to the state government. Nonetheless, the Court did allude to potential criteria that would ensure that the measures were not "arbitrary or oppressive."[62] Specifically, the Court noted that smallpox was "prevalent" within the city, and that it was "increasing."[63] The two-fold determination of disease prevalence and rising incidence was sufficient to affirm mandatory vaccination as a "necessary" order to protect the public's health.[64]

Despite HPV's differences from other infectious diseases (e.g., influenza), its nature, prevalence, and incidence satisfies the Court's test in *Jacobson v. Massachusetts* and meets the contemporary definition of a public health emergency. Over 20 million individuals in the U.S. are infected, and 6.2 million new cases of HPV infection occur annually.[65] Moreover, by the age of 50, approximately 50 percent of *all* sexually active men and women will have acquired HPV at some point in their lives.[66] The fact that HPV infection is at present the most common sexually transmitted infection reiterates the *imminent* nature of the threat and the need for an effective public health response.

3. Mandatory vaccination requirements are not affected by distinctions between non-sexually and sexually transmissible diseases

Distinctions between sexually and non-sexually transmitted diseases should not influence a determination as to whether a vaccine should be mandatory. In addition to the argument in subsection (1) that HPV infection constitutes a public health emergency, other blood borne, sexually transmitted diseases are currently subject to mandatory vaccination. Furthermore, HPV poses a similar—if not greater—threat than such diseases.

The Hepatitis B virus, like HPV, is spread through sexual contact but the Hepatitis B vaccination is mandated for school children nationwide. Laws in 44 states mandate Hepatitis B vaccination for children entering elementary schools, and 34 states require vaccination for adolescents in middle school.[67] In fact, HPV can be distinguished on multiple grounds from Hepatitis B, in each instance warranting a more plausible reason for mandating vaccination.

HPV is more prevalent, has a higher incidence, and is more easily transmissible than Hepatitis B. Whereas Hepatitis B currently infects 73,000 individuals in the U.S., over 20 million individuals are infected with HPV.[68] Additionally, 60,000 new infections of Hepatitis B occur annually, compared to 6.2 million HPV infections.[69] Finally, Hepatitis B is transmitted when blood from an infected person enters the body of another; thus, condom usage is paramount to protect against infection.[70] On the other hand, HPV can be spread merely by genital contact.

While the severity of any illness should not be undermined, it should be contextualized within the broader public health objectives and interventions. To be sure, Hepatitis B is a severe illness that is asymptomatic in approximately 30 percent of individuals and may lead to lifelong infection, liver cancer, or even death.[71] The risk of progressing to chronic infection is heavily age-dependent, occurring in 2 to 6 percent of persons over age 5, and up to 90 percent of infants.[72] Moreover, chronic infections are the cause of 80 percent of primary liver cancer.[73] While decreasing the risk of transmission is important, the CDC has attributed sharp declines in Hepatitis B rates from

1997 to 2007 as a result of "widespread use of vaccines."[74] In light of its uncertain prevalence and potentially deleterious consequences, mandatory vaccination is a reasonable precautionary measure.

In like manner, the case for HPV vaccination is compelling. Against a backdrop of certainty as relates to HPV prevalence, ease of transmission, and potential development into cervical cancer, vaccination is an (albeit limited) precautionary measure. Ultimately, attempts to determine a threshold of severity may be subjective and enable individual state legislatures to proceed down a slippery slope. On an international level, there are instances of peculiar characterizations. In its reservation to the revised International Health Regulations concerning international public health threats, the Indian government indicated that it would consider "the whole territory as infected whenever yellow fever has been notified," but provided no standard for determining when the burden or impact warranted a national declaration of emergency.[75] In the U.S., a single case of any disease has never resulted in a declaration of emergency at a state or national level. Still, as demonstrated by the Texas Executive Branch in bypassing its legislature and issuing an executive order mandating HPV vaccination, a potential public health threat may give way to alternative—however unreasonable—determinations. Ultimately, the severity of a public health problem should be measured by its present impact, for example disease prevalence, as well as its existent threat. Nonetheless, there is considerable public health and legal support to analogize HPV to other STDs, like Hepatitis B, in determining whether mandatory vaccination is an appropriate public health intervention.

4. Minimum orb of protection is consistent with, but not a function of, the state's parens patriae authority

The doctrine of *parens patriae* recognizes the authority of the state in its capacity to provide protection to those unable to care for themselves.[76] The Supreme Court has also recognized a state's constitutional authority to exercise the *parens patriae* power when a child's mental or physical health is in danger. In *Parham v. J.R.*, the Court assessed the constitutionality of a Georgia statute that enabled parents to voluntarily admit their children to mental health hospitals.[77] The Court held that the statute was unconstitutional for lack of an objective finding by a neutral fact-finder that the child had satisfied a medical standard of admission.[78] Nonetheless, the state's interest in affording procedural safeguards (i.e., due process) and securing the best interests of the child does not automatically override parental decision-making. When a child's health is jeopardized, a state may exercise constitutional control over parental discretion. Still, the Court found that parents "can and must make those decisions" related to a child's need for medical treatment and care.[79] The decision, however, must withstand a healthcare provider's "independent examination and medical judgment."[80] Clearly, parental discretion is not absolute or unreviewable, but a state may not interfere absent a bad faith showing that a decision has jeopardized a child's mental or physical health.

The case of *Parham v. J.R.* and the Court's rationale for upholding parental discretion is distinguishable from state efforts to implement a mandatory vaccination schedule. The quintessential issue is whether an adolescent's failure to become vaccinated constitutes a threat to the *public's health*. In *Parham v. J.R.*, the *health* threat—mental illness—was limited to the child and could not be transmitted to another person. Of course, a mentally ill individual may pose a threat to the safety of another, but the state authority to confine the individual would stem from the police powers. Such coercive measures are analogous to state action during a public health emergency.

As discussed above in subsection (1), an influenza pandemic may warrant state governments to quarantine or isolate individuals who are exposed to, or infected with, the virus. In doing so, however, the state does not assume responsibility in lieu of parental decision-making as relates to the provision of seeking medical care. While both measures secure population health, the legal authority that must be invoked is distinct. Therefore, vaccination simply provides a minimum orb of protection that is consistent with—but not a function of—the state's *parens patriae* authority that otherwise defers to parental decision-making in securing the best interests of the child.

5. Legislative efforts to encourage HPV vaccination fall short of state governments' prerogative to protect the public's health

The importance of educating the public is an often overlooked, yet essential function of state governments and delegated authorities. Education ensures that the public receives objective information, and encourages healthy choices that promote and protect population health. Regulation of images that did not contain truthful information in tobacco advertising, for example, was invaluable in curbing smoking trends. It was found that such images "did not impart any objective information about the product," and could actually mislead the public by underplaying the harms of smoking and its associated risk with lung cancer.[81]

Given the low levels of HPV awareness (as discussed in Part I(B)(1)), educating the public, and particularly adolescents, of HPV infection is vital to encourage vaccination (whether voluntary or mandatory) and engage in healthy lifestyle choices. Unfortunately, of 42 states recommending HPV vaccination, only 22 addressed supporting an educational campaign. In Table 8.1, I reviewed the 27 total education-supporting bills to determine whether they targeted the general public, adolescents, or both; as well as an assessment of how many bills had been enacted into law.

While less than half of all jurisdictions (22) introduced legislation supporting HPV education, the passage of bills that did support educational campaigns was no less promising. Initially, 11 bills were introduced supporting general education campaigns and 16 bills targeted adolescents in particular

Table 8.1 State bills supporting HPV education in schools and the public

State	Public Awareness Campaign	School Sex Education Campaign	Enacted into Law (Yes/No)	
			Public Campaign	School Campaign
Arizona	S.B. 1437	–	No	–
Colorado	–	H.B. 1292	–	Yes
Connecticut	H.B. 6085	–	No	–
Florida	S.B. 660	–	No	–
Illinois	H.B. 115	H.B. 115	No	No
Indiana	–	S.B. 0327	–	Yes
Iowa	S.F. 326	S.F. 43	No	No
Kansas	–	H.B. 2227	–	No
Maine	L.D. 137	–	Yes	–
Michigan	–	S.B. 415	–	No
Missouri	–	S.B. 514	–	No
Minnesota	–	S.F. 243	–	No
New Jersey	S. 2286	S. 2286	No	Yes
New Mexico	–	S.B. 1174	–	No
New York	–	A.B. 2856	–	No
North Carolina	–	S.B. 260	–	Yes
North Dakota	H.B. 1471	–	Yes	–
Ohio	–	H.B. 81	–	No
Pennsylvania	H.B. 352	H.B. 845	No	No
Texas	H.B. 146	H.B. 1098	No	Yes
Utah	H.B. 358	–	Yes	–
Washington	–	H.B. 1802	–	Yes
Total	11	16	3(Y), 8(N)	6(Y), 10(N)

through existent school sexual education curriculums. Among the general education bills, however, only three were passed; in like manner, only six adolescent sexual education bills were enacted into law. Despite national attention, it is of grave concern that only six states have enacted laws that provide baseline information to adolescents and their parents of the risks of HPV and potential advantages of HPV vaccination. The dearth of legislative activity in support of educating the public illustrates the shortcomings of state governments and health educators to protect the public's health.

D. Initial reflection upon the arguments

Against a backdrop of low levels of public awareness and increasing sexual activity among adolescent females, it is likely that the prevalence and incidence of HPV will continue to rise. There is also sufficient evidence indicating that HPV infection may constitute a public health emergency. Even so, the severity of a public health problem is not dispositive. While state governments retain the legal authority to implement mandatory HPV vaccination, such efforts may be futile if unaccompanied by comprehensive education campaigns, especially if there is a recurrent risk. Empowering the general public—and particularly parents and adolescents—with vital information of the risks of HPV infection and the advantages of vaccination is essential to curb its spread and protect population health.

The arguments for (or against) mandatory vaccination, however, are more complex if we examine the issue not through the lens of what is legally permissible in the narrowest sense to vaccinate against HPV, but what may be effective in the broadest sense to ultimately reduce the incidence of cervical cancer. From this perspective, the legal arguments concerning mandatory vaccination are useful, but ultimately limited, in the furthering the broader debate on allocating resources, and to what degree, as relates to research and the potential targets, services, and criteria for evaluation of potential interventions.

II. Incorporating a social epidemiological framework to reduce cervical cancer

The nature and scope of issues related to HPV vaccination illustrates how societal norms, laws, and policies may affect decision-making on the part of physicians and patients. While exploring these issues may enhance our skills to become successful patient advocates, they evade an outstanding issue that neither Merck (the manufacturer of the vaccine) nor the public media has addressed: most women with HPV do not get cervical cancer.

Notwithstanding the efficacy of the vaccine, the role of non-HPV risk factors in HPV-induced carcinogenesis remains unclear. In this section, I argue in favor of a social epidemiological approach to address cervical cancer, and describe a multilevel framework and study to illustrate why the proposed hypothesis is consistent with the existent social and physiological context of disease. The purpose here, however, is not to prove a pathway of cervical cancer pathogenesis (quite frankly, I believe I have stretched the boundaries of plausibility as far as my own scientific reasoning goes). My intent is to illustrate how incorporating a social epidemiological framework enables us to widen the lens with which we scrutinize existent programs and policies, with profound implications for interpreting health-related laws and related obligations at the international, national, and subnational levels.

To be sure, the issues that are implicated encompass multiple disciplines, including epidemiology, law, politics, social norms, and ethics—though their role may contribute in a somewhat different manner than currently assumed. Clinical and (traditional) epidemiological evidence is based on studies of vaccine efficacy and duration of protection (i.e., five years) for the affected population (i.e., adolescent females who complete the three-dose series). Parental rights and the authority of public health departments are the central legal issues, while political will to enact legislation to direct resources for vaccination or education has been left to the purview of legislators. Finally, the role of providers in engaging patients to discuss the risks and benefits of vaccination is essential for optimal uptake. To date, the impetus to promote vaccination has been the common thread that unites these disciplines. I challenge this notion by discussing a subtle factor that also unites these disciplines, and is emerging as an equally powerful candidate as HPV to warrant our collective attention in its potential role in cervical carcinogenesis: stress induced-pathways preceding *and* following HPV infection that disrupts allostasis, exacerbates cervical dysplasia (treatment notwithstanding), and triggers disease onset.

A. Clinical and epidemiological backdrop

The incidence and prevalence of HPV infection and cervical cancer command national attention as a public health problem. Twenty million Americans are currently infected with HPV, with 6.2 million new cases, annually.[82] In 2008, 11,070 women were also diagnosed with cervical cancer, which causes approximately 4,000 annual deaths.[83] There are four high-risk HPV types that cause most cervical cancers (HPV-6, -11, -16 and -18), all of which are sexually transmitted.

Age is an important risk factor for many cancers, and cervical cancer is no exception. Most women are above age 30 when diagnosed, though the actual progression from HPV infection to disease onset is somewhat rare. Considering that 50 percent of sexually active persons acquire genital HPV at some point in their lives, and that 26.8 percent of U.S. women are currently infected with some form of HPV, the number of new cases is relatively small.[84] In fact, the immune system naturally clears up HPV within two years for 90 percent of cases for both high- and low-risk types.[85] For those cases that do develop, the mean time between initial infection and manifestation of invasive cancer is approximately 15 years, though the latency period ranges from months to years.

B. Rationale for, and likely role of, fundamental causes

Stress has been studied at both the macro and micro levels by sociologists and microbiologists, respectively. In particular, the hypothalamic-pituitary-adrenocortical (HPA) system and its role in the stress response have illustrated the effect of stress on immunologic function. A number of studies have suggested that stress has an impact on the immune response among patients with cervical cancer.

For women with cervical dysplasia, a precursor to cervical cancer, perceived stress has been associated with impaired T-cell response to HPV-16. Psychosocial interventions have also been associated with improved quality of life and adaptive immunity in women with cervical cancer. Together, these findings illustrate an important role of stress in mitigating the effects of cervical dysplasia and cancer. They also illustrate how *post-diagnosis* stress may prevent effective treatment and how psychosocial interventions may facilitate better clinical outcomes. Nonetheless, they do not resolve the issue of whether stress may play a *pre-diagnostic* role prior to, and subsequent to, HPV infection in the progression of disease onset.

The epidemiological evidence and social context suggest that stress may be involved in two plausible pathways leading to cervical cancer as (1) "stress as denial," functioning as an indirect social construct—manifest in attitudes and beliefs—on the part of individuals and providers that prevents vaccination uptake, and consequently resulting in behaviors that weaken the immune system and facilitate HPV infection (in the absence of vaccination), and/or (2) a necessary and sufficient cofactor following HPV infection—irrespective of vaccination status—that compromises allostasis, thereby triggering a mechanism that initiates carcinogenesis.

C. Pathway 1: Stress as denial: An indirect social construct prohibiting vaccine uptake

I speculate stress as denial to be a potential indirect causal pathway in cervical cancer carcinogenesis. Here, stress presents as a social construct that prohibits HPV vaccine uptake and results in heightened immunosusceptibilty to infection. My proposed pathway is illustrated in Figure 8.1.

Figure 8.1 is modeled after Bastani's 'health behavior framework' that appreciates multiple factors that influence individual uptake of HPV

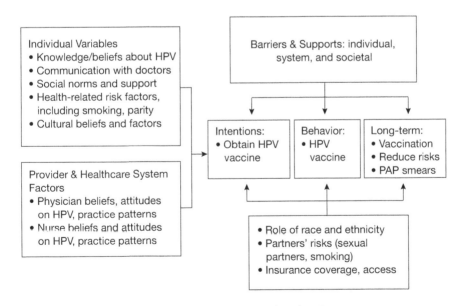

Figure 8.1 Model of pre-HPV infection stress-induced pathways

vaccination, including individual variables, provider and health system factors, and additional social characteristics (e.g., race, ethnicity, partners' risk factors, insurance coverage) that may influence short- and long-term behavior.[86] This (initial) model captures the first etiological pathway prior to HPV infection by elucidating the social and physiological aspects of individual and third-party variables. These factors may act independently, or interactively, in affecting behaviors, with direct effects on the immune system through (i) heightened protection against infection by undertaking the vaccine, or (ii) heightened risk of infection by refraining from vaccine uptake, coupled with engagement in high risk behaviors.

In the context of adolescent females, age 17 and under, and their parents, individual considerations may influence awareness and attitudes towards HPV. Specifically, issues affecting awareness may include knowledge about HPV infection, the vaccine, and beliefs; association between knowledge and vaccine uptake; as well as sources of knowledge and the role of the provider. Attitudes might include willingness to vaccinate adolescents; predictive variables based on ethnicity; and parental decisions on when (not if) to vaccinate.

The role of provider and health care system factors is also implicated, and may directly or indirectly influence patient attitudes and behaviors. Physician awareness of the association of HPV with cervical cancer, and any disparities among specialties (e.g., pediatrics, OB/GYN) would be particularly important in targeting gaps in patient awareness. Physician attitudes on discussing questions of sexuality, and the recommended age of vaccination would also influence vaccination uptake, considering that the national guidelines suggest vaccinating females, age 11 and above.

1. Specific findings on individual characteristics

In one survey, over 70 percent of individuals were aware that HPV is a sexually transmissible infection (STI), and 25 percent were aware that it was common.[87] Over 60 percent of individuals also knew the general purpose of a PAP test, with 72 percent aware that there was an HPV vaccine available. Notably, only 17 percent knew that the vaccine can protect against cervical cancer. It is often assumed that education about health interventions will result in higher uptake of the proposed behavior modifications. Even so, two independent studies reported conflicting accounts, with one finding an association between education and vaccination uptake; whereas the other suggested no increased acceptability of the vaccine.[88,89] A related finding was that only 25 percent of patients or parents received their information about HPV from physicians; most recipients received information from the media.[90]

Concerning attitudes, a number of studies report a general willingness (55–100 percent) of parents willing to vaccinate children, their low level of knowledge of the vaccine notwithstanding.[91] Hispanic women have the highest HPV-associated cervical cancer rates at 14.2 (per 100,000 females), then African-Americans (12.6), Caucasian (8.4), and Asian or Pacific Islanders (8.3).[92] There is, however, no conclusive data on why these disparities exist. Finally, 75 percent of parents likely to vaccinate before the child reaches 13, primarily for health and safety reasons; most common reason for those who did not was concern about encouraging sex.[93]

2. Specific findings on provider and system characteristics

Provider beliefs and attitudes are equally compelling in their potential to influence individual awareness and behaviors. While 98 percent of 300 pediatricians in a national survey knew that low-risk HPV types cause genital warts, only 66 percent of them knew that high-risk, oncogenic HPV type plays a causative role in cervical cancer.[94] Primary care physicians were least aware while OB/GYN were the most knowledgeable.[95] Among physicians supporting vaccination, the majority cited coverage of oncogenic HPV types, efficacy, safety, and prevention of cervical cancer. Still, many pediatricians report that they do not discuss questions of sexuality unless asked for a specific explanation of a specific clinical problem.[96]

To date, only one study has examined practice patterns concerning HPV. The researchers conducted a survey of Texas physicians, exploring attitudes and practices on (1) recommending vaccination for girls, aged between 11 and 12, (2) recommending vaccination for boys, aged between 11 and 12, and (3) determining whether they supported mandatory vaccination.[97]

They reported that less than half (46.5 percent) recommended vaccination for girls, 68.4 percent would likely recommend vaccination for boys, and 41.7 percent would favor mandatory vaccination. The primary physician-reported barrier to recommend vaccination was parental refusal owing to safety concerns (69.2 percent), followed by inadequate insurance coverage (67.2 percent), parental lack of education and understanding of HPV (65.2 percent), and refusal because of negative media reports (60.4 percent). For those who supported mandatory vaccination, 81.3 percent viewed it as an effective strategy for ensuring widespread uptake, especially for impoverished populations that would otherwise go unvaccinated. Notably, inadequate insurance coverage was also cited as the primary reason among physicians (73.0 percent) who *opposed* mandatory vaccination, followed by the public's poor understanding of the HPV vaccine (48.2 percent) and insufficient long-term data on safety (45.0 percent).

D. Stress, individual and provider/system characteristics, and behaviors

Together, the trends in individual and provider/system characteristics illustrate the social and physiological dimensions that may heighten risk of HPV infection. As a social construct, stress may underlie parental, individual, and even provider inhibitions about the vaccine, and transparent discussions of sexuality, and related health behaviors. As a result, there is a heightened atmosphere of denial, with the short-term effect of precluding vaccination uptake; and the secondary, long-term effect of exacerbating existent risks, stemming from sexual activity and related behaviors, for example smoking, which have also been associated with increased risk of cervical cancer.

Here, stress presents as an upstream determinant that has a direct effect on immunologic susceptibility by preventing vaccine uptake. The supposed objections by parents who thought the vaccine was not necessary, did not know enough about the vaccine, or reported that their children were not sexually active, are suspect. In fact, they do not readily comport with (1) the vaccine's demonstrated effectiveness, (2) readily available information on its efficacy and risks, and (3) the fact that over 46 percent of adolescents engage in intercourse, to merit such objections.

The role of these upstream social determinants cannot be overstated. Since no state law mandates HPV vaccination without an opt-out provision, patient, parental, and provider beliefs are determinative in securing vaccination, and engaging in health-promoting behaviors. As of 2010, while 25 percent of adolescents (aged 13–17) received one dose of the vaccine, only 11 percent completed the three-dose series.[98] Moreover, the rate of youths who ever had sexual intercourse (46 percent) in 2009 has decreased since 1991 (54 percent), but has remained constant from 2007 to 2009.[99] The vaccine's cost may be prohibitive in securing access, given the opinions of providers who favor (or even oppose) mandating or even recommending vaccination. The cost and insurance coverage of the vaccine may also be prohibitive ($375 to complete a three-dose series[100]), and was cited among providers who were both proponents and opponents of vaccination. Consequently, the general availability of the vaccine is not sufficient to protect against the risk of HPV infection.

E. Emerging, yet unspecified, role of microRNAs in stress and HPV-infection

Since HPV infection is implicated in the majority of cervical cancer cases, vaccinating someone against the virus would arguably moot any need to examine post-infection mechanisms. In other words, why explore a downstream pathway if an upstream determinant is effectively regulated? The answer, quite frankly, is that within every woman is a protective mechanism that precludes disease onset, *notwithstanding her HPV status*. Therefore, HPV infection is not necessary and sufficient for triggering subsequent carcinogenesis. If the precise pathway can be understood between infection, (recurrent) dysplasia, and disease onset, additional preventive measures can be taken. Moreover, the vast majority of women, aged 11 and over, has neither undergone vaccination nor completed the three-dose series. Identifying the interactive effects within the micro-, exo-, and meso-systems, coupled with the potential modification owing to longitudinal factors (e.g., age, infection, etc.), is consequently essential.

1. Pathway 2: Stress-induced miRNA disruption and recurrent cervical dysplasia

There is an emerging, yet unspecified, role of microRNAs in stress and HPV-infection. Unfortunately, the models proffered by the WHO (e.g., ecological model), Brofenbrenner's ecological systems theory, and related socio-ecological models do not capture the longitudinal dimension that are central to this secondary pathway. McEwen hypothesizes that behavior is inherently associated with a complex network of interactive mediators (e.g., neural, neuroendocrine, immune system), which govern allostasis and allostatic load, subsequently affecting effectors (e.g., cardiovascular system, adipose tissue, brain) that lead to disease outcomes (e.g., coronary heart disease, obesity, depression).[101]

The longitudinal dimension of behavior-induced anxiety that triggers the biological mechanisms are notably absent from McEwen's framework. This is in large part owing to the fact that the source of anxiety is unknown. Without some longitudinal marker, we assume that the host simply fails to adapt to potentially stressful challenges, disrupting allostasis, and concomitantly triggers a pathway that leads to disease onset. Using this approach, the time required to reach the threshold is of less interest than the actual threshold level. Therein lies our methodological fallacy. Cervical cancer has a mean latency of 15 years, which is initiated by infection, which arguably marks the first acute moment of stress on the host's system (whether that stress is compounded by social or individual characteristics is secondary), which has arguably altered the interactive mediators from a pre-infection state. The problem is that we don't know precisely how, or what specific changes may have occurred. During the subsequent interval post-infection, these changes are still occurring, but at a slow pace with no clinical manifestations (i.e., asymptomatic) that prevents us from examining their influence on the related effectors (i.e., the cervix).

My proposed (secondary) pathway takes account of this acute disruption and introduces this longitudinal dimension, as illustrated in Figure 8.2.

My framework does not require using cervical cancer as the primary outcome because, in fact, it may not be the dispositive indicator of the stress factor. Rather, the transition to dysplasia may trigger a feedback mechanism that effectively results in allostatic load, which leads to cervical cancer. The precise details and strength of this model are explained in further detail, below.

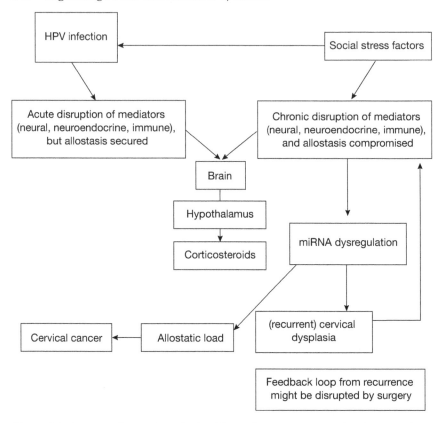

Figure 8.2 Stress as disruption of miRNA regulation, recurrent dysplasia, and
onse

2. The role of Micro-RNA regulation in stress, immunity, and cervical dysplasia

MicroRNAs (miRNAs) are a recently discovered group of noncoding RNAs that may regulate thousands of mRNA targets, which are implicated in the regulation of many biological processes. A growing number of miRNAs have been implicated in promoting or suppressing tumorigenesis in many tissues, indicating a potential role as a class of oncogenes or tumor suppressor genes. Their role in cervical cancer has also been demonstrated in a number of studies, ranging from general under- and over-expression of mi-RNA molecules in cervical tissues, to the precise impact of HPV infection on specific regulators. The role of a stress-mediated pathway for mi-RNA dysregulation, however, remains biologically plausible based on general and specific trends. One study found variation in two cancer-related miRNA molecules associated with brief psychologically stress-induced circumstances (the experiment involved academic stress in a pre/post test design and used blood tests to determine molecular expression).[102] It appears that no study has explored the association of stress-induced miRNA dysregulation and cervical cancer. Even so, there is evidence suggesting as much. A recent study examined whether stress was associated with immune response to high-risk HPV-16 (that causes cervical cancer) among women with cervical dysplasia.[103] After controlling for measures of health behaviors and stressful life events—which were not associated with T-cell response to HPV—the authors found that higher levels of perceived stress are associated with impaired HPV-specific immune response in women with cervical dysplasia. The reasons underlying this supposed paradox of a non-association of stressful life events with T-cell response to HPV, juxtaposed with a perceived higher level of stress associated with impaired HPV-specific immune response in women with cervical dysplasia, is readily explained by our model. The stressful events measured by the researchers were limited to events that occurred over the previous six months. Noting events over this shortened time interval, considering a 15-year latency, would be less likely to capture the acute and chronic contributions of disruption triggered by social factors, and their physiological consequences.

Another strength of this model is that it accounts for the occurrence (and recurrence) of cervical dysplasia as another point of intervention, which may explain the subsequent rarity of progression to cancer. As a precancerous condition, dysplasia is usually asymptomatic, but it can be detected by routine Pap smears that may indicate abnormal cells (a positive diagnosis can be followed up by a colposcopy-directed biopsy to confirm). While disparities exist based on race, education level, and age, the majority of women (70 to 80 percent), aged 18 and older, had a Pap test in the last three years. Once an abnormality is detected, numerous treatment options exist. Mild dysplasia may go away on its own, but otherwise patients may opt for cryosurgery, electrocauterization, laser vaporization, or a cone biopsy—absent which, 30 to 50 percent of cases would proceed onto invasive cancer. Even so, the risk of recurrence remains. One study estimated that treatment should clear up 90 percent of cases, but found that out of 352 patients, 37 (or 10.5 percent) had recurrence.[104] One explanation, per my proposed model, is that the feedback loop is effectively closed by treatment for most mild and moderate to marked cervical dysplasia (i.e., CIN I, CIN II). Of particular note is that the majority of recurrences (69 percent) were comprised of severe cases (CIN III), with the remainder (31 percent) including moderate to marked cases (CIN II). The invasion of the epithelium is what characterizes the different grades of dysplasia. It is conceivable that the feedback loop remains intact in more severe cases where surgical treatment does not eliminate the threat.

F. Brief proposal of a study that may explore the validity of the model

While the proposed model may satisfy numerous criteria (e.g., strength, consistency, temporality, biologic gradient, analogy, coherence), the experimental evidence is concededly lacking. As such, I hereby propose a brief study that may explore the validity of the model given the stress-induced pathways that may induce cervical carcinogenesis.

1. Hypothesis

Broadly, effective coping mechanisms are protective against stress-induced pathways that exacerbates cervical cancer dysplasia, *subsequent to* high risk HPV-infection, and are a necessary and sufficient cause of underlying cervical cancer pathophysiology. Here, stress is not suggested as a factor independent of HPV-infection, but a necessary cofactor that triggers the biological mechanisms that are further compounded by the feedback loop, which leads to allostatic load. Specifically, the physiological effect of acute and/or chronic stress interferes with microRNA regulation of a protective mechanism that secure allostasis, and whose dysregulation results in recurrent cervical dysplasia, which triggers a feedback loop that leads to allostatic load, prior to carcinogenesis.

2. Methods

The proposed methodology would entail a nested case-control design. One benefit of this approach is that the variable latency period (months to years) of cervical cancer suggests that controls selected at the time each case occurs or from the baseline cohort may yield some insight on the effect of acute versus chronic stress (presuming that chronic stress is associated with a longer latency period). The baseline cohort of my study would include women, aged between 25 and 40, with cervical dysplasia. This cohort is ideal because follow-up of earlier diagnoses of HPV infection among adolescent females, that is, aged between 15 and 24, would not necessarily yield any useful information. We already know that HPV-infection is a necessary but insufficient cofactor for cervical cancer. Rather, we ought to tease out the demographic variables and health behaviors, coupled with objective and subjective measures of stress (e.g., stressful events and perceived stress), and their association with under- or over-expression of mi-RNA molecules that are implicated in cervical dysplasia.

Recruited participants would include all women, aged between 25 and 40, diagnosed with cervical dysplasia residing in the city of Chicago (hospitals, other medical facilities, etc.) matched on age, sex, and geographic residence for at least 15 years prior to diagnosis (given that the average mean latency time is 15 years). Social and clinical stress indicators would be measured based on the models, above, including: partner migration habits, socioeconomic position, parity, and smoking habits (of the index patient and partner(s)). The number of potential sexual partners notwithstanding, the absence of the partner due to work or other factors may be associated with the index patient's stress. Inadequate insurance coverage to pay was the primary reason among physicians (78 percent) who opposed mandatory HPV vaccination and the secondary reason for opposing recommendation thereof (67 percent); ironically, it was the second highest reason among physicians (76 percent) who supported mandatory vaccination because they thought it would facilitate access for the poor. Smoking may be associated with a weakened immune system, or simply be an ineffective coping mechanism. A recent study indicated how teens see smoking as a mechanism to reduce stress in their family, and among their peers.[105] These co-factors may have an etiological role in the HPV-causal pathway vis-à-vis a weakened immune system, or they may simply be markers for a psychologically stress-induced pathway that, following HPV-infection, is necessary and sufficient to initiate disease onset.

3. Discussion of incorporating a social epidemiological framework

Adopting a social epidemiological framework has profound implications for allocating resources to reduce the burden of morbidity and mortality within a population. Relying on a single service (e.g., vaccination) that serves a particular demographic (e.g., adolescent females) is convenient for purposes of simplicity and outreach. Yet given the trends and factors associated with HPV-infection, provider knowledge and patient uptake, and factors associated with subsequent cervical cancer pathogenesis demand further scrutiny on how best to utilize epidemiology to reduce the overall rates of HPV and cervical cancer, the efficacy of the vaccine notwithstanding. The vast range of studies with varying strengths underlies the iterative nature of epidemiological practice, with studies examining potential associations alongside a myriad of confounding and interacting variables. Together with available resources, this accumulated data dictates the kind of studies that are employed, each one contributing additional knowledge that improves our understanding of an association and the underlying causal pathway. Based on this evidence, a host of primary, secondary, and tertiary preventive measures may be implemented. Adopting a social epidemiological approach is consistent with the broader framework of public health as a multi-disciplinary field that must leverage the knowledge and insight of different practitioners to address the overall burden of disease. In this context, the legal implications will not be limited to the mere permissibility of coercing the adoption of a particular practice (e.g., vaccine uptake), but a broader and more extensive scrutiny of applicable laws that may aid in the prevention of disease, and promotion of population health. It is incumbent on health advocates to recognize the complexity of the epidemiological backdrop upon which current policies are based; and scrutinize the underlying assumptions that ultimately allow disease trends to sustain.

Suggested further reading

Davidson, M.R. *et al.* (2010) MicroRNA-218 is deleted and downregulated in lung squamous cell carcinoma. *PLoS ONE* 5(9).: e12560. doi:10.1371/journal.pone. 0012560.

Haigis, M.C. and Yankner, B.A. (2010) The aging stress response. *Molecular Cell*;40:333–44.

Kawakami, K. *et al.* (2008) Low expression of (-glutamyl hydrolase mRNA in primary colorectal cancer with the CpG island methylator phenotype. *British Journal of Cancer*;98:1555–61.

Lanza, G. *et al.* (2007) mRNA/microRNA gene expression profile in microsatellite unstable colorectal cancer. *Molecular Cancer*;6:54–64.

Lee, R.C. *et al.* (1993) The c. elegans heterochronic gene *lin-4* encodes small RNAs with antisense complementarity to *lin-14*. *Cell*;75:843–54.

Lee, R.C. *et al.* (2001) An extensive class of small RNAs in Caenorhabditis elegans. *Science*;294:862–64.

Lee, Y.S. and Dutta, A. (2009) MicroRNAs in cancer. *Annu Rev Pathol.*;4:199–227.

Li, J.H. *et al.* (2011) MicroRNA miR-886-5p inhibits apoptosis by down-regulating Bax expression in human cervical carcinoma cells. *Gynecologic Oncology*; 120(1):145–51.

Li, J.H. *et al.* (2010) miR-30 regulates mitochondrial fission through targeting p53 and the dynamin-related protein-1 pathway. *PLoS Genet* 6(1): e1000795. doi:10.1371/journal.pgen.1000795.

Martinez, I. *et al.* (2008) Human papillomavirus type 16 reduces the expression of microRNA-218 in cervical carcinoma cells. *Oncogene*;27(18):2575–82.

Paranjape, T., Slack, F.J. and Weidhaas J.B. (2009) MicroRNAs: tools for cancer diagnostics. *Gut*;58(11):1546–54.

Pauley, K.M. and Chan, E.K.L. (2008) MicroRNAs and their emerging roles in immunology. *Ann. N.Y. Acad. Sci.*;1143:226–39.

Pereira, P.M. *et al.* (2010) MicroRNA expression variability in human cervical tissues. *PLoS ONE* 5(7): e11780. doi:10.1371/journal.pone.0011780.

Siebolts, U. *et al.* (2009) Tissues from routine pathology archives are suitable for microRNA analyses by quantitative PCR. *J Clin Pathol*;62:84–8.

Wang, X. *et al.* (2008) Aberrant expression of oncogenic and tumor-suppressive microRNAs in cervical cancer is required for cancer cell growth. *PLoS ONE* 3(7): e2557. doi:10.1371/journal.pone.0002557.

Wilting, S.M. *et al.* (2010) Methylation-mediated silencing and tumour suppressive function of *has-miR-124* in cervical cancer. *Molecular Cancer*;9:167.

Zhou, X. *et al.* (2010) Polymorphisms involved in the *miR-218-LAMB3* pathway and susceptibility of cervical cancer, a case-control study in Chinese women. *Gynecologic Oncology*;117:287–90.

9 Perspectives from the field

A conversation with John Kraemer,
J.D., M.P.H., Assistant Professor,
Georgetown University,
Washington, D.C.

Q.1 On scientific versus legal evidence

Q: The application of epidemiology to elucidate causality is very much an iterative process that relies on different kinds of studies to illustrate that an association is, in fact, real. If we can identify the correct factors as causes of disease, we can then modify those factors to prevent or control negative health outcomes. The Bradford Hill criteria offer an extensive list of criteria to establish causality, including (1) temporality, (2) strength, (3) dose-response, (4) replication, (5) biological plausibility, (6) consideration of alternative explanations, (7) cessation of exposure, (8) consistency with other knowledge, and (10) specificity. How can these criteria influence the legal standard of review to determine whether a proposed intervention or existing practice (and the attendant modification of alleged risk factors) is necessary to promote public health?

A: These criteria are good signposts for causality, but it is important to remember that they are not hard-and-fast rules. In fact, only temporality is necessary for a causal inference, and consideration of alternative explanations is, while perhaps not logically required, critical for research inferences to be given any weight at all. The others are often very useful, but a valid causal inference could exist without many of them being present. (And specificity is pretty much worthless outside the infectious disease realm, where causes are usually both necessary and sufficient.)

All that said, valid causal inferences about the etiology of a health problem and the effectiveness of solutions are critical for public health responses. Without being able to make a strong causal case for what one is proposing actually solving or mitigating a public health threat, it will be much harder for public health officials to assert convincingly that a particular control measure is justified and necessary for the public's health. And when public health measures infringe on liberty (as is the case for quarantine and isolation), authorities have to meet a fairly exacting standard of review to show that their action is both warranted by the importance of the threat being faced but also likely to solve that problem without limiting liberty to a greater extent than necessary.

Q.2 On the challenges of studying social determinants

Q: The rise of social epidemiology has prompted debate on how we, as a public health community, choose to employ our resources to identify causes of morbidity and mortality across the lifespan. Aside from the political decisions that must be made to determine how best to allocate those resources, are there any methodological challenges in utilizing epidemiology to examine broader social determinants of health as opposed to traditional studies that look at exposure to biochemical agents as opposed to income, education, or social capital?

A: Knowing how to classify and measure social exposures can be really tough. Most are difficult to conceptualize and validate (e.g., is SES measured by wealth, income, education, perceived status, etc.?) and highly inter-related. On top of that, many social determinants are correlated, so it is difficult to know if an observed effect between some social determinant and some outcome is real, confounded, or a proxy for something else. Exposures are often accumulated over a long time period and of relatively small effect. And then, of course, there is a great deal of ideology in this field—on both sides. (Of course, all of this can be true for environmental exposures too.) The best social epidemiology is deeply rooted in the social sciences, guided by social science theory and relying on our understanding of sociology, psychology, and other disciplines to determine what results are likely to be causal.

Q.3 On science, information sharing, and security

Q: You recently published an article in Science to address the U.S. government's response to findings by two research teams who were able to genetically modify H5N1 avian influenza viruses, making them capable of efficient respiratory transmission between ferrets. You explain the cause for concern since a small number of genetic changes might convert the zoonotic virus into a pathogen with dangerous pandemic potential with over a 50 percent human-to-human case-fatality rate. The government requested non-publication of key findings based on security concerns. You argue for a more transparent and balanced process undertaken by research institutions to enable information sharing for scientific benefits and public safety. What organization or adjudicatory body is best equipped to conduct a balanced review of the numerous implications (e.g., trade, safety, health) of scientific research?

A: There probably does not exist the perfect forum currently. Most of the existing fora are either tilted strongly in one direction or another (toward health, trade, or security)—where you stand does, to some extent, depend on where you sit—or they are intensely political. This may be an area where the academy or other relatively neutral actors might be able to start to build consensus, but I think it will be quite difficult for the current structures to arrive at answers that satisfy everybody.

Q.4 On the challenges of adjudicating international health disputes

Q: Do you envision scientists having a greater role outside of building the evidence base for the effectiveness of an intervention to contribute to ongoing debates—in trade, human rights, etc.—as either expert witnesses or perhaps establishing some basic level of scientific scrutiny when it comes to reviewing empirical evidence in a legal forum?

A: Hopefully, scientific rigor will be an important part of evaluating empirical evidence at the international level. Empirical claims are often quite persuasive to treaty monitoring bodies. Even outside of individual complaint mechanisms, many official and shadow reports submitted during countries' periodic review are full of empirical data, and it is important that these data are analyzed well because the stakes are often high. Take, for example, when trade and health are in dispute. If scientific data about health harms are discounted, serious harm can come to populations. On the other hand, if poor quality claims about risks to health are not rigorously examined, trade may be restrained without good reason—and that also does real harm to human development and, ultimately, health. The quality of empirical claims should always be analyzed.

Notes

1 Introduction to international law and global health

1 Jeffrey P. Koplan *et al.*, *Towards a Common Definition of Global Health*, 373 THE LANCET 9679 (2009).
2 The Constitution was adopted by the International Health Conference held in New York from 19 June to 22 July 1946, signed on 22 July 1946 by the representatives of 61 States (*Off. Rec. Wld Hlth Org.*, 2, 100), and entered into force on April 7, 1948.
3 Lawrence O. Gostin and Allyn L. Taylor. *Global Health Law: A Definition and Grand Challenges.* 1(1) PUBLIC HEALTH ETHICS 53 (2008).

2 A critical assessment of treaty-monitoring bodies: A case study of CEDAW's Optional Protocol

1 Lon L. Fuller, *The Forms and Limits of Adjudication*, 92(2) HARVARD L REV 353, 366 (Dec., 1978).
2 Convention on the Elimination of All Forms of Discrimination Against Women ("CEDAW"), Art. 5(a)–(b) (requiring that States Parties take measures to "ensure that family education includes a proper understanding of maternity as a social function . . .").
3 United Nations, *Fact Sheet—Goal 5: Improve maternal health* 1 (2008) *available at* http://www.un.org/millenniumgoals/2008highlevel/pdf/newsroom/Goal%205%20FINAL.pdf (last accessed September 25, 2012).
4 Fuller, *supra* note 1, at 357.
5 *See* International Covenant on Economic, Social, and Cultural Rights, Article 12; *see also* Social Charter of the European Union, Arts. 13, 16.
6 Additional Protocol to the European Social Charter Providing for a System of Collective Complaints, Art. 1 (1995).
7 International Covenant on Civil and Political Rights ("ICCPR"), Art. 2(b).
8 Optional Protocol to the International Covenant on Civil and Political Rights ("ICCPR"), Art. 5(b) (1966).
9 A.A. Cancado Trindade, *Exhaustion of Local Remedies Under the UN Covenant on Civil and Political Rights and its Optional Protocol*, 28(4) INT'L COMP L QUART 748–49 (Oct., 1979) (citing U.N. Doc. A/2929, ch. VII, 88, para. 1). *Id.*
10 *Id.* at 749.
11 Protocol, Art. 4(1) (emphasis added).
12 Protocol, Art. 5.
13 Protocol, Art. 7(4).

14 Case Concerning Avena and Other Mexican Nationals, 2004 I.C.J. 12 (Mar. 31, 2004); *see also* Karen Noelia Llantoy Huamán, Communication No. 1153/2003, U.N. Doc. CCPR/C/85/D/1153/2003 (2005).

15 Pardiss Kebriaei, *U.N. Human Rights Committee Decision in K.L. v. Peru*, 15 INTERIGHTS BULLETIN 151 (2006).

16 Rebecca J. Cook *et al.*, *Prenatal Management of Anencephaly*, 102 INTL J GYN & OBSTETRICS 303 (2008).

17 K.L. v. Peru at ¶ 3.1; see also ICCPR, Art. 2 (ensuring that an individual claiming a violation of a right shall have an effective remedy and, provided that the right is determined by competent judicial, administrative or legislative authorities, enforcement of the remedy when granted). *Id.* at 3(b)–(c).

18 *Id.* at ¶ 3.2; see also ICCPR, Art. 3 (declaring the equal right of men and women to the enjoyment of all civil and political rights).

19 *Id.* at ¶ 3.3; see also ICCPR, Art. 6 (providing that every human being has the inherent right to life).

20 *Id.* at ¶¶ 3.4–3.5; see also ICCPR, Art. 7 (ensuring that no one shall be subjected to torture or to cruel, inhuman or degrading treatment or punishment).

21 *Id.* at ¶ 3.6; *see also* ICCPR, Art. 17 (providing that no one shall be subject to arbitrary or unlawful interference with her privacy, family, home or correspondence).

22 *Id.* at ¶ 3.7; *see also* ICCPR, Art. 24 (declaring that every child shall have the right to such measures of protection as are required by her status as a minor, on the part of her family, society, and the State).

23 *Id.* at ¶ 3.8; *see also* ICCPR, Art. 26 (ensuring that all persons are equal before the law and are entitled without any discrimination to the equal protection of the law).

24 K.L. v. Peru at ¶ 3.6.

25 *Id.* at ¶ 3.3.

26 *Id.*

27 *Id.* at ¶¶ 3.4–3.5.

28 *Id.* at ¶ 6.3.

29 *Id.* at ¶ 6.4.

30 *Id.* at ¶ 6.5.

31 *Id.* at ¶ 6.3.

32 Cook *et al.*, *supra* note 16.

33 K.L. v. Peru at ¶ 6.3.

34 ICCPR, Art. 17.

35 K.L. v. Peru at ¶ 3.2(a).

36 *Id.* at ¶ 3.2(b).

37 *Id.* at ¶ 5.3 (emphasis added).

38 *See, e.g.,* The Mauritian Women Case, Communication No. 35/1978 (in which immigration laws were challenged that afforded free access to female spouses of Mauritian male citizens, but did not extend the same benefits to male spouses of Mauritian citizens who were females); *see also* Broeks v. the Netherlands, Communication No. 172/1984 (in which only married women could not claim continued unemployment benefits unless they proved that they earned over a certain proportion of the family's total income or were permanently separated from their husbands).

39 Cook *et al.*, *supra* note 16.

40 CEDAW, Art. 17(1).

41 CEDAW, Art. 18(1); *see also* Art. 21(1).

42 CEDAW, Art. 18(1)(a)–(b).

43 CEDAW, Art. 21(1).

44 *Id.*

45 Compilation of Rules of Procedure Adopted of Human Rights Treaty Bodies (hereafter "Committee Rules") HRI/GEN/3/Add.1 (April 18, 2002); see also CEDAW, Art. 19(1) ("The Committee shall adopt its own rules of procedure.").
46 CEDAW, Art. 22.
47 *See* CEDAW, Art. 18(2).
48 Committee Rule 45.
49 Committee Rule 46.
50 Committee Rule 47.
51 Claudia García-Moreno *et al., WHO Multi-Country Study on Women's Health and Domestic Violence against Women* (2005).
52 CEDAW, Art. 21(2).
53 *See, e.g.,* Commission on the Status of Women, *Report on the Forty-Third Session* (April 1, 1999).
54 *Id.* at iv.
55 *Id.* at 13.
56 John M. Paxman *et al., The Clandestine Epidemic: The Practice of Unsafe Abortion in Latin America,* 24(4) STUDIES IN FAMILY PLANNING 205 (July–August 1993).
57 Committee Rule 72(4).
58 Protocol, Art. 3 ("Communications shall be in writing and shall not be anonymous).
59 Protocol, Art. 2 ("Communications may be submitted . . . claiming victims of a violation of any of the rights set forth in the Convention . . .").
60 Protocol, Art. 4.
61 Vienna Convention on the Law of Treaties (hereafter "VCLT") (1969) (entered into force on January 27, 1980).
62 Richard K. Gardiner, Treaty Interpretation 12 (2008) ("It is now well established that the provisions on interpretation of treaties contained in Articles 31 and 32 of the [VCLT] reflect pre-existing customary international law . . .").
63 *Id.* at 15.
64 *Id.* at 17.
65 *Id.*
66 VCLT, Art. 31(1).
67 VCLT, Art. 31(2).
68 VCLT, Art. 31(2)(a)–(b).
69 VCLT, Art. 31(3)(a).
70 VCLT, Art. 31(3)(b).
71 ICESCR, Art. 12(2)(a).
72 Committee on Economic, Social and Cultural Rights, General Comment 14, E/C.12/2000/4 (August 11, 2000).
73 *Id.* at ¶ 21.
74 *Id.* at ¶ 34 (requiring that States abstain "from imposing discriminatory practices relating to women's health status and needs").
75 *Id.* at ¶ 12.
76 *Id.* at ¶ 14.
77 *Id.* at ¶ 2.
78 *Id.* at ¶ 14.
79 *Id.* at ¶ 22.
80 *Id.* at ¶ 34.
81 VCLT, Art. 32.
82 VCLT, Art. 32(a) (holding that resort to supplementary means is appropriate when the general means of interpretation "leaves the meaning ambiguous or obscure.").

83 VCLT, Art. 32(b) (holding that resort to supplementary means is appropriate when the general means of interpretation "leads to a result which is manifestly absurd or unreasonable.").

84 Committee, *Concluding Comments of the Committee on the Elimination of Discrimination against Women: Peru* at ¶ 24 (2007) (noting with concern "that illegal abortion remains of the leading causes of the high maternal mortality rate and that the State Party's restrictive interpretation of therapeutic abortion, which is legal, may further lead women to unsafe and illegal abortions.").

85 CEDAW, Art. 21 (providing that "The Committee shall, through the Economic and Social Council, report annually to the General Assembly of the United Nations on its activities and may make suggestions and general recommendations based on the examination of reports and information received from the States Parties. Such suggestions and general recommendations shall be included in the report of the Committee together with comments, if any, from States Parties.").

86 Background of general recommendations *available at* http://www.un.org/women watch/daw/cedaw/recommendations/index.html (last accessed September 25, 2012).

87 *Id.*

88 Report of the Committee on the Elimination of Discrimination Against Women (Fifth Session), Supplement No. 45 A/41/45 at ¶ 358 (April 4, 1986).

89 *Id.* at ¶ 359.

90 *Id.*

91 *Id.*

92 Report of the Committee on the Elimination of Discrimination Against Women (Thirteenth Session), Supplement No. 45 A/41/45 at ¶ 797 (April 4, 1986) (emphasis added).

93 *Id.*

94 CEDAW, Art. 21(2).

95 VCLT, Art. 31(1).

96 VCLT, Art. 31(2).

97 *See supra* note 86.

98 B.J. v. Germany; Yildirim v. Austria; Goekce v. Austria; and Salgado v. U.K./N. Ireland.

99 Kayhan v. Turkey; and Nguyen v. the Netherlands.

100 B.J. v. Germany.

101 Salgado v. U.K./N. Ireland.

102 A.T. v. Hungary; Yildirim v. Austria; and Goekce v. Austria.

103 Yildirim v. Austria; and Goekce v. Austria.

104 A.T. v. Hungary.

105 A.S. v. Hungary.

106 A.T. v. Hungary and A.S. v. Hungary.

107 B.J. v. Germany, Communication No. 1/2003, 31st Session (July 14, 2004) (alleging violations of Articles 1, 2, 3, 5, 15, and 16).

108 *See* A.A. Cancado Trindade, *Exhaustion of Local Remedies under the U.N. Covenant on Civil and Political Rights and its Optional Protocol*, 28 INT'L & COMP L QUART 734, 756 (1979).

109 Appendix to B.J. v. Germany, Krisztina Morvai and Meriem Belmihoub-Zerdani (dissenting).

110 B.J. v. Germany at ¶ 2.3.

111 *Id.* at ¶ 2.7.

112 *See* B.J. v. Germany at ¶ 5.9.

113 CEDAW, Art. 11(e).

114 CEDAW, Art. 16(c), (h).

115 B.J. v. Germany at ¶ 1.

116 A.T. v. Hungary, Communication No. 2/2003, 32nd Session (January 26, 2005).
117 *Id.* at ¶ 2.3.
118 *Id.*
119 A.T. v. Hungary at ¶ 1; *see also* CEDAW Arts. 2(a), (b), and (e).
120 A.T. v. Hungary at ¶ 1; *see also* CEDAW Art. 5(a).
121 A.T. v. Hungary at ¶ 1; *see also* CEDAW Art. 16.
122 The Vienna Intervention Centre against Domestic Violence and the Association for Women's Access to Justice v. Austria [hereafter "Yildirim v. Austria"], Communication No. 6/2005 (August 6, 2007).
123 Yildirim v. Austria at ¶ 12.1.3.
124 Yildirim v. Austria at ¶ 3.1; *see also* CEDAW, Art. 1, 3, and 5.
125 The Vienna Intervention Centre against Domestic Violence and the Association for Women's Access to Justice v. Austria [hereafter "Goekce v. Austria"], Communication No. 5/2005 (August 6, 2007).
126 Goekce v. Austria at ¶ 12.1.3.
127 *Id.*
128 A.T. v. Hungary at ¶ 9.2.
129 A.T. v. Hungary at ¶ 9.3.
130 *Id.*
131 CEDAW General Recommendation 21.
132 A.T. v. Hungary at ¶ 9.4.
133 *Id.*
134 *Id.* at ¶ 9.5.
135 Brenda A. Miller and William R. Downs, *Violence Against Women*, WOMEN AND HEALTH 529 (2000).
136 CEDAW, Art. 5(a).
137 CEDAW, Art. 16.
138 CEDAW, Art. 2.
139 CEDAW, Art. 16 (requiring non-discrimination in all matters relating to marriage and in particular ensure equal rights (a) to enter into marriage, (b) to choose a spouse, (c) during marriage and its dissolution, (d) as parents in matters relating to their children, (e) decide freely on the number and spacing of their children, (f) in regards to guardianship, (g) as husband and wife, e.g., choosing a family name, profession, and occupation, and (h) of ownership, enjoyment, and disposition of property).
140 Kayhan v. Turkey, Communication No. 8/2005 (January 27, 2006).
141 *Id.* at ¶ 3.1; *see also* CEDAW Art. 11(a)–(d).
142 Turkey, 2nd and 3rd State Party Reports 5 (1996).
143 *Id.* at 6.
144 Turkey, 4th and 5th State Party Reports 30 (1996).
145 Kayhan v. Turkey at ¶ 2.8.
146 Kayhan v. Turkey at ¶ 7.7.
147 *Id.*
148 Turkey, 2nd and 3rd State Party Reports 58 (1996).
149 Turkey, 4th and 5th State Party Reports 8 (1996).
150 *Id.* at 33.
151 Kayhan v. Turkey at ¶ 2.4.
152 A.S. v. Hungary, Communication No. 4/2004, 36th Session (August 14, 2006).
153 A.S. v. Hungary at ¶ 2.3.
154 *Id.* at ¶ 3.1; *see also* CEDAW Arts. 10(h), 12, and 16(1)(e).
155 *Id.* at ¶ 11.5.
156 Anita Danka, *In the Name of Reproductive Rights; Litigating before the U.N. Committee on the Elimination of Discrimination Against Women*, 4 ROMA RIGHTS QUART 34 (2006) (emphasis added).

157 RUTH R. FADEN AND TOM L. BEUCHAMP, HISTORY AND THEORY OF INFORMED CONSENT 3, 8–9 (1986).
158 A.S. v. Hungary at ¶ 11.2; *see also* Committee, General Recommendation 21, *Equality in Marriage and Family Relations* (13th Sess., 1994).
159 A.S. v. Hungary at ¶ 11.2.
160 *Id.*
161 CEDAW, Art. 10(h).
162 LARS ADAM REHOF, GUIDE TO THE TRAVAUX PRÉPARATOIRES OF THE UNITED NATIONS CONVENTION ON THE ELIMINATION OF ALL FORMS OF DISCRIMINATION AGAINST WOMEN 120 (Martinus Nijhoff Publishers: 1993).
163 *Id.* at 121 (emphasis added).
164 *Id.*
165 *Id.*
166 CEDAW, Art. 12.
167 CEDAW, Art. 12(2).
168 A.S. v. Hungary at ¶ 11.3; *see also* Committee, General Recommendation 24, *Women and health*, ¶ 22 (20th Sess., 1999).
169 REHOF, *supra* note 162, at 145.
170 *Id.*
171 *Id.*
172 A.S. v. Hungary at ¶ 11.3.
173 CEDAW, Art. 16.
174 Protocol, Art. 2.
175 A.S. v. Hungary at ¶ 11.4.
176 CEDAW, Art. 16(e).
177 Nguyen v. the Netherlands, Communication No. 3/2004, 36th Session (August 14, 2006).
178 CEDAW, Art. 11(2)(b).
179 *Id.* at ¶ 10.2.
180 *Id.* at ¶ 6.4.
181 *Id.* at ¶ 10.5.
182 Muñoz-Vargas v. Spain, Communication No. 7/2005 (August 9, 2007); *see also* CEDAW, Art. 2.
183 Muñoz-Vargas v. Spain at ¶ 2.4.
184 CEDAW, Art. 2(c).
185 CEDAW, Art. 2(f).
186 Muñoz-Vargas v. Spain at ¶ 13.8.
187 Muñoz-Vargas v. Spain at ¶ 11.5.
188 Muñoz-Vargas v. Spain at ¶ 12.2.
189 *Id. See also* Protocol, Art. 4(2)(b).
190 Muñoz-Vargas v. Spain at ¶ 13.7.
191 *Id.* at ¶ 13.9.
192 *Id.*
193 *Id.*
194 *Id.*
195 *Id.* at ¶ 13.10.
196 *Id.* at ¶ 13.13.
197 *Id.* at ¶ 7.3 (emphasis added).
198 CEDAW, Art. 2(f).
199 N.S.F. v. U.K./Northern Ireland, Communication No. 10/2005 (June 12, 2007).
200 *Id.* at ¶ 2.14.
201 *Id.* at ¶¶ 2.2–2.3.
202 *Id.* at ¶ 7.3.

203 Salgado v. U.K./Northern Ireland, Communication No. 11/2006 (January 22, 2007).
204 *Id.* at ¶¶ 2.2–2.3.
205 *Id.* at ¶ 1; *see also* CEDAW, Art. 9(2).
206 Salgado v. U.K./Northern Ireland at ¶ 8.4.
207 *Id.* (emphasis added).
208 REHOF, *supra* note 162, at 108 (emphasis added).
209 *Id.*
210 *Id.*
211 *Id.* at ¶ 8.5.
212 *Id.*
213 CEDAW, Art. 5(a).
214 *See generally* CEDAW, Arts. 7, 10, and 11.
215 CEDAW, Art. 12.
216 Protocol, Art. 4(1).
217 *See* CEDAW, Art.2(2).
218 CEDAW, Art. 12(2).
219 REHOF, *supra* note 162, at 306.
220 *Id.* at 146 (emphasis added).
221 *Id.*
222 CEDAW, Art. 5(b).
223 *See, e.g.,* Art. 5(b) ("it being understood that the interest of the children is the primordial consideration in all cases").
224 Committee Response to State Party Reports, 12th Sess., 70 (1994).
225 *Id.* at 438.
226 *Id.* at 181.
227 *Id.* at 329.
228 *Id.* at 391.
229 Committee Response to State Party Reports, 13th Sess., 66 (1994).
230 *Id.* at 120.
231 *Id.* at 244.
232 *Id.* at 301.
233 *Id.* at 347.
234 *Id.* at 405.
235 *Id.* at 675.
236 *Id.* at 761.
237 *Id.* at 490.
238 Protocol, Art. 7(4).
239 K.L. v. Peru, at ¶ 9.
240 *Id.* at Art. 13.
241 K.L. v. Peru, at ¶ 4.
242 Committee, *Concluding Comments of the Committee on the Elimination of Discrimination against Women: Peru* at ¶ 24 (2007) (concerned "that the recommendations of the Human Rights Committee in K.L. v. Peru . . . were not adhered to by the State Party).

6 Trade and health: Emergent paradigms and case studies in infectious diseases: An emerging paradigm shift

1 World Health Organization, *Cumulative Number of Confirmed Human Cases of Avian Influenza A/(H5N1) Reported to WHO, available at* http://www.who.int/influenza/human_animal_interface/H5N1_cumulative_table_archives/en/index.html (last accessed May 4, 2012).

2 *Indonesia Wants Legal Pact on Sharing H5N1 Samples*, CIDRAP NEWS, *available at* http://www.cidrap.umn.edu/cidrap/content/influenza/panflu/news/mar1407indo.html (last accessed May 4, 2012).

3 World Health Organization, *Agreement Reached on Influenza Virus Sharing, Intellectual Property*, News Release, May 23, 2007, *available at* http://www.who.int/mediacentre/news/releases/2007/wha02/en/index.html (last accessed May 4, 2012).

4 P. Capella, *Countries Adopt Stopgap Deal on Flu Virus Sharing*, WHO, May 30, 2007.

5 BBC NEWS, *Jakarta Bird Flu Deal Questioned*, *available at* http://news.bbc.co.uk/2/hi/asia-pacific/6337435.stm (last accessed May 4, 2012).

6 *See* News Release, *supra* note 3.

7 C. J. L. Murray *et al.*, *Estimation of Potential Global Pandemic Influenza Mortality on the Basis of Vital Registry Data from the 1918–20 Pandemic: A Quantitative Analysis*, THE LANCET 368, 2211–18 (2006).

8 *See* World Health Organization, *supra* note 1.

9 World Bank Policy Brief, *Improving Indonesia's Health Outcomes*, January 2005, *available at* http://siteresources.worldbank.org/INTEAPREGTOPHEANUT/Resources/health.pdf (last accessed May 4, 2012).

10 Centers for Disease Control and Prevention, *Interim Pre-pandemic Planning Guidance: Community Strategy for Pandemic Influenza Mitigation in the United States*, February 2007, *available at* http://healthvermont.gov/panflu/documents/0207interimguidance.pdf (last accessed May 4, 2012).

11 *Id.*

12 *Declaration on the TRIPS Agreement and Public Health*, Section 4, 2001, *available at* http://www.wto.org/english/thewto_e/minist_e/min01_e/mindecl_trips_e.htm (last accessed May 4, 2012) [hereinafter cited as *Declaration*].

13 *Id.*, at Section 5(b)–(c).

14 World Health Assembly, *Revision of the International Health Regulations*, WHA 58.3, at Article 18(1).

15 *Id.*, at Section 5(2).

16 D. P. Fidler and L. O. Gostin, *The New International Health Regulations: An Historic Development for International Law and Public Health*, JOURNAL OF LAW, MEDICINE & ETHICS 34(1), 85–94, at 93 (2006).

17 *See Declaration*, *supra* note 12, at Section 5(b) (2001).

18 World Trade Organization, *TRIPS and Pharmaceutical Patents*, Fact Sheet, September 2006, *available at* http://www.wto.org/english/tratop_e/trips_e/tripsfactsheet_pharma_2006_e.pdf (last accessed May 4, 2012).

19 Council for TRIPS, *Decision on the Extension of the Transition Period under Article 66.1 of the TRIPS Agreement for Least-Developed Country Members for Certain Obligations with Respect to Pharmaceutical Products*, June 27, 2002, *available at* http://www.wto.org/english/tratop_e/trips_e/art66_1_e.htm (last accessed May 4, 2012).

20 Council for TRIPS, *Implementation of Paragraph 6 of the Doha Declaration on the TRIPS Agreement and Public Health*, August 20, 2003, *available at* http://www.wto.org/english/tratop_e/trips_e/implem_para6_e.htm (last accessed May 4, 2012).

21 *Id.*

22 Notice of Motion in the High Court of South Africa, Case Number 4183/98, Pharmaceutical company lawsuit (42 applicants) against the Government of South Africa (ten respondents), *available at* http://www.cptech.org/ip/health/sa/pharmasuit.html (last accessed May 4, 2012).

23 K. Samson, *Drug Companies Withdraw AIDS Lawsuit*, UNITED PRESS INTERNATIONAL, April 18, 2001.

24 World Health Organization, *South Africa Unveils National HIV/AIDS Treatment Programme*, News Bulletin, January 2004, *available at* http://www. who.int/bulletin/volumes/82/1/news.pdf (last accessed May 4, 2012).

25 World Health Organization, *Sub-Saharan Africa, Fact Sheet, available at* http://www.who.int/mediacentre/factsheets/fs360/en/index.html (last accessed May 4, 2012).

26 World Health Organization HIV/AIDS Media Centre, *Global AIDS Epidemic Continues to Grow, available at* http://www.who.int/hiv/mediacentre/news62/ en/index.html (last accessed May 4, 2012).

27 *Id.*

28 Statement of complaint submitted by H. Tau *et al.* vs. GlaxoSmithKline South Africa (PTY) Ltd *et al., available at* http://www.section27.org.za/wp-content/ uploads/2010/10/TauvGSKevidenceAndLegalSubmissions.pdf (last accessed May 4, 2012).

29 Treatment Action Campaign, *The Competition Commission Complaint: Questions and Answers, available at* http://www.tac.org.za (last accessed May 4, 2012).

30 Settlement agreement entered into by H. Tau *et al.* and Glaxo-SmithKline South Africa (PTY) Ltd *et al.*, at 4, *available at* http://www.tac.org.za (last accessed May 4, 2012).

31 *See Revision of the International Health Regulations, supra* note 14, at Article 1(1).

32 *Id.*, at Article 18(1).

33 *See Declaration, supra* note 12, at Section 4 (2001).

34 *Id.*, at Section 5(c).

35 World Health Organization, *WHO Issues a Global Alert about Cases of Atypical Pneumonia*, News Release, March 12, 2003, *available at* http://www.who.int/ mediacentre/news/releases/2003/pr22/en/ (last accessed May 4, 2012).

36 World Health Organization, *Severe Acute Respiratory Syndrome Press Briefing, available at* http://www.who.int/csr/sars/2003_04_02/en/ (last accessed May 4, 2012).

37 L. Hawryluck *et al.*, *SARS Control and Psychological Effects of Quarantine, Toronto, Canada*, EMERGING INFECTIOUS DISEASES 10(7), 1206–12 (2004).

38 M. ROTHSTEIN *ET AL.*, QUARANTINE AND ISOLATION: LESSONS LEARNED FROM SARS 9 (2004).

39 H. MARKEL, QUARANTINE! 60 (1997).

40 ASSOCIATED PRESS, *Drug-Resistant TB Stain Raises Ethical Dilemma*, April 2, 2007, *available at* http://www.msnbc.com (last accessed May 4, 2012).

41 J. W. LEAVITT, TYPHOID MARY 58 (1996).

42 J. Hodge, D. Bhattacharya, and J. Gray, *Legal Preparedness for School Closures in Response to Pandemic Influenza and Other Emergencies, available at* http://www2a.cdc.gov/phlp/docs/Legal%20Preparedness%20for%20School%2 0Closures%20in%20Response%20to%20Pandemic%20Influenza.pdf (last accessed May 4, 2012).

43 D. Woodward and R. D. Smith, *Global Public Goods and Health: Concepts and Issues, in* GLOBAL PUBLIC GOODS FOR HEALTH 9 (R. Smith, D. Woodward, R. Beaglehole, and N. Drager eds, 2003).

44 J. Giesecke, *International Health Regulations and Epidemic Control*, in *id.*, at 199.

45 *Moore v. Regents of the Univ. of California*, 51 Cal.3d 120 (Cal. 1990).

46 Centers for Disease Control and Prevention, *Key Facts about Avian Influenza (Bird Flu) and Avian Influenza A (H5N1) Virus, available at* http://www. cdc.gov/flu/avian/gen-info/facts.htm (last accessed May 4, 2012).

47   World Health Organization, *Cumulative Number of Confirmed Human Cases of Avian Influenza A/(H5N1) reported to WHO, available at* http://www. who.int/influenza/human_animal_interface/H5N1_cumulative_table_archives/en/index.html (last accessed May 4, 2012).
48   *See Revision of the International Health Regulations, supra* note 14, at Article 32 (2005).
49   *See* MARKEL, *supra* note 39.
50   National Intelligence Council, *National Intelligence Estimate: The Global Infectious Disease Threat and Its Implications for the United States*, ENVIRONMENTAL CHANGE & SECURITY PROJECT REPORT, Issue 6 (Summer 2000), *available at* http://www.dni.gov/nic/PDF_GIF_otherprod/ infectiousdisease/infectiousdiseases.pdf (last accessed May 4, 2012).

8   Epidemiology and the challenge of regulating social determinants of health

1   Centers for Disease Control and Infection (CDC), *A Closer Look at Human Papillomavirus* (January 15, 2008).
2   *Id.*
3   Eileen F. Dunne *et al.*, *Prevalence of HPV Infection Among Females in the United States*, 297 J AMER MED ASSN 813, 816 (2007).
4   Food and Drug Administration, Press Release, *FDA Licenses New Vaccine for Prevention of Cervical Cancer and Other Diseases in Females Caused by Human Papillomavirus* (June 8, 2006).
5   CDC Genital HPV Infection Fact Sheet, *available at* www.cdc.gov/std/ hpv/stdfFact-hpv.htm (last accessed September 25, 2012).
6   Advisory Committee on Immunization Practices, *Quadrivalent Human Papillomavirus Vaccine*, 56 MORBIDITY AND MORTALITY WEEKLY REPORT 16 (March 23, 2007).
7   *Id.*
8   National Conference of State Legislatures, *HPV Vaccine—Updated December 2007*.
9   *Id.*
10   VA. CODE. ANN. § 32.1–46 (A)(12).
11   Dunne *et al.*, *supra* note 3 (study determined prevaccine population-based prevalence of cervicovaginal HPV in the U.S. by performing HPV DNA testing on self-collected vaginal swabs among females participating in the National Health and Nutrition Examination Survey (NHANES) 2003–2004); *see also* Centers for Disease Control and Prevention, *QuickStats: Prevalence of HPV Infection among Sexually Active Females Aged 14–59 Years, by Age Group— National Health and Nutrition Examination Survey, United States, 2003–2004*, 56(33) MORBIDITY AND MORTALITY WEEKLY 852 (August 24, 2007).
12   Iviva Olenick, *Roughly Half of Teenagers are Sexually Active; Few Have Multiple Partners*, 30(5) FAMILY PLANNING PERSPECTIVES 250–51 (Sept.–Oct., 1998) (citing Moore, K.A. *et al.*, *A Statistical Portrait of Adolescent Sex, Contraception, and Childbearing* (Washington, D.C., 1998)).
13   The Henry J. Kaiser Family Foundation, *National Survey of Adolescents and Young Adults: Sexual Health Knowledge, Attitudes and Experiences* 14 (2003).
14   *Id.*
15   National Youth Risk Behavior Survey, *Percentage of Students who had Sexual Intercourse with One or More People During the Past Three Months* (2005).
16   The Henry J. Kaiser Family Foundation, *National Survey of Adolescents and Young Adults: Sexual Health Knowledge, Attitudes and Experiences* 14 (2003).
17   *Id.* at 15.

18 *Id.* at 14.
19 National Youth Risk Behavior Survey, *Percentage of Students who ever had Sexual Intercourse* (2005).
20 *Id.*
21 *Id.*
22 Kristin Moore *et al.*, *Nonvoluntary Sexual Activity Among Adolescents,* 21(3) FAMILY PLANNING PERSP 110 (1989) (citing examples of health problems, including unwanted pregnancies, childbearing, and high incidence of venereal disease).
23 Ramesh Raghavan *et al.*, *Sexual Victimization Among a National Probability Sample of Adolescent Women* 36(6) PERSP ON SEXUAL AND REPRODUCTIVE HEALTH 225 (2004).
24 *Id.* at 228.
25 *Id.*
26 *Id.* at 227.
27 Joyce Abma *et al.*, *Young Women's Degree of Control over First Intercourse: An Exploratory Analysis,* 30(1) FAMILY PLANNING PERSP 12 (1998).
28 Tom Luster and Stephen A. Small, *Sexual Abuse History and Number of Sex Partners Among Female Adolescents,* 29 FAMILY PLANNING PERSP 204 (1997).
29 D. Montano *et al.*, *STD-Prevention Counseling Practices and Human Papillomavirus Opinions Among Clinicians with Adolescent Patients—United States, 2004,* 55(41) MORBIDITY AND MORTALITY WEEKLY 1117-20 (October 20, 2006).
30 ORC Macro, *STD Communications Database: General Public Focus Group Findings—Final Report* 21 (February 2004).
31 *Id.* at 22.
32 Rebecca Anhang *et al.*, *News Media Coverage of Human Papillomavirus,* 100(2) CANCER 308 (2003).
33 *Id.*
34 Maghboeba Mosavel and Nadia El-Shaarawi, *"I Have Never Heard of That One": Young Girls' Knowledge and Perception of Cervical Cancer,* 12 J HEALTH COMM 707, 716 (2007).
35 Heather Baer *et al.*, *Knowledge of Human Papillomavirus Infection Among Young Adult Men and Women: Implications for Health Education and Research,* 25(1) J COMM HEALTH 67 (2004).
36 Eva Yacobi et al., *University Students' Knowledge and Awareness of HPV,* 28(6) PREVENTIVE MEDICINE 535 (1999).
37 *Id.*
38 LAWRENCE O. GOSTIN, PUBLIC HEALTH LAW 183 (2000).
39 U.S. CONST. amend. X.
40 Jacobson v. Massachusetts, 197 U.S. 11 (1905).
41 *Id.* at 29.
42 Zucht v. King, 260 U.S. 174 (1922).
43 *Id.* at 176.
44 *Id.*
45 INSTITUTE OF MEDICINE, THE FUTURE OF PUBLIC HEALTH 146 (1988).
46 *Id.*
47 INSTITUTE OF MEDICINE, THE FUTURE OF THE PUBLIC'S HEALTH IN THE 21ST CENTURY 4 (2002).
48 *Id.*
49 Turning Point Public Health Statute Modernization Collaborative, *Turning Point Model State Public Health Act* (2003).

50 The Center for Law and the Public's Health, *The Turning Point Model State Public Health Act—State Legislative Matrix Table* 1 (2007).
51 The latter definition of "public health emergency" is modeled after the Model State Emergency Health Powers Act (2001), developed by the Center for Law and the Public's Health, and *available at* http://www.publichealthlaw.net/.
52 Turning Point Public Health Statute Modernization Collaborative, *supra* note 49, at 20.
53 Angie A. Welborn, *Mandatory Vaccinations: Precedent and Current Laws* CRS REPT FOR CONGRESS 3 (January 18, 2005).
54 LAWRENCE O. GOSTIN, PUBLIC HEALTH LAW 183 (2000); *see also* JOHN M. LAST, A DICTIONARY OF EPIDEMIOLOGY 84 (2001).
55 Centers for Disease Control and Prevention, *Polio Vaccine—What You Need to Know* 1 (2000).
56 *Id.*
57 Centers for Disease Control and Prevention, *Mumps In-Short* 1 (2007).
58 *Id.*
59 Associated Press, *School Bans Students Without Mumps Shots* (Dec. 6, 2007).
60 Turning Point Public Health Statute Modernization Collaborative, *Turning Point Model State Public Health Act* 25 (2003) *available at* http://www.public healthlaw.net/.
61 Centers for Disease Control and Prevention, *Interim Pre-Pandemic Planning Guidance: Community Strategy for Pandemic Influenza Mitigation in the United States* 10 (2007).
62 Jacobson v. Massachusetts, 197 U.S. 11, 38 (1905).
63 *Id.* at 27.
64 *Id.* at 28.
65 CDC Genital HPV Infection Fact Sheet, *available at* http:www.cdc.gov/.
66 *Id.*
67 Centers for Disease Control and Prevention, *Achievements in Public Health: Hepatitis B Vaccination—United States, 1982–2002*, 51(25) MORBIDITY AND MORTALITY WEEKLY 549 (June 28, 2002).
68 Centers for Disease Control and Prevention, *Hepatitis B Frequently Asked Questions* (2006) (based on 2003 data).
69 Centers for Disease Control and Prevention, *Hepatitis B Fact Sheet* (2007) (based on 2004 data).
70 *Id.*
71 *See supra*, note 68.
72 *Id.*
73 Hepatitis B Foundation, *Hepatitis B and Primary Liver Cancer, available at* http://www.hepb.org/.
74 Centers for Disease Control and Prevention, *Acute Viral Hepatitis Cases Down; Hepatitis A and Hepatitis B at Lowest Levels Ever Reported*, Press Release (March 15, 2007) *available at* http://www.cdc.gov/.
75 World Health Organization, *State Parties to the International Health Regulations* (2005) *available at* http://www.who.int/.
76 BLACK'S LAW DICTIONARY 1145 (8th ed., 2004).
77 Parham v. J.R., 44.2 U.S. 584 (1979).
78 *Id.* at 603.
79 *Id.*
80 *Id.* at 604.
81 LAWRENCE O. GOSTIN, PUBLIC HEALTH LAW 169 (2000).
82 Centers for Disease Control and Prevention, *HPV Vaccine Monitoring, available at* http://www.cdc.gov/std/hpv/monitoring-rpt.htm (last accessed September 25, 2012).

83 Centers for Disease Control and Prevention, *Cervical Cancer Statistics, available at* http://www.cdc.gov/cancer/cervical/statistics/ (last accessed September 25, 2012).

84 Centers for Disease Control and Prevention, *Genital HPV Infection – Fact Sheet, available at* http://www.cdc.gov/std/hpv/stdfact-hpv.htm (last accessed September 25, 2012).

85 *Id.*

86 Bastani, R. *et al, Integrating Theory into Community Interventions to Reduce Liver Cancer Disparities: The Health Behavior Framework*, PREVENTIVE MEDICINE 50, 63–67 (2010).

87 Herzog *et al.*, *Initial Lessons Learned in HPV Vaccination*, GYNECOLOGIC ONCOLOGY 109, S4–11 (2008).

88 Ferris D.G., *et al.*, *Midadult Women's Attitudes about Receiving the Prophylactic Human Papillomavirus Vaccine.* J LOW GENIT TRACT DIS 11(3), 166–72 (Jul 2007).

89 Dempsey *et al.*, *Factors that are Associated with Parental Acceptance of Human Papillomavirus Vaccines: A Randomized Intervention Study of Written Information about HPV*, PEDIATRICS 117(5), 1486–93 (May 2006).

90 Herzog *et al.*, *supra* note 86 (citing Tracking MBC, 11/13/06-4/29/07).

91 Brewer NT *et al.*, *Predictors of HPV Vaccine Acceptability: A Theory-Informed, Systematic Review*, PREV MED (June 2007).

92 Centers for Disease Control and Prevention, *HPV-Associated Cervical Cancer Rates by Race And Ethnicity, available at* http://www.cdc.gov/cancer/hpv/statistics/cervical.htm (last accessed September 25, 2012).

93 Constantine N. and Jerman P., *Acceptance of Human Papillomavirus Vaccination Among Californian Parents of Daughters: A Representative Statewide Analysis*, J ADOLESC HEALTH 40, 108–15 (2007).

94 Daley *et al.*, *A National Survey of Pediatrician Knowledge And Attitudes Regarding Human Papillomavirus Vaccination*, PEDIATRICS 118(6), 2280–89 (2006).

95 Herzog *et al.*, *supra* note 86 (citing GSK. HPV Vaccine Physician Tracking Study—Wave 6, 4th Post-Gardasil Launch Report for GlaxoSmithKline; 2007).

96 Esposito, S. *et al.*, *Pediatrician Knowledge and Attitudes Regarding Human Papillomavirus Disease and Its Prevention*, VACCINE 25(35), 6437–46 (Aug 29, 2007).

97 Kahn, J.A. *et al.*, *Human Papillomavirus Vaccine Recommendations and Agreement with Mandated Human Papillomavirus Vaccination for 11-to-12-Year-Old Girls: A Statewide Survey of Texas Physicians*, CANCER EPIDEMIOLOGY BIOMARKERS PREV 18(8), 2325–32 (2009).

98 Hitt, E., Complete HPV immunization rates low in the United States, *2010 National STD Prevention Conference*, abstract LBb, presented March 10, 2010, *available at* http://www.medscape.com/viewarticle/718413 (last accessed September 25, 2012).

99 Centers for Disease Control and Prevention, *Sexual Risk Behaviors, available at* http://www.cdc.gov/HealthyYouth/sexualbehaviors/ (last accessed September 25, 2012).

100 Planned Parenthood, *HPV Vaccine (cost), available at* http://www.planned parenthood.org/health-topics/stds-hiv-safer-sex/hpv-vaccine-19345.htm (last accessed September 25, 2012).

101 McEwen, B.S., *Stress, Adaptation, and Disease. Allostasis and Allostatic Load*, ANN N Y ACAD SCI. 840, 33–44 (1998).

102 Gidron, Y., *Influence of Stress and Health-Behavior on miRNA Expression*, MOLECULAR MEDICINE REPORTS 3(3), 455–57 (May–June 2010).

103 Fang, C.Y. *et al.*, *Perceived Stress Is Associated with Impaired T-Cell Response to HPV16 in Women with Cervical Dysplasia.* ANN. BEHAV. MED. 35, 87–96 (2008).
104 Leguevaque, P. *et al.*, *Predictors of Recurrence in High-Grade Cervical Lesions and a Plan of Management, EJSO* 36, 1073–79 (2010).
105 Scales, M.B. *et al.*, *Adolescents' Perceptions of Smoking and Stress Reduction,* HEALTH EDUC BEHAV 36(4), 746–58 (2009).

References

Ali, Shaheen Sardar (2000) *Gender and Human Rights in Islam and International Law: Equal Before Allah, Unequal Before Man?* London: Kluwer Law International, 20.

Bankole, Akinrinola (1998) Reasons Why Women Have Induced Abortions: Evidence from 27 Countries. *International Family Planning Perspectives* 24;3: 117.

Convention on the Elimination of All Forms of Discrimination Against Women, intro., *opened for signature* March 1, 1980, 1249 U.N.T.S. 13; United Nations Treaty Collection, Status, Convention on the Elimination of All Forms of Discrimination Against Women.

Daily News and Analysis, *Delhi HC for realistic solution to deal with teenage marriage* (August 12, 2010).

Duggal, R (2004) The Political Economy of Abortion in India: Cost and Expenditure Patterns. *Reproductive Health Matters* 12: 130.

Fernea, Elizabeth Warnock and Bezirgan, Basima Qattan (1977) *Middle Eastern Women Speak.* Austin, TX: University of Texas Press, 29.

Ganatra, Bela and Hirve, Siddhi (2002) Induced Abortions Among Adolescent Women in Rural Maharashtra, India. *Reproductive Health Matters* 10;19: 76.

Ganguli, Kisari Mohan (1896) *The Mahabharata.* New Dehli, India: Munshiram Manoharlal Publishers Pvt. Ltd., 3(42); 277.32, 281.36.

Jayadeva (2008 [12th century]) *Gita Govinda* (Sanskrit) C. John Holcombe (tr.). Ocaso Press.

Government of India (1993) *Declaration and Reservation to CEDAW.*

Government of India (1999) Initial Report of States Parties: India, CEDAW/C/IND/1:3.

Indian Penal Code (1860) [1911]. Section 292(1).

Islamic Republic of Pakistan (1948) Constitution of the Islamic Republic of Pakistan §§ 14.1, 25(1), 37(e).

Jain, Vanita (2004) Unsafe Abortion: A Neglected Tragedy. Review from a Tertiary Care Hospital in India. *Journal of Obstetrics and Gynaecology Research* 30;3: 197.

Law Publishers (India) Pvt. Ltd (2003) *Gour's Empowerment of Women in India* (2nd ed.).

Medical Termination of Pregnancy Act, The (1971) § 3(2)(i–ii).

Merriam-Webster's Collegiate Dictionary, 11th Ed. (2003). Springfield, MA: Merriam-Webster.

Muddupalani (republished in 1972) *Radhika Santawanam* (Telugu).

Muddupalani (2011) *Radhika Santawanam* (English), Sandhya Mulchandani (tr.). New Delhi, India: Penguin Books India.

National Institute for Population Studies (NIPS), Government of Pakistan (2001) *Preliminary Findings of Pakistan Family Planning and Reproductive Health Survey 2001.*

Nussbaum, Martha (1999) *Sex and Social Justice.* New York: Oxford University Press, 41.

Optional Protocol to the Convention on the Elimination of All Forms of Discrimination against Women, *adopted by resolution* Oct. 15, 1999, 2131 U.N.T.S. 83.

Pakistan Penal Code (XLV of 1860), §338.

Population Council (2004) *Unwanted Pregnancy and Post-Abortion Complications in Pakistan: Findings from a National Study*, 29.

Ravindran, T.K. Sundari and Balasubramanian, P. (2004) "Yes" to Abortion but "No" to Sexual Rights: The Paradoxical Reality of Married Women in Rural Tamil Nadu, India. *Reproductive Health Matters* 12;23: 88.

Rehan, N. (2003) Attitudes of Health Care Providers to Induced Abortion in Pakistan. *Journal of Pakistan Medical Association* 53: 293.

Republic of India (1948) Constitution of the Republic of India §15.

Rogers, W., Ballanthyne, A. and Drapper, H. (2007) Is Sex-Selective Abortion Morally Justified and Should it be Prohibited? *Bioethics*;21(9):520–24.

Saleem, Sarah and Fikree, Fariyal F. (2001) Induced Abortions in Low Socio-Economic Settlements of Karachi, Pakistan: Rates and Women's Perspectives. *Journal of Pakistan Medical Association* 51;8: 275.

Saleem, Sarah and Fikree, Fariyal F. (2005) The Quest for Small Family Size Among Pakistani Women: Is Voluntary Termination of Pregnancy a Matter of Choice or Necessity? *Journal of Pakistan Medical Association* 55: 291.

Samar Ghosh v. Jaya Ghosh (2007) Appeal (civil) 151 of 2004. Supreme Court of India (March 3, 2007).

Sathar, Zeba A. (2007) Estimating the Incidence of Abortion in Pakistan. *Studies in Family Planning* 38;1: 11.

Singh, Susheela (2006) Hospital Admissions Resulting from Unsafe Abortion: Estimates from 13 Developing Countries. *The Lancet* 368: 1887.

United Nations Population Fund (1999) *Key Actions for the Further Implementation of the Programme of Action of the International Conference on Population and Development.*

United Nations Population Fund (2004) *The World Reaffirms Cairo: Official Outcomes of the ICPD at Ten Review*, 83.

van Buitenen, J.A.B. (1971) *Mahabharata 1(2).* Chicago, IL: University of Chicago Press, 235.

World Health Organization (2007) *Unsafe Abortion: Global and Regional Estimates of the Incidence of Unsafe Abortion and Associated Mortality in 2003* (5th ed.).

Zilberberg, Julie (2007) Sex Selection and Restricting Abortion and Sex Determination. *Bioethics* 21;9: 517.

Index